Praise for *Welsh Witchcraft*

"A delightful blend of wit, wisdom, and practicality, Welsh Witchcraft provides an intimate yet engaging exploration into the magic and lore of Wales from a homegrown perspective. Mhara brings to the table not only her own personal lived experience and in-depth research, but also welcomes the reader to discover Welsh Witchcraft for themselves. The beautifully crafted exercises are inspiring and accessible—for both the novice and experienced practitioner alike. This book expertly illuminates Welsh Witchcraft as a living, breathing practice steeped in folklore, myth, and magic."

—Laura Tempest Zakroff, author of
Weave the Liminal, Sigil Witchery, and *Anatomy of a Witch*

"I am deeply appreciative of Mhara's *Welsh Witchcraft*—a thoroughly enjoyable and insightful introduction to the magical traditions, mythology, customs, sacred loci and otherworldly presences of her native landscape. It is a book fully capable of guiding the reader towards developing a workable and personal magical practice drawn from and inspired by the timeless and eldritch landscapes of Wales."

—Gemma Gary, author of *Traditional Witchcraft* and *The Black Toad*

"*Welsh Witchcraft* offers extensive insight into the rich history of Welsh magical practice. Mhara has a magical way with words that draws the reader in … She takes you on a fantastical journey through the pages; delving into the roots of Witchcraft that lay deeply intertwined within Welsh mythology, folklore and culture."

—CCJ Ellis, author and illustrator of *Welsh Monsters & Mythical Beasts*

"A delightful introduction to Welsh Witchcraft which takes readers on a tour of all of the essentials of belief and practice from the perspective of someone who has lived them. The style is engaging and the author deeply knowledgeable on the subject, giving readers a text that is both entertaining and thorough. Highly recommended."

—Morgan Daimler, author of *A New Fairies Dictionary*

"Mhara Starling breathes life into the long, magical history of Wales so many of us think we already know. Her writing is tender, clearly cherishing each tale, spell, and exercise. *Welsh Witchcraft* is utterly overflowing with Starling's passion and personal connection to the material … Mhara Starling is an absolute gift to the community and I'm thrilled future generations will have her as a guide."

—Fire Lyte, author of *The Dabbler's Guide to Witchcraft*
and host of the *Inciting A Riot* podcast

"Starling gifts the world with a cauldron of wisdom and a profound insight into the magical heritage and landscape of Wales. This is a book created from deep, personal practice and the love of land and culture … This book bridges the gap between the ancient and modern and brings authentic, practical Welsh Witchcraft to the table of modern magical traditions. Starling is a powerful new voice that is sure to inspire a generation."

—Kristoffer Hughes, Chief of the Anglesey Druid Order,
author of *From the Cauldron Born* and *Cerridwen*

"Starling presents a modern approach to a magical practice that is rooted in the mythology, folklore, and cultural traditions of Wales. This is a gift of a book; both well-researched and magically sound, it is also a love letter to the land, history, and spirit of Wales … With a commitment to well-sourced legends and long-standing tradition, *Welsh Witchcraft* bridges the gap between static collections of folklore and modern-day seekers hungry for authentic, relevant, and culturally alive magical practices. Highly recommended!"

—Jhenah Telyndru, MA, founder of the Sisterhood of Avalon and author of
Avalon Within and *The Mythic Moons of Avalon*

"Mhara Starling has written a beautiful, authentic guide to Welsh Witchcraft … Written by a Welsh Witch from a first-hand perspective, this is a valuable volume for readers that study a Celtic or Traditional Witchcraft path. Mhara has filled this book with a beautiful array of mythology, folklore, plants, spells, and Welsh knowledge."

—Annwyn Avalon, author of *Water Witchcraft*
and *The Way of the Water Priestess*

WELSH
WITCHCRAFT

About the Author

Mhara Starling was born in North Wales, raised on the Isle of Anglesey, and is a native Welsh speaker. She is a transgender woman who has been practicing witchcraft from a very young age, and her witchcraft videos on TikTok have more than a million views. Mhara is a celebrant and a tarot reader, and she runs moots, gatherings, and open rituals. She was featured in the BBC Wales documentary series *Young, Welsh and Pretty Religious.*

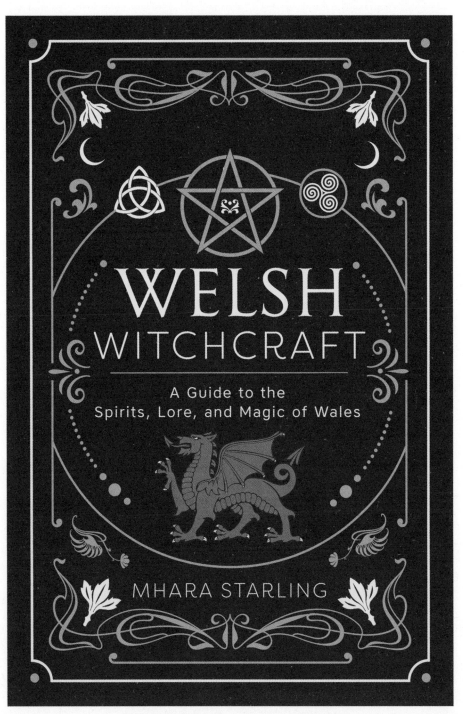

WELSH WITCHCRAFT

A Guide to the
Spirits, Lore, and Magic of Wales

MHARA STARLING

Llewellyn Publications • Woodbury, Minnesota

First Edition
Fourth Printing, 2022

Cover design by Kevin R. Brown
Editing by Marjorie Otto

Llewellyn Publications is a registered trademark of Llewellyn Worldwide Ltd.

Library of Congress Cataloging-in-Publication Data (Pending)
ISBN: 978-0-7387-7091-8

Llewellyn Publications
A Division of Llewellyn Worldwide Ltd.
2143 Wooddale Drive
Woodbury, MN 55125-2989
www.llewellyn.com

Printed in the United States of America

This book is dedicated to
Matthew Scott Lewis,
My one constant, thank you for always being there for me, fy nghariad.
And
Mam, my mother,
For loving me unconditionally.

Contents

Exercises

Acknowledgments

Initially, I would like to thank every Pagan, Witch, and curious mind who over the last decade or so has quizzed me on Welsh Paganism, magic, and Witchcraft. It is your curiosity that sparked the initial idea for this book. I am so proud to be sharing a glimpse into the magical practises of my land with the world. However, this book would not exist without the exceptionally powerful love and patience of many people who are near and dear to me.

I send my thanks, first and foremost, to Kristoffer Hughes, my mentor through the process of writing this book and the initiator of my inspiration. It was you who truly introduced me to a Paganism that is Welsh in spirit back in my tumultuous teen years and you who inspired me to embrace my culture, my language, my land. Without your support, advice, and recommendations, I have no idea how I could have ever even formulated the idea for this book. Thank you.

I would also like to send my love and thanks to Matthew Scott Lewis. We have taken on the world together for so long, and you are the one true constant in my otherwise chaotic life. You make my world more magical day by day. Thank you for listening to my woes and fears, and quelling them in a way only you ever could. It is you who empowered me to share my voice and stand firm in the knowledge that someone out there would want to read what I would write.

There are numerous people I would like to thank and acknowledge. To Julie Franklin, for inspiring my Witchcraft in a way no other Witch ever has; sleep well, Lettuce To Suzie Kincla, for giving me a safe place to grow when I needed one, and being an amazing new friend who I hope will be in my life for many moons to come. To the team at the magical shop in Chester. To my best friend, Kyara, who inspired me to write when I was following a path that was not suited to me whatsoever. And finally, to my ever-loving and supportive mother, for your unconditional love and all you have ever given me. Thank you all.

Introduction

The culture of Wales is packed to the brim with pure, unadulterated magic. Many modern-day inhabitants of Wales would rarely describe their culture as magical, and yet within the language of the land, the regional folklore and myth, and the beauty of the landscape, magic is ever present. Who could ever deny Wales' magic, when the emblem of the *Cymry*, the people of Wales, is the mighty red dragon. Wales, or *Cymru* as it is known by its native Welsh speakers, is a land rich with a legacy of myth, legend, superstition, and intrigue.

It is of no wonder then, that a land so very rife with magical potential would also be the historical home of a variety of magical specialists. Magical practitioners, magicians, soothsayers, and healers who delve into the magical arts have operated within Wales for centuries. Some would believe that the magical arts native to Wales would have ceased to exist long ago, lost to the mists of time. However, magic never left this land. With the popularity of Neopaganism rising steadily year by year, more people today are turning to Wales' Pagan past to influence, inspire, and inform their spiritual pathway. With the interest in Wales' ancient Pagan past, it is of no wonder that people are also discovering the rich array of magical arts that have been practised on Welsh soil over the last thousand years or so as well.

The purpose of this book is to present my personal exploration into Witchcraft and magical practises, which is specific to my native land, Wales. The pages of this book include an exploration of both modern Celtic spirituality and traditional Welsh folk magical practises. I will also explore how modern Celtic spirituality, inspired by the continuum of myths, legends, and lore of the land, and a knowledge of Welsh folk magic, can be transferred into a modern Witches' practise. Dotted throughout the pages of this book, I will present my personal magical practises and discuss how a knowledge of Celtic myth and traditional Welsh folk magical practises has informed them, presenting a fresh approach to Witchcraft with a spirit that is wholly from the land of the red dragon.

The main purpose of this book is simple: to introduce you to the rich and deeply interesting array of magical practises that stem from the Celtic region of what is today known as *Cymru*, or Wales. The history of magic and Witchcraft in Wales is absolutely fascinating and can easily inspire any modern-day Witch. It is my belief that a deeper understanding of the history of Witchcraft and magic can truly propel a modern Witch's craft. By understanding the continuum of beliefs, practises, and individuals who led Witchcraft to the shape in which it is understood today, we, as modern Witches, can truly begin to understand the vast implications that embracing the longstanding traditions of Witchery has. My goal here is not to present some old, ancient tradition of Witchcraft to you. This book is very much an exploration of historical accounts of Witchcraft and magic, the folklore associated with magic in Wales, and an insight into how a modern-day Witch might incorporate a knowledge of these things into their practise. This is in keeping with the spirit of many streams of what is known today as "traditional Witchcraft." Modern traditional Witches pull on folklore, history, and regional superstitious beliefs to inform and construct their practises, as opposed to following the modern mythos found in many Neopagan traditions of Witchcraft. This book acts as an insight into a region-specific history and lore associated with magic and Witchcraft. Much of what you will find within the pages of this book may not align with Neopagan, eclectic streams of Witchcraft such as Wicca, as I am not Wiccan. The Witchcraft presented in this book follows the magical traditions of both Celtic Paganism and historical magical practises originating in Wales.

What does it mean to be a Witch today? The pages of this book will explore Witchcraft and the very archetype of the Witch as found in the Celtic legends and folklore of Wales and Britain, as well as among folk beliefs stretching back over the past few millennia. Many people today don the label of "Witch" with pride and integrity. How times have changed from the days when claiming to be a Witch might have earned oneself a death sentence. One of the key elements of being a Witch today is being an individual who is empowered, who takes matters into their own hands, and knows the power they hold. They employ this empowered understanding of their own intrinsic power in order to cause change and work their magic in the world. A Witch is unapologetic in nature, wholly authentic to who they are and what they desire. At its core, however, a Witch is simply someone who practises Witchcraft. You will find lists upon lists in various media pointing to "signs" that you may be a Witch at heart. The fact of the matter is that the only true signs of being a Witch are that you practise Witchcraft, and that you label yourself as a Witch. It is very much as simple as that. Of course, by choosing to carry the label of "Witch" with you, you are entering a continuum of magical practitioners and specialists, who have, whether by choice or not, also been referred to by that term.

A Witch is a complex archetype, simultaneously feared and revered. Witches are the stuff of nightmares, and the stuff of dreams, all wrapped up into one. Contrary to what many might believe, being a Witch does not require any specific religious beliefs. Being a Witch and being religious are two entirely separate things. You can be both religious and a Witch, or one or the other. Throughout history, Witches have come from a variety of cultures and beliefs. In fact, much of what we now know of as the archetype of the Witch stems from the lore formulated in predominately Christian periods of history. Many of the traditional healers—wise women and cunning folk that are often conflated as being the predecessors of the modern-day Witch—were indeed Christian, or of a similar faith, rather than Pagan as most Witches today are. The practises explored in this book cannot be neatly compartmentalised as being purely Pagan in nature. The path of the Witch in Wales was historically a crooked path, not quite Pagan, yet not quite Christian either. It is easy for modern practitioners of Witchcraft to dismiss Christianity as having no bearings on modern magical practise, and yet the historical folk magical practises of Wales and indeed Britain drew upon Christian theology. The charms, spells, and magical workings that are recorded in historical documents often seem Christian on the surface, and yet there is also an element of archaic, pre-Christian knowledge within them. Brushing aside any discomfort we have with Christianity, the church, and the God of the Christians, we cannot entirely ignore the vast influence Christianity has had on Wales' and Britain's culture and people for centuries. I invite the reader of this book to sweep away any preconceived ideas they may hold regarding the folk magician and the Witch's role within Christianity. Things are rarely binary in nature, and moving forward in this book the reader may find it useful to bear that in mind.

The archetype of the Witch will be continually explored throughout this book, and the history associated with the Witch touched upon too. Within Welsh and Celtic myth we have a myriad of magical practitioners to turn to as guides to lead us down the path of magic. None greater, I would be so bold as to say, for the Witch than the Witch goddess herself, Cerridwen. However, it must be noted that this book does not draw purely upon the texts of Welsh mythology. There are numerous books, most with a Druidic expression, that explore the myths, such as those of the Mabinogi, and how they relate to modern Paganism. This book is for the folk magicians, the modern-day cunning folk and the Witches. Not only will we delve into those sacred texts and myths, which inspire many Pagans today, but we will also explore the rich abundance of magical specialists who operated throughout Wales and their specific practises.

A core principle I have found that the majority of Witches hold is the ability to question everything. Witches continually learn and develop their knowledge. I hope that this book offers an insight into a Witchcraft born of a Celtic land, and that it inspires others to take on the mantle of the student of magic, and conduct their own investigations into the same fields. My hope is that this book aids in continuing your magical study, and facilitates that constant desire and drive to learn and explore.

It would not be too far a stretch to assume that the majority of Witches who feel drawn to this book would classify themselves as Celtic Witches. Meaning, that they are Witches who operate within a Celtic expression through their practises. The Welsh Witch's magic is fuelled and inspired by the myth, legend, and lore found among the various Celtic nations. Whether you have a genetic connection to the various lands where a Celtic culture was found, or whether you are simply drawn to the lore, legend, languages, and practises of all that encompasses "Celtic," this book is for you. It is to further your investigations and explorations into the very heart of Celtic magic.

Who Am I?

I feel it is important this early on to introduce myself to you and elaborate on what the content of this book has to do with me on a personal level. I identify myself today as a Welsh, Celtic Witch. My practise is what many would describe as being in keeping with the spirit of modern traditional Witchcraft. I am far from an eclectic Witch; I do not tend to dip my toes into a variety of world traditions. Instead, my Witchcraft is very much in tune with the land I walk upon. My practise is inspired by the continuum of folklore, legend, traditions, and beliefs found intertwined into the land in which I was born. I was raised on an island, and one steeped in magical history and mythology. Ynys Môn, or as it is known in English: The Isle of Anglesey. This island has not only been marked as an island sacred to the ancient Druids, but it is also littered with stories of fairies, Witches, magic, and wonder. It is no wonder then that I feel such a sense of pride and devotion to my land. Ynys Môn is often referred to as *Môn, mam Cymru*, translating to mean "Môn, mother of Wales." I was told while growing up that this is due to the fact that the majority of food consumed in Wales is grown on the island. However, to me, as an Earth-loving Witch, there is nowhere I feel closer to our divine mother goddess than on my mystical island home. Therefore, referring to Ynys Môn as the mother of Wales speaks to the very essence of my spiritual and magical practise.

I was born into a Welsh-speaking family, and Welsh is indeed my native language. My language is very important to me, and aids me in feeling connected to my ancestors and to the spirits of the land itself. My family has no specific ties to Witchcraft or Paganism, at least as far as I am aware. My late paternal grandmother had a keen interest in divination and often practised various forms of divination, such as tea-leaf readings. I have heard whispers here and there that she had an interest in Witchcraft, but other than those faint whispers, as far as I can deduce, I am the first Witch of my family. I am lucky in that I was never raised particularly religious, and so I was able to begin my explorations into Witchcraft and spirituality from a very young age. My first encounter with Witchery came about when I was a preteen. I came across a dusty little spell book buried underneath a pile of books in a secondhand store. I still own the spell book to this day, and it is very much a Neopagan introductory guide to spells and Witchcraft. At that young age I was obsessed with attempting the spells in this book. It did not take long for my interests to pique, as I frantically searched for any fragments of information I could find on magic. Initially my path was very much Neopagan and eclectic, as I explored the intricacies of Wicca and modern Pagan Witchcraft. However, it was not until I was sixteen years old that my true path began to unfold before me. At this age, I stumbled upon an article that mentioned an order of Druids operating near my home on Anglesey. I met with the chief of this order, and that is when I was introduced to Welsh Celtic Paganism. I was already familiar with the various myths and legends of Wales. Growing up attending Welsh-speaking schools I was introduced to the tales of the Mabinogi and various other folk tales from a very young age. However, I could never predict that these myths and legends would be the key to a deeper level of spiritual and magical exploration that awaited me. From that moment on, I began devouring all the information I could on Celtic mythology and began to forge spiritual connections to regional deities and spirits.

I considered turning to Druidry, as the majority of the Pagans I met who operated within a Celtic expression seemed to lean toward that path. However, something never felt right about devoting myself entirely to being a Druid. I found the most comfort and empowerment within Witchcraft. And whilst yes, Witchcraft and Druidry can work seamlessly hand in hand, I still have yet to this day felt drawn to immersing myself down the path of the Celtic Druid. Perhaps one day I shall, but for now, I am very much happy being the solitary, modern traditional Welsh Witch that I am.

It did not take long after I began studying the myth and legend of my land for me to begin questioning what role Witchcraft played in Wales, both historically and in this modern day and age. The history I found was ever so rich! Wales is a land ripe with magical practises, magical specialists, and folkloric traditions. This book is a glimpse into much of what I have discovered over the years of studying, as well as being an insight into how I have incorporated what I have learnt into my personal magical and spiritual practises today.

I am a Witch who is intensely passionate about Celtic magic. My magic is informed by the legends of old associated with this land, as well as the magical practitioners throughout history whose practises I attempt to uphold whilst keeping in touch with my modern sensibilities. The beauty and majesty of the sacred landscape upon which I was raised inspires me and my devotions to its local spirits and deities daily. I am a Witch, but also a *Swynwraig*, and this book will delve into the intricacies of what exactly that means.

Why Do I Feel This Book Is Needed?

One of the driving forces that led me to write this book was the frustrations I felt at attempting to find a book of this nature. There simply is not a diverse range of voices discussing Celtic Witchcraft, especially not Witchcraft that is inspired by Welsh traditions and practises. Even among the various books available that delve into various aspects of Welsh Celtic Paganism, very few are written for Witches and magical practitioners, and fewer still are written by people who were raised and have lived within the culture these practises stem from. I would even be so bold as to say that many books concerning Welsh Celtic Paganism and spirituality are in fact written by those who have yet to even step foot upon the land. However, there is something to be said about hearing the information directly from those who not only have read and studied these traditions, beliefs, and practises, but who also connect regularly with the spirits of their land of origin. Within my personal experience, I have also found that there is certainly a demand for this knowledge to be shared, and be easier to access. I run a variety of events and gatherings of a spiritual and Pagan nature, and people desperate to connect with their Welsh ancestry and regional magical practises often bombard me, begging that I point them toward more resources that explore Celtic Witchcraft and spirituality. There is certainly a drive recently among Witching circles to connect our magical practises with our ancestral roots, and a desire to connect deeper with the spirits and deities of our land, which I believe is absolutely beautiful to see.

How to Use This Book

The main purpose of this book is to share the information that I have learnt over the years concerning the magical practises specific to my land. It is meant to act as inspiration and a springboard for you to enable yourself to forge your own pathway into your own unique studies. Much of what you will read in these pages has become the very foundation of my magical practise, and has empowered me to construct a Witchcraft that is wholly authentic to me.

Dotted throughout the book are a variety of exercises, spells, rituals, and meditative tasks. I urge you to try to partake in most, if not all of them. They will aid you in engaging with the material on a deeper, visceral level. You may choose to read through this book from cover to cover initially, and then come back to it so that you may immerse yourself fully in the practical elements provided. You know what works best for you, but I implore you to take full advantage of both the theoretical knowledge I share with you and the practical elements. Many of the spells and rituals are snippets of my personal grimoire, and I humbly present them to you. In saying that, however, I do not expect you to practise every single practical element included within this book exactly as instructed. The beauty of Witchcraft is that it is a deeply personal endeavour. I openly invite you to deconstruct the spells and rituals included, alter them to suit you and your desires. We all have a uniquely individualistic approach to magic, and adding that personal element will be highly beneficial to you.

This book acts as a springboard. Perhaps some of the topics mentioned within these pages are completely new to you, or perhaps they are areas of study you have already delved into before. Either way, I hope that my perspective on the topics at hand will inspire you to further your exploration. My words act merely as a guide, introducing you to them and, hopefully, enticing you to dig deeper. Once you have finished this book paw through the bibliography and the further reading section at the back. Find further resources to extend your knowledge. There is also a glossary at the back of this book of common Welsh words and names used throughout this book. The glossary provides tips on how to pronounce the words, as I am aware not all who read this book will be Welsh speakers.[1]

Open Practise

I would assume that most who felt drawn to this book have some form of connection to Wales, the culture, and the land in some capacity. However, when writing this book, I began pondering whether being Welsh, having Welsh ancestry or being immersed in the Welsh culture is at all important to exploring a Welsh Celtic spirituality. To put it simply and bluntly, no, it is not inherently important at all. Of course, it is beneficial, but not a necessity. I will not deny that being immersed in the culture will help propel a Welsh Celtic spiritual practise, but the Welsh Celtic culture is not a closed practise. Being Celtic in my view has very little to do with ancestry, blood, race, or location. Being Celtic is a state of mind, a way of living, a way of believing.

Unfortunately, the cruel and ridiculous notions of racism and elitism have found their way into modern Paganism lately, with certain individuals and groups attempting to fuel the notion that their race is somehow superior. I cannot abide this way of thinking; it is dangerous and wrong. I refuse to believe that a sense of racial superiority is simply a matter of personal opinion. No race or culture is superior; we are simply different.

Different, however, is when indigenous cultures and faiths deem their practise as "closed" practises, especially to the descendants of the people who oppressed and colonised their cultural practises to begin with. I completely stand by any cultures, traditions, and indigenous people across the world who wish to keep their practises closed to those outside the culture. However, as a Welsh woman, a native Welsh speaker, whose ancestors are mostly Welsh and who was born and bred in Wales, I welcome anyone. I

---

1. A guide to many of the Welsh language elements spoken about in this book will also be featured on my YouTube channel; search "Mhara Starling" on YouTube.

welcome any individual who wishes to partake in our culture, our traditions, our history, and our beliefs. To be perfectly honest, I completely believe that the more people who start not only acknowledging that Wales exists but who also explore and celebrate our traditions, practises, and ways of life, the better. It saddens me greatly when I come across people from across the world who barely know Wales is its own country, not to mention a country with its own language, cultural identity, and history.

Welsh Celtic Paganism, spirituality, and magic is open to you regardless of whether you have an ancestral link to our culture. Regardless of whether you speak fluent Welsh. Regardless of where you are in the world. Regardless of how you look.

I intended for this book and the practises spoken of within to be accessible to all. Whether you have ancestral links to any of the Celtic nations, or whether you feel intuitively drawn to the Celtic practises and beliefs despite having no known ties to the nations that are considered Celtic today. This book welcomes you with open arms, and sees you as wholly valid. If anything, as someone who lives and breathes within a modern Celtic culture, I thank you for showing this continuum such reverence and respect.

This book acts as my personal devotional offering to the spirits of my land, my ancestors, and those magical specialists of the past who continue to inspire, empower, and inform my practise daily.

✪ EXERCISE ✪
Constructing a Sacred Focal Space

Magical practitioners employ a variety of methods to aid the mind in concentration and focus. We are able to utilise tools such as wands that are an extension of our bodies, and a focal tool. We construct magical working circles in order to construct a metaphorical landscape within which our magical working is all that matters. A powerful element utilised in many a Witch's craft is the altar. Altars act as a focal point for our devotions and workings. Some practitioners construct altars in honour of certain spirits and deities they work with. Others construct altars as physical representations of their practise. Within this introductory exercise, you will construct an altar specifically to aid you in fully immersing yourself to the contents of this book.

Every altar should be unique to the practitioner that constructs it; therefore the instructions here may seem vague. That is entirely purposeful, as I expect you to fill in the gaps and employ your own unique perspective into constructing this focal space.

I recommend that the altar be somewhere that you can easily sit near, somewhere that you feel comfortable and capable of performing various exercises such as meditations, spell craft, and reflective exercises. The primary focus of constructing this altar is to create a focal point to aid you in performing the exercises and in reflecting on the topics discussed in this body of work.

Decorate the altar to your liking; however, in order to keep in touch with the practises we'll delve into, I suggest your altar include the following:

- A cauldron
- A wand
- A lantern or candle holders
- Candles

You may also find it useful to include something to burn incense in, and enough negative space to place this book down upon the altar when you are not reading it.

Once you have constructed the altar, return to it to perform the various exercises found throughout the pages of this book. Keep the altar up until you are done reading this book and exploring its themes.

Chapter 1
Finding a Welsh Witchcraft

This book has a predominant focus on Witchcraft, as Witchcraft is my area of expertise. I identify primarily as a Witch, a practitioner of magic. Witchcraft is an art to me, and I express myself through it. My Welsh identity and my identity as a Witch are not separate; they are connected by very intricate webs. My practise enables me to connect with my Welshness and Celticity; my Welshness and Celticity help me connect to magic which I engage with through the means of Witchcraft. Throughout this book you will see that I will discuss aspects of modern Witchcraft as well as Welsh Celtic Paganism and spirituality, and of course how to link the two things together. Before we begin to delve into the intricacies of Witchcraft, and how one might explore Witchcraft through a Welsh Celtic lens, let me begin by explaining in further detail how my personal spiritual and magical practises operate.

I do not adhere to the notion that labels are purely restrictive and harmful. As someone who holds her Welsh identity and her identity as a Witch with pride, as well as someone who found community and fulfilment in accepting and acknowledging the fact that I am transgender, labels have always been things of beauty and empowerment for me. It is easy to see labels as restrictive and negative when you do not rely on them for a sense of community and self-acceptance. But when you have grown up in a world thinking you are "broken," "wrong," or "strange," finding a label that helps solidify that no, you are none of those things, and in fact there are many others in this world who feel the same as you, is exhilarating. Yes, labels that have been imposed upon you by others' perceptions are very much harmful and negative. However, there is a big difference between someone placing you into a box and making judgements about who you are against your will, versus finding terminology that allows you to not only accept yourself, but also reach your true potential.

Therefore, I wear many labels with absolute pride. I am a Witch, plain and simple. I am personally not inspired to refer to myself in any other way such as "grey Witch," "kitchen Witch," or "green Witch," etc. However, I completely respect and admire those who find solace and comfort in those labels. Nevertheless, personally I am simply a Witch. Being a Witch to me means standing in my own intrinsic power, and connecting with the ancestral knowledge that has been passed down throughout my culture, my ancestry, and my land. Beyond being a Witch, I am also Welsh, which in turn of course means that I am Celtic. Being a *Cymraes* (a Welsh woman) gives me a similar sense of pride that being a Witch does. Historically the Welsh have been suppressed, ignored and overlooked and yet our language, our culture, and our land still stands proudly and boldly. When I go visit my mother and family and I hear the Welsh language trailing from their mouths with such ease and comfort, I cannot help but feel connected to something old, resilient, and powerful. Witchcraft provides those same emotions for me, and that is why I proudly and boldly call myself a Welsh Witch.

I am not Wiccan. Many assume these days that all Witches must be Wiccan, but that is far from true. Though my practise undoubtedly holds elements of Wicca, as Wicca was a pioneering religion in the resurgence of modern Witchcraft and helped set the building blocks for many Witches that would follow. I do not, however, align with the Wiccan religion. I have a reverence and respect for it, but my Witchcraft is very much a formulation of my own and is not tied down to any specific religion. Some might be tempted to compare my practise to that of traditional Witchcraft, and I would be inclined to agree that my methods of working align much more with that frame of mind. My practise is informed by the folkloric practises of my land, I often work with an entity known as the "Witches' Devil," and I do not adhere to the rules of more Neopagan traditions. Nevertheless, I still hold a few concerns over publicly referring to myself as a traditional Witch. To claim the term "traditional" in many people's opinion, is to imply a long-standing, old, and ancient tradition. I make no such claims. My grandmother was rumoured to be a Witch—she certainly practised divination and had an inclination toward magic—but none of my beliefs were passed down to me through a hereditary or cultural tradition. I very much formulated my practise entirely myself. It must be noted that "traditional" does not always necessarily mean an antiquated, ancient lineage of Witchcraft—no, traditional Witchcraft within my personal definition simply means that I incorporate elements of traditional folk magic, folklore, and beliefs that are specific to my native landscape into my craft.

I am a Welsh Witch, a *Swynwraig* who is informed by the rich folklore, mythology, and history of my land. My Witchcraft is rooted in a reverence for my culture, my native language, and the landscape in which I was raised.

What Is a Witch?

There is no one universally agreed-upon definition of what exactly a Witch is. The concept of the Witch will vary depending on culture, tradition, and personal belief. I must make it clear that whenever I discuss what exactly it means to be a Witch, it must be noted in the reader's mind that this is purely my own perception, experience, and belief. Those who turn to Witchcraft are often asked what exactly drew them to practise such a thing. For me, and for many others who are like-minded, Witchcraft is a form of empowerment and wisdom that we stand firmly and proudly within. Being a Witch to me means living a life of integrity, power, wisdom, and of course living with a constant thirst for knowledge. A Witch is not someone who wallows in self-pity, consumed and controlled by their inner demons. A Witch stares their inner demons in the eyes and says to them, "I am, and always will be, stronger than you." At its core, that is what Witchcraft has always been about. In various cultures around the world, Witchcraft was the art of the oppressed, the silenced, the unseen, and the judged. Witchcraft was an art that was utilised by those who felt they were powerless, to instil a feeling of control into their otherwise persecuted existence. It is no shock that those who are marginal-ised are heavily drawn to modern Witchcraft today: women, queer people, people of colour, anyone who has lived a life where an intrinsic aspect of who you are has evoked fear and confusion in the majority. I myself am a trans-gender woman, and Witchcraft does grant me a sense of empowerment that this life otherwise has not.

Witchcraft has always been associated with folk magic and folk customs. Rural areas have also often been associated with Witchcraft, Paganism, and Heathenism. To no surprise at all, the people and places largely associated with Witchcraft have often been the oppressed, poor, marginalised people and areas.

Some may believe that Witchcraft is an illusory tool to distract the oppressed from their ordeals and lack of privilege and power in the world. Yet, throughout history, those who wield privilege have feared the magical practises and beliefs of the very same folk they looked down their nose at. Why fear something that supposedly is not real? Why go to an extreme effort to try to stamp out a practise that yields no results? Perhaps the ruling classes were always aware of the power and potency of magic.

Witchcraft in some ways has always been a method of taking oppression, hatred, and intolerance and proving that despite the cards life may have dealt us, we still have power.

The Witch is a figure of fear, yet undoubtedly also one of power. Not power as in the same power that money, titles, and privileges grant you, but power of the hidden and secret arts. To be a Witch is to dance in the shad-ows, peel back the veil which most folk say you should never dare peel back, and to learn the hidden knowledge of the realms of spirit and of nature.

Though people feared the Witch, many also respected them. Local charm-ers, soothsayers, conjurers, and diviners were often approached to help folk in various ways. Whether it was to help with the crops, heal their ailments, divine the future and aid them in making decisions, or setting a curse upon their ene-mies. People travelled from all over to seek the help of a well-respected, com-petent magical practitioner.

Witchcraft speaks of a way in which humans connect to and engage with magic.

Magic has always existed throughout human history, especially in the British Isles and in communities of the modern Celtic regions, such as those of Wales. Magic exists all around us; it is a powerful spiritual energetic force that pulsates throughout the seen and unseen worlds. It is a connective energy, one that connects all life, all consciousness, and all energy together. Magic is not supernatural; it is the very essence and spirit of the natural world. By utilising an understanding of magic and practising magical arts such as Witchcraft, one can tap into this energy and inflict change in accordance with exertion of will. Everything in this universe is connected: you are connected to each and every person you pass in your day-to-day routine. A practitioner of magic knows this and uses it to their advantage.

Magic is not an inaccessible, complicated force that only a select few are capable of harnessing. We all have the potential to tap into our magic, our connection to the universe. There are various methods of engaging with magic, Witchcraft being one of the most common. Witchcraft is by nature a very folksy, accessible method of connecting to and engaging with magic. Modern Witchcraft is being fused today with the practises of more structured traditions of magic, and this may lead many to believe that in order to practise Witchcraft today you must own a certain array of magical tools, or learn about the magical uses of various herbs and stones. Though it is intensely useful to learn about correspondences, it isn't entirely required to practise Witchcraft. Witchcraft ranges from complex, intricately planned ritualistic methods of working right down to more simplistic methods. I have met Witches who plan their magical workings months in advance, ensuring they have the correct herbs and tools, and that they are working in accordance with the movements of celestial bodies such as the moon and stars. However, I have also met Witches who claim that their method of working is much less structured, some even stating that the most they do is light a candle and stare at it whilst projecting their desires into the universe. Regardless of the method, most of the Witches I know are adamant their spells work and so I find credence in all methodologies.

With Witchcraft being very much associated with poorer, dishevelled, and oppressed people throughout history, it is difficult to imagine that a large collection of expensive and handmade tools as well as a cupboard filled to the brim with as many herbs as possible are necessary to be a successful Witch. I like to imagine that most Witches of old would have used whatever was available to them at the time. My personal method of engaging with magic and practising Witchcraft is very much a modern mixture of ceremonial, ritualistic magic and more down to Earth, accessible, intuitive magic. I find joy in sometimes planning a magical working meticulously down to the last detail, colour coordinating my altar cloth and ritual attire as well as using the appropriate herbs. However, I also find great power and strength in spontaneous, informal, intuitive magic when and if the situation arises. Through personal experience, I would never argue that one method works better than another does; it simply depends on the nature of the working. Whatever the method of engaging with magic, the core reason one would turn to magic is usually that they desire to have a say in the outcome of a situation.

On the Topic of "Baneful" Magic

Many Witches today would lead you to believe that Witchcraft is very much pure, light, and ethically sound in nature. Countless books will teach you that most Witches have no interest in causing harm, and that if they do universal forces will rain down upon them negatively with great judgement. Whether they call it karma, the threefold law, or another spiritual ideology which imposes the notion that spells and magic used in anger or to harm another will be met with severe backlash, the basic notion is that Witches are timid, kind, and above all else are morally sound. However, history tells a completely different story.

Historically speaking, curses, hexes, and baneful magic are intrinsic elements of Witchcraft's history. Whether it be that within lore Witches cursed a person or household that offended them in some way, or whether people sought out a professional conjurer to curse their enemies, the Witches of the past were not afraid to weave their magic for either positive or negative means. Some may say that this is simply propaganda perpetuated by the church and other people in power who sought to stamp out Witchcraft and folk magic under the guise of spiritual enlightenment. However, there are numerous accounts of cunning folk and other occult and magical practitioners casting baneful magic in the name of a client who paid them for their services.

I believe it is of vital importance that modern Witches do not decide their views on topics such as baneful magic based on the rules and notions of prominent figures who established their own Neopagan traditions in the mid-twentieth century. Instead, I believe we should all be exploring morality and ethics for ourselves. Many people lean on concepts such as that of karma as proof that practises such as cursing, hexing, or casting what would be considered baneful magic is morally reprehensible and will result in some form of backlash to the practitioner. Karma is a belief system that has often been bastardised by modern Western spiritual methods of thinking to be some cosmic entity that punishes wrongdoers and rewards those who live a life that is morally and ethically sound. This is not the original meaning of karma, and as someone who is not from a culture that leans into the karmic belief systems I will not attempt to try and define the true meaning; it is not my place to do so. The issue with the idea that there is some cosmic entity existing somewhere in the universe judging each and every individual for their actions day by day, is that it is very similar to the idea of the Christian God. Many Witches leave certain religions, such as Christianity, only to then impose very similar ethics and values upon themselves but under a different guise. A Christian might refuse to hurt someone on the notion that it will send them to hell, a modern Witch who has been taught the ideology of the Western bastardised concept of karma will refuse to harm someone due to not wanting to be met with a negative reaction.

In no way am I implying that modern Witches should harm people through magical means. I am simply asking you, the reader, to consider ethics and morality. In my experience life does not operate in a purely good or bad, binary way. I believe any Witch should meditate on that and truly delve into their own views on the topic. Many modern Witches claim a reverence for the natural world, but the natural world can be undeniably cruel and harmful at times—but often the cruel nature of Mother Earth opens the door for things to improve. Within my personal practise I do not believe in the threefold law, karma, or in any ideology that perpetuates that there is a cosmic entity in the universe who is specifically judging my every move and deciding whether I will be rewarded or punished for it. I do curse, I do hex, when necessary and appropriate based on my own moral values. Of course, I do believe in cause and effect, and in connectivity; the idea that everything we do is connected to the rest of the universe. However, it is not as clear-cut as simply thinking curses are intrinsically bad or negative. As someone who has dealt with bigotry, hatred, and abuse, I am not ashamed of the fact that in the past I have worked what many would call baneful magic against my oppressors, abusers, and against the intolerant barriers that attempt to squash me down. I refuse to believe that utilising my magical art to fight against the aspects of my life I otherwise have very little control over is inherently evil. I also do not believe that throwing "love and light" at all obstacles will fix everything. Anger, sadness, grief, pain, and trauma are all immensely powerful energies that can be utilised beautifully in protective ways. The ways of my ancestors were not forged in love, light, bliss, and blessings; therefore, neither are mine.

Would many Witches agree with my morals? No, absolutely not. However, my practise is not theirs it is my own, just as yours is completely your own. You must decide your own moral values. I urge you not to follow rules and ethics set out by others; question morality, question the rules, meditate on them and come to your own conclusions and ideals. Knowing yourself is vitally important to most spiritual practises, and by questioning and constructing your own view on morality, you are in turn expanding your understanding of your own inner workings and solidifying your practise.

The Debate of Antiquity vs. Authenticity

Modern Witchcraft is a fickle thing. Many aspects of modern Witchcraft are sold to novice practitioners as "ancient" and "old," yet they are about as ancient as Coca-Cola or sliced bread. There is an obsession among many modern Witches with the notion that antiquity is the purest sign of authenticity. The older, more ancient a practise is, the more authentic and true it must be. This can be seen in the ways in which many state they turn to "traditional" Witchcraft rather than Neopagan religions such as Wicca because it is "older" and therefore more "authentic." However, authenticity and truth does not stem from whether something is antiquated and ancient.

As a Witch who draws most of her practises from studying the ways of the past, folk traditions and cultural practises tied to my ancestry, one might assume that I believe my path to be ancient, and traditional. However, my path is one that I have forged myself; it is as old as I am. I am inspired by my ancestors, by my culture, and by the Witches and magical practitioners who pioneered before me. Nevertheless, I am without a shadow of doubt a modern practitioner living in a modern world. I often fear that Witches of today are so caught up in antiquity, ancient beliefs, and traditions that they are ignoring the here and now. Witchcraft, just as anything else in this world, must evolve and adapt with the times, and it has. Very few practises utilised by Witches today actually stem from ancient Pagan antiquity despite what some may believe. However, does that make those practises any less authentic? Not at all.

A discussion on authenticity and antiquity is very much prominent and important when writing about Celtic spirituality. I will never claim in the pages of these books that I am attempting to discuss an ancient tradition of Welsh Celtic Witchcraft. Many of the things I discuss in this book may be inspired by folklore, history, and mythology of Celtic Wales, but I am presenting them as tools to help build and formulate a wholly modern, new tradition. Keeping in touch with the old whilst embracing and accepting the new.

Exploring Witchcraft in Wales

Welsh folklore and myth is steeped in magic, Witchcraft, and fairy lore, and now that we have explored Witchcraft in the broader context, we can narrow our focus onto the beliefs, legends, and tales of Witchcraft in Wales.

Witchcraft is not a religion; that I am certain is clear to most who might be reading this. As mentioned earlier, Witchcraft is a method in which people connect to and engage with magic, and that method is not restricted to a specific faith. Most modern Witches operate in a very Pagan method of working their magic and incorporating their beliefs into their craft; however, historically Witches and magical practitioners have come from all walks of life, all faiths and beliefs. Speaking of Wales specifically, most magical practitioners in Wales over the last millennium and a half would probably have been Christian, or operating in a very similar belief system to Christianity at least. In fact, many conjurers, wise men, and soothsayers of Welsh history were said to have achieved their magical abilities through divine intervention, prayer, and connection to God.[2] Wales' magical nature however, has also been associated strongly with its inherent Celtic Pagan past. Throughout history, English folk, as well as various invaders into Wales, have perceived Wales as being a dark, barbaric, and uncivilised place where old folk traditions that they believed survived from the pre-Christian era of Wales still persist to this day. A place where so-called "backward" practises are commonplace and Witchcraft both good and bad are practised freely.[3]

Witchcraft has long been associated with Paganism, though most of what we perceive as Witchcraft today stems from a period in time long after the Druids roamed the hills and mountains of Wales. However, it is not inherently necessary to be Pagan in order to practise Witchcraft. I personally operate in what can be described as a Pagan expression, as I pull inspiration mainly from Celtic Pagan practises and of course, from the mythology of my land which undoubtedly predate Christianity. However, there is nothing to say that a Witch could not practise without being Pagan.

Witchcraft is very much a practise or craft first and foremost, and your beliefs can either colour or play no role whatsoever in those practises. From a very Welsh way of thinking Witchcraft is an art, and just as with any form of art, it can be expressed in whatever way you deem fit. The most important thing about Witchcraft is that it remains authentic to who you are.

Most Witches today operate within a Pagan frame of thought, or at least that has been my personal experience. Especially within the world of Celtic spirituality, people wear the term "Pagan" with the utmost pride. It helps one feel a closeness with the ancient world, a time before the coming of Christianity to the shores of Britain. A time of tribal connections and unbound magic, where humans lived at one with the natural world, relying on nature to provide food, shelter, and sustenance. Though it is unlikely any Pagans of the ancient world actually referred to themselves as Pagan, it was a term

---

2. Hutton, *The Witch*.

3. Suggett, *A History of Magic and Witchcraft in Wales*.

coined by the Christian Roman Empire. Originally, it would have been a derogatory term used to denote that those who practised polytheism and refused to bow down to the newer Christian faith were lesser. In this modern day and age, Paganism is predominately used to describe Neopagan belief systems, the term denotes a belief in the power and divinity of nature, and most Pagans today are either pantheistic or polytheistic.

Welsh Celtic spirituality is very much mostly Pagan in nature today, with people who practise within a Welsh Celtic belief system turning to the deities found in Welsh myth, which have origins in Wales' pre-Christian past. The landscape of Wales makes it very difficult for one not to have a deep affinity for the beauty and power of nature, as the land is rugged and filled with natural wonders. Dotting the land are ancient monoliths and monuments, from burial chambers and cairns to standing stones and stone circles. It is easy to see Wales as a chiefly Celtic, Pagan country, though it must be emphasised that the standing stones and ancient structures found all over Wales pre-date the Celtic inhabitants of this land.

Wales is also strongly associated with Druidry, with *Ynys Môn* (or Anglesey) being the last stronghold of the Druids on the British Isles. The Romans wrote of the Druids of Anglesey with utmost fear and disbelief—if the Romans are to be believed, the Druids were wild, untamed, and delved into various fearful magics. With so many associations with ancient Paganism and the Druids of old, it is no wonder that most people who feel a pull toward Welsh Celtic spirituality fall deeply into modern Druidry.

As I have previously mentioned, my personal practise focuses mostly on Witchcraft and magic, as opposed to being druidic in nature. This does not necessarily mean I will not eventually allow myself to traverse down the path of Druidry. However, can one be both? A Druid and a Witch? I cannot think whyever not. It is a popular misconception that the difference between modern Pagan Witches and modern Druids, is that Witches practise magic whilst Druids do not. This is completely false. I have noticed through experience that Druids from Wales tend to be more inclined toward magic than their counterparts in England; however, magical practise blends beautifully into a Druidic practise. If we look to the mythology of Wales as well as the historical accounts of the Druids as recorded by the Romans, we will find that Wales is a land of magicians, sorcerers, and weavers of magic. I believe it would be somewhat foolish to attempt a connection with this land, this culture and ignore magic when it is so interwoven into the soil. Many of my friends who are Druids happily call themselves a Witch as well; as we touched upon earlier Witchcraft is not a religion. As an art or practise, Witchcraft can be intertwined into any belief system. One does not have to choose between being a Druid and being a Witch if they do not wish to.

Magical Specialists and the Terminology of Magic in Wales

The Welsh language holds a magic of its own, being a language that stretches back through the centuries and persevered throughout countless attacks. A practitioner of Witchcraft pulling inspiration from the Welsh Celtic cultural continuum might find it highly beneficial to incorporate the Welsh language into their practises. In this section, we will take a look at some of the magical terminology of Welsh magic and Witchcraft.

Magic is very much at the core of Wales' cultural history, which is not very surprising when one considers how the country's flag is literally a large and dramatic red dragon. Surprisingly however, it is somewhat difficult to discuss Witchcraft specifically in Wales, as the concept of a "Witch" is rather alien to the Welsh stream of thought. That is, the English concept of what the word "Witch" entails is difficult to attach to Wales. In fact, the Welsh language barely even has an adequate word for a "Witch." Some would argue that the Welsh word for Witch is *Gwrach*, as that is the term most commonly used among modern Welsh speakers and I have met very many a Witch from Wales over the years who identify as a *Gwrach*. I, however, do not find this term appropriate to describe a Witch, and historically the Welsh language agrees with me. Very rarely outside of modern novels and older fairy tales and folklore will you find any mentions of actual practitioners of magic in Wales being called a *Gwrach* or *Gwrachod*. The etymology of the word *Gwrach* shows us that historically this word originally meant "repulsive," "old," "ugly," and "odd."[4] *Gwrach* might have been a word that was used to

---

4. Bevan, *Geiriadur Prifysgol Cymru*, 1696.

describe hideous and foul creatures such as warty toads or slimy slugs. It also became a rather derogatory term for an elderly woman, very similar to "hag." A *Gwrach* when compared to the term Witch today is more specifically a term used to describe the fantasy, grotesque image of a Witch from fairy tales and was never historically used in accusations of Witchcraft or at trials. In fact, when the Witch hysteria hit Wales, albeit at much lower levels as mentioned earlier, Welsh courts took to calling accused Witches a "*Wits*" or "*Witsh*," an obvious adaptation of the English word Witch.[5] Despite the fact that the word Witch is a difficult one to express in the Welsh language, there are very many terms found in the Welsh language to depict a practitioner of magic and Witchcraft.

As a Welsh practitioner of magic who is also a native Welsh speaker, when conversing in my native Welsh I much rather refer to myself as a "*Swynydd*" or "*Swynwraig.*" *Swyn* in modern Welsh usage would translate roughly to mean "charm" though is often used to also mean "spell." It is an intrinsically magical term that encapsulates Welsh cultural magical practise. A *Swynydd* is someone who works magic, a very literal translation into English being "charmer," but fits much better than *Gwrach* would for a modern practitioner of Witchcraft. "*Swynydd*" being a gender-neutral term, as well as a plural form (charmers) for a charmer, with "*Swynwraig*" being feminine and "*Swynwr*" being masculine.

Witchcraft is another term that is somewhat difficult to fully translate into the Welsh language; however, there are a few words that fit beautifully. Among many of my Welsh-speaking circles, I have heard people translate *Witchcraft* into *Gwrachyddiaeth*, the prefix of that word being of course *Gwrach-*, which as we mentioned is used widely in modern Welsh to mean Witch but does not quite encapsulate what a Witch is. The suffix of the word being *-iaeth*, which is the Welsh equivalent of *-ology*, as in words such as *egyptology*. It is a term that works for those who are not of a Witching nature, but I much prefer the term *doethgrefft*, which literally translates to *wisecraft*, which goes well with the idea that Witchcraft is the "craft of the wise." In a modern Witchcraft context, *doethgrefft* is the best and most suitable term for

---

5. Suggett, *A History of Magic and Witchcraft in Wales.*

Witchcraft; however, there are alternatives that can be found in Welsh antiquity such as *Swyngyfaredd*.

We have already touched upon what *Swyn* is, and how a *Swynydd* is a charmer, or in modern terms would fit very well as meaning a practitioner of magic and Witchcraft. The name for the practise of utilising *Swyn* would be "*Swyngyfaredd*." In fact, most Welsh dictionaries today would translate "*Swyngyfaredd*" as meaning Witchcraft, sorcery, or magic. Therefore, if *doethgrefft* is not to your taste, "*Swyngyfaredd*" is another highly useful term that is quintessentially Welsh in nature.

Other terms for magical and occult practitioners in Wales include:

Dewin

A *dewin* in the modern Welsh usage is synonymous with the English term "wizard," and in most modern Welsh would be used as a literal translation for wizards. However, in Welsh a *dewin* can also mean a prophet, with the term being associated with numerous figures, from the infamous Merlin to the three magi of the biblical nativity tale.

Consuriwr

A *consuriwr* is a wise man, an occultist or practitioner who gains knowledge of magical and mystical practises through books and study. The word is a direct translation or loan word based on the English "*Conjurer.*"

Rheibiwr/Rheibes

This is a term that is used to speak of a Witch, sorcerer or magical practitioner who works baneful magic to harm others. *Rheibiwr* being male, and *rheibes* being female. They are often said to perform various bloody sacrifices and are often suggested to be working with the devil or similar demons.

Awenydd

An *awenydd* is much more similar to the oracles of ancient Greece, or soothsayers. They were individuals who would enter a trancelike state to aid people in making decisions or answering a question. The *awenyddion* were said to mutter phrases that would seem like nonsense while they were deep in trance, but from this nonsense, a message would be found for their clients. In modern usage, I have encountered a few Welsh people who refer to themselves as *awenyddion*, claiming it means they have a strong affinity to the concept of Awen, the energetic force of divine inspiration.[6]

Personally, I choose to identify myself as a *Swynwraig* who practises *Swyngyfaredd* or *doethgrefft*. These terms from Wales' folk magical history match the closest with a modern-day Witch.

✸ EXERCISE ✸
Knowing Thyself

Before we ever gain any adequate understanding of the world around us, and how we operate within it, we must first ask the question:

"Who am I?"

To know oneself is an integral aspect of any spiritual journey. We must remain conscious of the fact, however, that we evolve over time and our perspective of who we are can alter drastically. As we have already touched upon, labels can be exceptionally powerful things. Some despise labels for their restrictive qualities, whilst others find refuge in the spirit of kinship and compassion they can provide. Regardless of your opinion on labels, we all wear them day by day. We all have a label that we are proud of: mother, feminist, Witch, spiritualist, magician, etc. What this exercise aims to do is aid you in exploring who you are, and why you may choose to don certain labels. What power they might provide you, and what energies they evoke within the depths of your spirit.

For this exercise, you will need:

- A notebook and pen
- An envelope
- A calm, quiet environment
- An incense that you prefer to burn

---

6. Suggett includes a chart outlining the common terminology of magical practitioners in Wales in *A History of Magic and Witchcraft in Wales.*

Find a space that calms your mind, and make yourself comfortable. This may be an opportune time to utilise the altar you constructed in the first exercise found at the end of the introduction of this book. Take with you a notebook and pen. Light your favourite incense, and if you wish, make yourself a soothing cup of tea. The main goal is to enter a state of pure comfort and relaxation, a state that will allow you to ponder and reflect without allowing any distractions from the outside world to take grip of your mind.

Take a look at these questions:

1. Who am I?
2. What am I most proud of about myself?
3. What labels do I carry with me day by day?

Ponder over those questions for a moment. Close your eyes, take deep, healing breaths, and truly reflect on your answers.

Who are you? This is an exceptionally difficult question to answer, but rest assured; there is no right or wrong answer. This exercise is not a test; it is an insight into your inner workings. What thoughts, words, images, or memories does your mind evoke when asked the question of who you are? Without hesitation, write down your intuitive answers to that question.

What aspects of yourself are you most proud of? Reflect on all you have achieved in life. All the little and big things you have done that have led you to where you are now. Worry not about what society may think is a worthwhile thing to be proud of; answer honestly and sincerely. It is imperative that for the purposes of this exercise you remain honest, transparent, and authentic.

What labels do you carry with you day by day? This is a more thought-provoking question. Often, we do not think too much about our labels. We all have them, though. Perhaps a label you attribute to yourself is mother, sister, brother, or father. Perhaps the label you are most proud of is your profession; are you a nurse? A doctor? A teacher? Or perhaps you see yourself as a spiritualist, a Witch. Take heed of all the labels you carry with you day by day. Worry not about the labels others place upon you; focus solely on those labels you feel a sense of pride in and place upon yourself freely. Write them all down.

Finally, reflect on the labels you have listed as an answer to the last question, list them, and write a short sentence beneath each one that describes why those labels are important to you. For example:

Witch

Witches are empowered, strong, and consistently true to themselves.

Once you have finished writing the answers to these questions, and have finished the final task, do not read over your answers. Instead, tear out the piece of paper with your answers written on them and fold it up. Place it in an envelope and seal the envelope. Label the front of the envelope with the phrase "Who am I?" Then, place the envelope in a safe place where you will not easily lose it.

Come back to the envelope after some time has passed. It is up to you how long you leave it for. Perhaps you feel drawn to leave it for a week, a month, six months, or even a year. Whatever you decide is completely your prerogative. Read over your answers once time has passed, and reflect on how much you have changed. You may even feel inspired to repeat this exercise after reading your answers, and track how much you have changed. We are powerful beings with the ability to change our perspectives repeatedly. Knowing ourselves is exceptionally important to any spiritual practise, and self-reflection is a powerful took in aiding us to learn more about who we are as individuals.

The answers you wrote in response to those questions, if answered intuitively and authentically, provide an insight into who you believe yourself to be beyond the façades of day-to-day life. This exercise hopefully provides you with an insight into your own perspective of yourself.

To Live a Life of Enchantment

My practise is not a hobby or side project that I put on hold when the "real world" calls for me. Being a Witch, and a Welsh Witch at that, is ingrained into every aspect of my being. To live a life filled with magic and wonder is to live a life filled with joy. I believe it is imperative that Witches not only practise Witchcraft, but also live it. Fully living Welsh Celtic Witchcraft is consistently strengthening your connection to the land. It is seeing the magic in the everyday. It is feeling the power of the Awen day by day, in everything that inspires you and speaks to your soul. Ultimately, the primary focus of modern Welsh Celtic Witchcraft I believe should be a focus on sacred connectivity. To stand in your power as a Witch is to connect with the power of all Witches who have come before you. To stand in your power as someone who is drawn to Celtic spirituality is to connect with the resilience and strength of spirit found among the people of the various Celtic regions. Celtic magic is old, transformative, and accessible. A Witch who draws on the power of the Celtic cultural continuum is a Witch who senses these connections day in and day out. See the magic in the everyday, and live a life of pure enchantment.

Chapter 2

A Brief History of
Magic and Witchcraft in Wales

The Welsh Celtic cultural continuum has a long history of interesting and thought-provoking magical practises. The history of Witchcraft itself in Wales is one that is steeped in mystery, intrigue, and of course for a modern-day Witch, inspiration. We are at heart a culture that is inherently magical. For any magical practitioner wishing to embed aspects of Welsh Celtic magic into their practise, a grasp on the complex and intricate history of magic in the region is exceptionally beneficial. This chapter aims to outline a brief history of magic in Wales. Magic that is Celtic in nature.

I would first like to make it clear that I am not a historian, nor an anthropologist. I am purely a Welsh Witch who has spent many years delving into the rich folkloric and magical practises of my native land. Much of my understanding of the history of magic within this land-scape comes from what I have learnt over the years whilst living in the country, what I was taught about my country in school, and what I have read from reputable historians on the topic of Witchcraft and Paganism. My aim with this chapter is not to provide an exhaustive and compre-hensive history of magic and Witchcraft in Wales. That has already been done by those much more qualified than I am. What I aim to provide here is a brief outline of magical practises native to my land. I hope to inform you on the history of Welsh magic so that you may in turn inform your practise. I very much recommend, if the history intrigues you, that you continue to explore this topic via the works of renowned historians and anthropologists in the field.

What I can provide is an insight into the historical magic and Witchcraft found in Wales from the perspective of a modern-day Witch.

Pagan Wales

When one thinks of pre-Christian, Pagan Wales, the initial thought is likely to think of all things Celtic. However, it is important to note that Wales was not always Celtic. Pre-Celtic, prehistoric landmarks dot the country, from intricate burial chambers, to striking standing stone monuments that are just as impressive as the infamous Stonehenge in England. These striking megalithic monuments are an insight into the mysterious lives of the earliest inhabitants of this land. Unfortunately, very little is known regarding why these monuments were built, what exactly they were used for, nor how the people of that time lived or what they believed. I would wager a guess, however, that these monuments made from enormous slabs of stone, and the soil of the land, is proof that the people of prehistoric Wales had a deep connection to their landscape. Around the period of 1000 BCE, the Celts arrived in Britain and the culture of Wales shifted to become the Celtic history we appreciate today.[7]

It would be near impossible, and rather shortsighted to explore magic and Witchcraft in Wales without first mentioning the Pagan history of this Celtic land. The leading figures in the history of Paganism in Wales of course were the infamous Druids. Druids existed in most Celtic regions in the pre-Christian era. They were learned, important figures who acted as spiritual advisors, community leaders and were commended for being exceptionally knowledgeable and wise.

---

7. Green & Howell, *Celtic Wales*, chapter 2.

The Isle of Anglesey, or Ynys Môn, is believed to have once been a centre of Druidic studies between 100 BCE and 60 CE. It is theorised to be a place where Druids from all across Europe took a pilgrimage to in order to learn and develop their skills and knowledge. Ynys Môn certainly feels like a place that was held as a highly sacred place. Even today, the island is packed to the brim with natural wonders, and a magic of its own. Even if Môn was not a centre for Druidic study, it is certainly considered one of the last great strongholds of the Druids of Britain. The ancient Roman historian Tacitus wrote a detailed account of a great battle around 60 CE, between the Romans and the Druids of Anglesey.[8]

The Druids were not considered meek, mild old men as one would imagine spiritual leaders to be today.[9] No, Roman accounts speak of how the Druids stood at the forefront of the battles, leading their people into exhilarating fights. Tacitus wrote of how the Druids evoked immense fear among the Roman armies, a feat in and of itself. How powerful and scary must one be to strike fear in the hearts of the soldiers of Earth's most potent armies at the time? The Druids were said to throw curses, spells, and magical attacks at the Romans. Thrashing their bodies wildly, praying to their gods and making sacrifices upon the shores of Môn in an attempt to send the army on their way.

Unfortunately, for the Druids and the inhabitants of the island, the Romans broke through their fear and charged onto the island, triumphing over their "barbaric" enemies. Accounts speak of numerous blood-stained altars across Anglesey, where the Druids conducted their gruesome magical rites.[10] The Romans eradicated the Druids after the battle of Anglesey.

It must be remembered that the victors often write history. Unfortunately, Druids operated in an oral tradition and nothing of substance is truly recorded about them beyond the accounts of the Roman invaders. Even today among many historians and anthropologists, there is a shroud of mystery surrounding Druids and their ways. People often refer to how the Romans mentioned bloody sacrifices carried out by the Druids; however, there is very

---

8. Green & Howell, *Celtic Wales*, chapter 3.

9. Ibid.

10. Hutton, *Blood and Mistletoe*, chapter 4,

little historical evidence beyond the Romans' word to truly authenticate that they did indeed practise sacrifice on the regular. The Romans sought to eradicate the Druids from power, and supposedly succeeded in eradicating them from existence too. It is doubtful they would ever speak highly of their enemies, and it may be that their prejudices and fearmongering aided in propelling their soldiers to easily eradicate them, committing mass genocide on the shores of Wales.

We may never fully understand the ancient Druids, their ways and practises. However, if the records by the Romans are anything to go by we do know that they were spiritual leaders, magical practitioners, and had a closeness to the gods of the old world that regular folk did not have. The ancient Druids continue to inspire many modern Pagans and Witches today, and many modern interpretations of Druidry exist worldwide.

Welsh Magical Specialists

Wales may have lost its Druids and its old ways in the wake of the Roman invasion. However, the loss of the Druids did not mean that Wales became a land devoid of magic. Magical practises were still very much commonplace in Wales in the centuries to follow. Magical specialists existed across Wales and sometimes folk would travel far and wide, even from England, to seek audience with renowned soothsayers and magical specialists who would aid them in cursing their enemies. Let us take a look at some of Wales' most notable types of magical specialists.

Awenyddion

Just as many in our modern day and age seek out psychics to help them make decisions, people of history did so too. Particularly in Wales, there were people known as "*awenyddion*," meaning "the inspired people." The *awenyddion* were similar to soothsayers, or oracles. People would travel to seek an audience with an *awenydd* in hopes that they would help them divine an answer for them. Perhaps people would come to them with their burning, most difficult questions and decisions in life. Their methodology of divining was unique and interesting; they would enter a trancelike state, and would move as if possessed by a spirit or divine entity. This was undoubtedly terrifying and intriguing for the clients. As they shook and moved with unnatural, spiritual movements, they would shriek and scream all manners of words and prophecies, which at first would make absolutely no sense to the client. Within these mumbles, shrieks, and screams, however, one would find an answer to their question. The knowledge the client desired would be deciphered from the babbling. The *awenyddion* were, for the most part, Christian, with most claiming that their powers came from divine intervention. They were gifted the ability to divine the future due to their unwavering piety to their god. They would often call upon the holy trinity as well as various saints before divining for their clients.[11]

Swynydd

The *Swynydd*, which can also be referred to as simply *Swyn*, were the standard folk who were learned in various magical practises, divination, healing and herbal arts. *Swynydd* were very much what one might think of when we speak of the wise men and women who lived in the community and helped their neighbours through magical means. Most *Swynydd* had ordinary jobs, weaving clothing or wool, making butter and cheese and so forth. One fine example of a *Swynydd* is Gwen ferch Ellis,[12] the first woman to have been executed for Witchcraft in Wales. Gwen ran a market stall selling linen cloths, which she spun herself. Beyond her mundane wares at her stall, she would also dispense tinctures, poultices, and potions from her market stall. These concoctions were used to help heal ailments, predominately animal ailments; many farmers took the healing potions for their livestock. Gwen never asked for money in return for her concoctions; instead it was very much an "I help you, you help me" system. The folk who took her healing medicines were kind enough to return the gesture in the form of food, clothing, and the likes. As well as these poultices and potions, Gwen also helped people find lost

---

11. Hutton, *The Witch*.

12. The word *ferch* means "daughter" in the Welsh language. Historically, Welsh children followed a patronymic naming system, meaning they took their father's name as a surname. Daughters would be (Name) ferch (Father's name) and sons would be (Name) ap/ab (Father's name). So, Gwen is Gwen ferch Ellis: Gwen *the daughter of* Ellis. You will see this often in this book, in names such as: Gwyn ap Nudd, or Mabon ap Modron.

objects and would heal the sick through the use of spoken charms. Gwen stated herself that she learnt the power of charming via her older sister.[13]

A *Swynydd* is probably the most similar magical specialist from Welsh history to a modern-day Witch. This is why I personally refer to myself as a *Swynydd* or *Swynwraig* (female *Swynydd*). A much more flattering term than the misconstrued, repulsive term *Gwrach*.

The *Swynydd* of Wales can be compared to the charmers that operated throughout Britain, though a significant difference being that *Swynydd* tended to be learned in various magical arts, and as such were in some ways a fusion of charmers and cunning folk. However, as the name *Swynydd* suggests, they were very well known for their use of *Swynion*: spells or charms.

The use of charms can be found throughout Britain, and a detailed look into charms and how to utilise them will be provided later in this book. Charms were spoken prayers or incantations used mostly for healing both humans and animals. Charmers usually had their own specific method of utilising the charm, whether simply speaking the charm aloud, writing them onto pieces of paper, or rubbing an afflicted area whilst chanting the charm. Many charmers learnt their charms hereditarily, usually with the charms being passed down from mother to child. The prayers were very much Christian in nature, though sometimes you would find certain lines from the charms that seem archaic and as though it were some form of survival of a pre-Christian prayer.

These are but two examples of magical specialists found throughout Wales' history. These people served their communities well, healing the sick and providing much-needed magical services.

The Witch Hunts in Wales

We are all aware of the Witch hysteria that ravaged Britain, Europe, and of course various locations in America, such as the infamous Salem. It is difficult to read about the cruelty inflicted upon innocent people due to what we in the modern world might consider unfair and nonsensical superstition and fear. The way in which accused Witches were often tortured via excruciating

---

13. Suggett, *A History of Magic and Witchcraft in Wales*.

methods causes one's skin to crawl and can evoke feelings of sadness and anger. We are privileged in this day and age to be able to stand firmly in our practises with pride, never truly having to fear persecution for simply doing what sets our soul afire. Wales, like most of Europe, does have a history of Witchcraft accusations, trials, and executions. However, the history of Witch hunting in Wales is one that often baffles scholars in the field of Witchcraft in late medieval and early modern Europe. Let us delve into the complex world of Witch hunting, the trials and the executions in Wales as well as some of the beliefs and practises surrounding Witchcraft and magic among the Welsh.

To the shock of many, Wales was relatively untouched by the Witch craze that had a firm and deadly grasp on England and the lowlands of Scotland around the seventeenth century. People were very rarely accused of Witchcraft in Wales, fewer still went on trial, and again even fewer were convicted and executed. The very few cases of Witch trials in Wales has left very many academics and scholars scratching their heads in confusion for a very long time. Wales borders England, a country torn to shreds by the mass fear surrounding Witches and their supposed evil deeds. Why then, was Wales left virtually untouched?

It is worth emphasising once more, that Wales did not even have a definitive grasp of what exactly a "Witch" was in the same way England did. In England the definition of what a Witch was, who could be a Witch, and what they did was clear and concise. Yet, Wales struggled to fully understand the notion of Witches. This is clear in the fact that when, on the rare occasions, Witch trials were held and held in Welsh at that, those accused of being a Witch were not accused of being a *Gwrach*, which is what most modern Welsh speakers would say is "Witch" in Welsh. Instead, those accused of being Witches were referred to as a "*Wits*" or "*Witsh*." This was an obvious borrowing of the English *Witch*.[14]

However, why were Witch trials so very rare in Wales compared to England and other European countries of this time? The answer to that question can be summarised as: Wales was a very different place with a very different culture. Just as it is today.

---

14. Burns, *Witch Hunts in Europe and America*, 315.

Welsh folk of the late medieval period through to the early modern period, especially those living in rural Wales, had a very strong belief in what we would now understand to be fairies. In our modern world, it is easy for us to see fairies as wonderfully whimsical creatures, small and dainty, beautiful and elegant. When one mentions the word *fairy* today, it evokes imagery of Tinker Bell from J. M. Barrie's *Peter Pan*. We envision lovely and delicate flower fairies with their butterfly wings and flower petal skirts. The fairies of Wales' history, however, were vastly different. Fairies were mischievous, scary, and downright violent at times. The belief in fairies and their mischief was much more extreme in Wales than in England. People went out of their way to protect themselves from the fae, or at the very least do as much as possible so as not to offend them. The belief in fairies in Wales could have played into why Witch trials were so rare in Wales. In England, if your livestock suddenly fell dead, or if your child was struck with a sudden strange fever, it was easy to blame those things on the evil doings of Witches who were in league with the devil. In Wales, however, these sudden bouts of rotten luck and unexplained events were more likely to have been blamed on the fairies.[15] One would assume that they might have offended the fae in some way, and so they would focus their energies on protecting themselves for the future rather than trying to blame a local individual who was a bit of an outcast.

Another explanation, and one that makes the most sense to me, is that Welsh folk understood magic to be very different to the Church of England's concept. Throughout England it was very much believed that all forms of magic, whether done for good or bad, were primarily the work of the devil and therefore worthy of being stamped out of existence. In Wales, however, the *Swynydd*, the charmers and the diviners, were respected and loved by their communities. Those who practised *Swyngyfaredd* were a vital part of the community. Offering healing charms, helping to find lost items, and making ointments and potions for sick animals. Many of these magical specialists were very much Christians, attending church and even calling upon God, Jesus, and Mary in their charms and incantations. It would be difficult

---

15. Hutton, *The Witch*.

for the Welsh to perceive these prominent and vital figures in the community as harmful Witches.

It must be said however, that in the few cases of Witch trials and executions there are in Wales, many of those convicted tended to have a history of being charmers, healers, and diviners.[16] Usually, they would be accused of using their magical abilities to harm someone, or curse someone in some capacity. Being accused of Witchcraft was very rarely done on a whim in Wales. It would be the outcome of an accumulation of accusations and incidents that led people to being accused of Witchcraft. It is not as simple as the narrative of the lonely, eccentric widow being blamed for someone's misfortune that we have come to envision when thinking about the Witch hunting of England, Europe and America.

It is also interesting to note that the places which Witch trials were more common in Wales tended to have a higher population of English folk living there. Highly anglicised areas were more likely to be struck by numerous Witchcraft allegations.[17] This denotes that a belief in malicious, evil Witchcraft was much more commonplace among the English than the Welsh. It was also more likely for a local charmer to be accused of Witchcraft after going to the aid of higher-class, rich folk rather than staying within their poorer community, as was the case with the first Witch to be executed in Wales, Gwen ferch Ellis.

The people of Wales were very obviously under the belief that magic could be utilised for healing, blessings, and good things. They did not view all forms of magic as purely satanic and evil. *Swynwyr* were vital parts of Welsh communities, providing their charms, ointments, and divining skills to the common folk.

Dynion a Gwragedd Hysbys

Following in the tradition of the *Swynydd*, and the charmers of past, the eighteenth and nineteenth century saw a rise in cunning folk. The idea of who and what the cunning folk were matches identically with the *Swynydd*; they

---

16. Ellis, "Conjurations, Enchantments and Witchcrafts."
17. Hughes, *Cerridwen*, 111.

were members of the community who offered magical services. Cunning folk would usually offer all manners of services from finding lost possessions, divining the future, providing counter-magical talismans and spells to ward off curses and hexes brought on by malicious Witches, and even occasionally cursing your enemy for you. In Wales, cunning folk were known as "*Dynion a Gwragedd Hysbys*" meaning "Cunning men and women" (*Dynion* is the Welsh word for "men," whereas *Gwragedd* is the Welsh word for women). Male cunning folk were much more common than their female counterparts, and so the term *Dyn Hysbys* (cunning man) is seen much more frequently than *Gwraig Hysbys* (cunning woman).

Cunning folk were usually exceptionally learned, boasting grand collections of numerous books pertaining to the occult, astrology, astronomy, herbalism, and magic. Many believed that cunning folk gained their magical skill from their bountiful books. Keeping a journal or a personal grimoire was a common practise for cunning folk. In Wales, their journals were dubbed as a *Llyfr Cyfrin,* which translates to *Mystic Book* or *Book of Secrets.* Within their journals, they would keep their most useful charms, spells, and folk magical knowledge. Heredity was no issue within the cunning folk practises, as most learnt their craft themselves through the means of books rather than it being a practise passed down through family.[18]

Among modern Pagans and Witches, cunning folk are often referred to as being the Witches of the past. Modern Witches do very much practise in a very similar way to the cunning folk of the past; however, cunning folk certainly did not see themselves as Witches. In fact, cunning folk were often perceived as being the enemy of Witches. Providing the common folk with charms, spell bottles, talismans, and blessed objects that would help to protect them from the influences of Witches. Nineteenth-century folklorists labelled cunning folk as "white Witches"; however, no cunning folk nor their clients actually referred to themselves as such. It was more common that they would refer to themselves as wizards.[19]

---

18. Hutton, *The Triumph of the Moon,* 91.
19. Hutton, *The Triumph of the Moon,* 85.

Modern Witchcraft in Wales

In his spectacular and deeply important book *"Triumph of the Moon,"* Ronald Hutton briefly touches on a magical tradition in Wales based on the isle of Anglesey. This magical tradition predates Wicca, and the very little information we have of it is riveting and intriguing. The group supposedly operates within different circles, meeting together at sacred ancient sites across the island. The group is said to have worshipped Gwydion, as well as his three divine sons. Learning of this group via reading Hutton's work was jaw dropping for me as a Witch who comes from the isle of Anglesey. I had never heard of them, yet once I began asking my family and friends suddenly more and more people mentioned they had heard of them. From what I understand, the group was called *Cylch Cyfrin*, which translates to mean "The Mystic Circle." The rumours and whispers surrounding the group make them out to be a secret Pagan cult—run exclusively by powerful women, who were often feared by locals across the island to be Witches. In reality, according to those who have met members of the group in the past, the group is supposedly much less formal and organised. What can be ascertained is that *Cylch Cyfrin* certainly existed, whether as an organised cult full of magical practitioners that spans back deep into the nineteenth century, or as an informal post-war collective. The group would certainly appear to be Druidic and Celtic in their expression, having Gwydion as their main point of worship.

What truly intrigues me are the more sinister rumours surrounding the group. Hutton describes in *Triumph* how the group were said to have made a powerful powder concoction of local plants, which was blown into their enemies' faces. This sinister powder would induce cardiac arrest in the victim, killing them almost instantly. This is unlikely to be true, and probably purely fearmongering. Yet still deeply intriguing and wild that a group might have been feared so intensely.

Local lore maintains that *Cylch Cyfrin* did indeed meet at sacred sites, lakes, and holy wells. Specifically, they were known to meet at *Mynydd Bodafon* (Bodafon Mountain) and had at least a handful of incantations and spells within the tradition.[20]

---

20. This is local lore, as maintained by some inhabitants of Anglesey today.

What this shows is that magical traditions and practises continued even into twentieth-century Wales. Highlighting that the fire that is Welsh magic is thoroughly inextinguishable. Traditions and practises may change, evolve, and move with the times, but they are still here and still very much alive.

During the latter half of the twentieth century, Wicca took a hold on Britain and various covens began operating throughout England and Wales. This continued through to the twenty first century. I know via local knowledge that while I was growing up on the isle of Anglesey there were at least two formal covens within driving distance from my home.

In modern Wales, Witchcraft and magic can be found everywhere. Whether you find a spiritualist expression in the development circles and groups held in village halls and churches around the country or you venture into the moots held at local pubs. Modern Wales has its handful of Witches, Pagans and magical practitioners. It saddens me somewhat, that in my personal experience most Witches within Wales know very little of the magical legacy Wales holds. I have met numerous practitioners who work with Greek, Egyptian, and even Irish deities and have very little to no knowledge of the continuum of myth, magic, and Witchcraft we have here on our very shores. That is one of the primary forces that set me onto the task of writing this book. My hope is that more and more Welsh Witches will yearn to learn more of their culture and local practises. I also wanted this information to be known to the world, and so if you are reading this from across the sea I thank you heartily for allowing the magic of the Welsh into your heart and mind.

Welsh Traditional Witchcraft

Most modern Witches in Wales operate within either a purely eclectic, solitary method or Wiccan form of practise. This is how I began my path into Witchcraft, by initially being as eclectic and well-rounded as possible. In my teens, I was very much intrigued by Wicca, though very quickly moved away from Wicca to practise a more solitary form of magic. Nevertheless, I always felt that something was amiss. I read the books of pioneers in English and Cornish traditional Witchcraft and thought how remarkable it was that they were pulling inspiration from their local folkloric and magical history.

I wished and hoped for the same within the Welsh context. Lo and behold, it is certainly possible to practise a craft that is wholly Welsh.

As I said earlier in this book, I am somewhat cautious about calling myself a "traditional" Witch as that implies a sense of heredity. However, traditional does not necessarily need to mean hereditary or passed down. At a local moot a few years back, we discussed what exactly "traditional" might mean when within the context of Witchcraft. We concluded that traditional purely means that something must be repeated and passed on by word of mouth to someone else.

As this entire chapter has proven, Wales has an extraordinary amount of magical history. I learnt about the history of magical practise in Wales through reading, learning, and practising, as well as via meeting wonderful Witches and Pagans in Wales. Now I am passing on the knowledge I have collected to you.

My personal practise today, my magical art, is inspired and influenced by the magic and Witchcraft of Wales' past. Is my practise traditional in the sense that I practise exactly what my Welsh ancestors practised before me? Not remotely. However, I am using what resources I have to revive the traditions of the past. Fusing the knowledge I have of traditional forms of magical practise with a devotion for the myths and deities of Wales.

It has been proven time and time again, that many practises today that label themselves "traditional" are very unlikely to be surviving continuous practises from antiquity. Much of what we see as traditional today is revisionist in nature, a reconstruction of what has been to suit modern sensibilities. Even the modern Druids of Britain do not claim an ancient lineage; much of their practises come from the reconstruction of Druidism by figures such as Iolo Morganwg. However, antiquity does not equal authenticity; a practise or tradition can be completely devoid of any ancient legacies and yet still be completely authentic.

So, what would Welsh traditional Witchcraft be? Quite simply, it would be Witchcraft that is drawing on the folk magic practises and magical traditions of Wales' past. To be a Welsh Traditional Witch today is to follow in the footsteps of the *Swynwyr*, the cunning folk, the Druids of old, and the charmers, utilising the resources we have possible to revive a Witchcraft that is wholly Welsh in nature.

To walk the path of the Welsh Witch is to connect with the land, learn about and honour the Welsh spirits and deities, and utilise our knowledge of Welsh folk magic.

✹ EXERCISE ✹
Honour Those Who Came Before

As modern magical practitioners, we are the accumulation of a continuum of individuals who have practised magic before us. We often read their teachings, their knowledge, and their experiences to help inform and construct our own practises. As we have touched upon in this chapter, history is rife with various practitioners who went by many titles and labels, and worked in a variety of expressions. We feel the influence they have had on our modern magical practises day by day. There is a great strength and power to be had in honouring their magical endeavours and explorations, in understanding all that we owe them for aiding in expanding the conversation on magic today. Witches, conjurers, cunning folk, healers, wise folk, wizards: They have all paved the way throughout the centuries and illuminated the path ahead for those of us today. In time, we will also influence, inform, and inspire a new generation of magical practitioners. Just as we honour our ancestors of blood and bone, we may also choose to honour those who paved the way for our magical traditions and practises.

This ritual exercise aims to provide a base ritual, which you can alter as you deem fit, to honour those who came before, those magical pioneers we owe so very much of our practises to. Those who inspire us, and provided us with an abundance of essential knowledge. This ritual can be utilised as a complete ritual in its own right, or could be incorporated as an enhancer to spell work, or other rituals.

Step 1: Take yourself away to a place that is special to you. Witches work their magic best in liminal spaces, and in spaces that they feel at full ease and comfort. You may choose to take yourself to a place that you know has a history of magical practise: an ancient monument, an old churchyard, a dense forest. However, the beauty of this ritual is that it can be done wherever and whenever. Even within the comfort of your own home.

Step 2: Once you have found your working space, make yourself comfortable and prepare yourself for magical working. Breathe deeply, close your eyes, and allow yourself to enter a magical mind set. When you feel ready, with your eyes still closed, flood your mind with the knowledge you have of magical specialists and practitioners of the past. Utilise the information you have read within this chapter. Think of the cunning folk whom common, mundane folk would employ to find lost objects, break baneful magic cast upon them, or ward their homes from negative magical attacks. Think of the wise women and charmers whom people employed to aid in healing their ailments. Think of the awenyddion, the soothsayers people travelled from far and wide to seek an audience with so that they might bestow wise prophecies unto them in order to aid them in making decisions. Spend a few minutes breathing deeply and filling your mind's eye with visions of what these magical specialists gave unto their communities. How particularly important they were to the common folk who could not afford to go to conventional doctors or physicians. Consider what integral aspects of the community these people were. Above all else, consider how the workings and knowledge of these folk have influenced and aided modern magical practitioners to pioneer the practises you utilise today. The strength of their magical specialism has been carried down to you. You are influenced by their ways. You now carry the torch they once did. When you feel that you have spent enough time pondering over these images and concepts, light your white candle and say aloud:

I light this candle in honour of those who came before me,
The magical specialists who paved the way for my practises to exist.

Step 3: Now is the time to call upon those specialists who came before you to aid in enhancing your magical competency and potentiality. To utilise yourself as a channel which the information, wisdom, and knowledge they acquired over their time of practising and aiding their communities may flow through and into the world. You carry the mantle now. Raise your arms skyward and say with pride:

I call upon the knowledge, the wisdom, and the power
of those who came before me.

Witches, cunning folk, Druids, prophets, and soothsayers of old.

Be here with me,

Aid in my magical workings this night.

I channel your wisdom and knowledge,

I honour your influence on our modern magical practises.

I carry the mantle; I now continue the work you once gave so
much of yourself to.

Be here with me,

Enhance my competency and skill.

Be here now.

Feel the energies of those who came before joining you. Their spirit surrounding you, enhancing your magical workings. You are tapping into the continuum of magical specialists who pioneered this legacy of magical practise. Sense their influence in your everyday workings, and honour their contributions to magic, as we know it today.

As mentioned before, this ritual may be utilised on its own, as a standalone ritual that aids in empowering you to embrace those webs of connectivity that flow between you and magical specialists of old. Alternatively, this ritual can be added into any other ritual or magical working as a means of enhancing your work. Pair it with the rituals found in the practical Welsh Witchery chapter later in this book for potent, powerful magical workings.

The important aspect of this ritual is to empower you to stand firm in the knowledge that you are one of the latest in a continuum of magic workers and weavers who have been an integral part of many communities across the world for centuries. Their knowledge and wisdom helped to formulate the practises we as modern Witches utilise today, and their spirit can be energetically tapped into in order to enhance your practises.

Chapter 3

The Sacred Landscape

Hiraeth. It is a Welsh word that is exceptionally difficult to translate fully. Because it is not simply a word, it is a feeling, an emotion. *Hiraeth* might be translated in dictionaries as being homesickness, nostalgia, or yearning. However, *hiraeth* is so much more. *Hiraeth* is that intense feeling of a depth of connection to a place, time, or emotion that is either just out of reach or lost to you. I feel *hiraeth* when my feet do not rest upon the shores of my island home. Being in Wales is a feeling like no other. It is home. It is sacred. It is magic. You can also feel *hiraeth* however, for a place that you have never been. I often meet people from outside of Wales who seem to be adamant that they "miss" the sacred landscape of Wales regardless of whether they have been here or not. Some may attribute this feeling to past lives, or ancestral ties. Regardless of why people feel this intense *hiraeth*, Wales is undoubtedly a country that has an extraordinarily sacred landscape.

This chapter will explore the sacred landscape of Wales. A connection to the land is an intrinsic element of my practise, and I would like to share that with you. This book deals with an exploration of folk magic, myth, and lore that originates in what is today known as *Cymru*, or Wales. In order to truly understand the intricacies of the practises, the magic, and the legacies of myth that permeate the practise of the Celtic

Witch, it is first important to have at least a decent understanding of the Celtic landscape.

The land of the red dragon is a land of pure beauty. With mountains that pierce into the skies above, beaches and coastlines that boast geological structures to take one's breath away, and deep, dark forests where one would expect to easily fall through a portal into a magical fairy dimension with ease. Wales has everything.

Wales is a country, a Celtic country filled with people who are proud of their culture and heritage. Sitting to the West of England, with the Irish Sea on the Northern and Western parts, Wales is truly a unique land. Language is at the heart of what makes Wales so unique. The Welsh language, after all, is boasted as being one of Europe's oldest surviving languages.

Every inch of Wales is steeped in myth, magic, and legend. With a landscape so rugged, untamed, and impressive it is no wonder that the ancient folk of this land were so inspired to tell tales of mystical beings, ferocious beasts, and courageous heroes.

Even some of the most popular myths and legends worldwide have their origins in this land. The legends of King Arthur and the great wizard prophet Merlin, known in Welsh as Myrddin, stem from here.

As magical a land as Wales may be, it is sad to think that the country is often overlooked and misunderstood. Often misunderstood as being simply a "part of England," the Welsh identity is often belittled. I remember the shock and confusion of many of my friends from overseas when I explained to them that Wales is indeed its own country, with its own Celtic language, culture, and history that is very much separate from England. Even among those with an affinity for all things Celtic, Wales seems to be among the least popular of Celtic nations. A simple internet search of books detailing Celtic Paganism will reveal that numerous resources are available detailing Irish Celtic spirituality, and almost the same can be said of Scottish. Yet, finding very much information regarding Welsh Celtic Paganism and spirituality is rather difficult. Regardless, Wales is a resilient nation. After centuries of suppression and of being overlooked, you would expect the culture, language, and identity of the Welsh to have been snuffed out by now. Yet we are still here, still proud, still singing the songs of our ancestors and telling the tales of our land.

I am proud to have the privilege of sharing the culture of my ancestors, and my hope is that this book helps those with a connection to Wales to further their interest and learn more of our rich cultural heritage. This land is one that teems with powerful mythology, quirky folklore, and a magic that is wholly unique. In this section of the book, we will explore the magical landscape of Wales. From the tales of the Mabinogi, to the fairy tales that fill me with great delight. From the sacred lakes and wells, to the magic of the Welsh language. This chapter will provide an insight into the magic of Wales as a nation, and how you can connect with it, regardless of where you might be in the world.

What Does It Mean to Be Celtic?

The culture and language of Wales is Celtic. However, what exactly does it mean to be Celtic? Contrary to popular belief, the term "Celtic" does not refer to any particular bloodline or race of people. There is also no such thing as one homogenous Celtic culture. The term Celtic refers to an array of diverse cultural groups found scattered around various parts of northwest Europe. The only thing that connects Celts to one another is language and certain shared cultural practises. The Celtic languages are split into two distinct groups, Gaelic and Brythonic. I have heard numerous people outside of Welsh culture imply that Welsh is a "Gaelic" language or culture, but that is not true. The Gaelic languages refer to the native language of the people of Scotland, Ireland, and the Isle of Man. Welsh is a Brythonic language, just like Cornish and Breton, which can be found in Cornwall as well as in Brittany in the northwest of France. We are all Celtic: Ireland, Scotland, Wales, Cornwall, and the Isle of Man along with various other areas in northwest Europe. We all have cultural similarities, and our languages are part of the same family. Aside from these connections however, there is very little else to connect Celts. There is no standard way a Celt will look, despite what some people may believe. We are a collection of tribes who migrated across many lands over time. The Celtic culture is not stagnant or attached to any single location today. There are people with a connection to the Celts across the world. Due to the nature of Celts being more so a cultural group connected by language, modern Celtic spiritualties are open for all to explore. You do not need any specific ancestry or blood relations to connect with what it means to be Celtic.

The word Celtic is pronounced with a hard "k" sound at the beginning. As in: "Kell-tick."

Connectivity to Land

A vital aspect of my personal practise, my magical art, is a strong connection to the land I am on. I would be as bold to say that connectivity to the land in which you are residing is a vital element of magical practise. How do we expect to work magic effectively if we do not know the resources available at hand, the folklore of the area we are working in, and the spirits who reside there? A connection to the land is not simply feeling at one with the trees, the stones, and the Earth beneath our feet. It is immersing yourself in the culture, the stories and the people that call the land their home.

An affinity for nature is a strong motif among modern Witches. I have yet to meet a Witch who is not awestruck by the moon, and feeling their best when they are exploring a dense forest. An affinity for the land is the first step to embracing your connection to it. Humans today love the notion of escaping into nature, as if nature is some separate aspect of this world that we are not a part of. Nevertheless, we are nature, we are natural beings just as any tree, insect, or animal is. Connecting with nature does not require you to venture miles away into a rural, quiet woods where only the sounds of birds and bees are present. Connecting to nature all around you can also mean appreciating the trees that line the road on your street. Learning the names of the shrubs and bushes in your garden. Watching the birds that fly past your window each morning, noon, and night. I find nothing more magical than seeing moss or weeds growing through a crack in the cement in a busy city. I see it as the resilient and persevering energies of nature, breaking through even the strongest and most potent of barriers.

Having grown up on Ynys Môn, I consider myself highly privileged. I grew up in a council house, in a terraced row of homes. Behind our home, however, were miles upon miles of fields, woods, and open countryside. Cattle grazed happily in the distance. If you were to walk a mile north of my home, you would find yourself in the depths of the countryside, surrounded by farms and woods. To the West was the coastline; the beach was only a mere ten-minute walk from my front door. Continue travelling to the south, past the sand dunes and winding country roads, and you would eventually find yourself in dense woodland and forests. In addition, a short trek to the east led you to a beautiful lake known as *Llyn Coron* surrounded by meadows and fields. This was my playground growing up. I spent most of my childhood exploring the landscape. Growing up in such a rural area where everyone knew everyone, we were allowed to explore to our hearts content. Much of my time was spent on the banks of the river, on the cliffs overlooking the *Eryri* mountain range,[21] or cycling up hills past fields. It was very easy to feel at one with nature and with the landscape when that was my personal playground. A world where land, sea, and sky blended in perfect harmony together.

Nowadays I live in a city, and it is sometimes difficult to feel at one with the land here. Nevertheless, the city holds a magic entirely of its own. The river that runs through the city has a history of being associated with various spirits, deities, and legends of old. Every summer I watch swarms of bees fly through the city and to the meadows in the southeast. The city has a host of wonderful creatures such as bats, herons, and foxes, to name a few. Connectivity to the spirits of the land and to the natural world is not reserved for those who live in rural areas.

Magic of the Language

Language is at the heart of Wales. The Welsh language is a language of poetry, magic, and antiquity. There is a saying that I heard repeated often as a child growing up in Wales, *"Cenedl heb iaith, cenedl heb galon,"* which translates to mean: "A nation without language, is a nation without heart." This statement is in many ways a poetic battle cry, which emphasises the importance of preserving the native language of this nation. I am fortunate to be a native speaker of *Cymraeg* (Welsh), having grown up surrounded by it. My mother, father, grandparents, and siblings all speak Welsh fluently as a first language.

---

21. Snowdonia.

I was taught through the medium of the Welsh language all the way through to high school. It was not until I graduated high school and entered college that my education switched from being mostly in Welsh to mainly English. My native language is vitally important to my practise, and to my magic. I do not believe it is necessary to be a fluent Welsh speaker to fully connect with the magic of the Welsh landscape, however; learning as much of the language as possible would help tremendously.

Wales' culture is very much oral in nature. The ancient Druids and inhabitants of Wales never wrote anything down pertaining to their beliefs and practises. It was all passed down through the beauty of the language. Many of the myths, legends, and practises of Wales are very much lost to the mists of time. Thankfully, many also survived, being recorded by monks.

The Welsh language is one that activates a sense of connection to something ancient, powerful, and resilient. Though the language as we know it today has only existed since around the sixth century, it is the descendant of the Brythonic, Indo-European Celtic language spoken by the Britons during the Iron Age.[22] Like any language, it has evolved over time, changing to suit modern sensibilities. The magic of the language, however, persists to this day. Ask any Welsh speaker today how they feel about the language, and they will undoubtedly tell you that there is a magical, poetic quality to the language. What many may not be aware of however, is that the Welsh language does indeed have magical, sacred, ceremonial origins. The origins of the Welsh language are steeped in a history of Indo-European magical ceremony, conducted by bards and poets. Verse would be utilised in *Cymraeg's* ancestral language in ceremonies surrounding the making of monarchs, and in the building of communities.[23] At heart, the very rules embedded into Welsh verse that have remained unchanged for centuries, the vocabulary and syntax that has aided in formulating Welsh into what it is today, has origins in archaic forms of ceremonial magic. The language of Wales was developed by bards and magicians, and as such is embedded with a magical quality that is inseparable from our modern language.

---

22. Davies, *The Welsh Language.*
23. Conran, *Welsh Verse.*

The magical quality of the Welsh language can be found in the rules of Welsh verse. For example, a *cynghanedd* is the harmonious quality found within a line of verse. Without a good grasp of how to incorporate stress, alliteration and rhyme into a line of verse, it lacks harmony. Then an *englyn* or a set of *englynion* focuses on the metering of poetic verse, the counting of syllables and the use of rhyme. As I have already established, verse would be utilised in archaic ceremonial magic. Words had a magic of their own and were weaved by the bards of the ancient Celtic world. With the power of words, bards could invoke ancestral strength, form bonds among the community, create monarchs, and transform people's perspectives. As modern magical practitioners who work within the Welsh cultural continuum, we can still tap into this transformative magic via the Welsh language. *Englynion* and *cynghanedd* are essentially powerful forms of spellwork. The right words used in the right patterns can evoke potent transformative magic.

Beyond the magical qualities of the Welsh language, the language is also intrinsically precious to many of the modern inhabitants of Wales. There is an effort that is growing year by year to preserve the language, which is now spoken by fewer than a million people. Over the centuries Welsh has been a language that has taken numerous beatings. English rule sought to stamp out the language time and time again in history. From laws back in the sixteenth century literally banning the language, to more modern instances of children in schools being punished for utilising their mother tongue. Beyond suppression, the anglicisation of Wales with numerous English speakers moving to Wales did not help in aiding the language's survival either. Yet against all odds, the language persists. *Ry'n ni yma o hud!* (We are still here!), as the famous Welsh song goes. It is important that we preserve the language, as it is an aspect of our Welsh identity, and carries so much culture and tradition.

The resilient nature of the Welsh language is something I can easily relate to the resilient nature of Witchcraft. Magical practises have long been misunderstood and judged, and those who delve in the magical arts have long been ridiculed, and at times persecuted. Nevertheless, just as with the Welsh language, magic persists to this day. It is as though both Witchcraft and the Welsh language are flames that are not easily snuffed out.

One element of Wales that I am always overjoyed by is the sense of community found within the language. I will not be as naïve as to try and say that bigotry and intolerance does not exist in Wales; it certainly does, as I have been a witness to it and have been on the receiving end of it occasionally. However, there is a sense of family and kinship that comes from speaking the Welsh language that is difficult to explain. I remember meeting a young man when I was travelling through Thailand, who at first seemed to be judging me and keeping his distance. The moment he learnt I was Welsh and a native Welsh speaker, we started conversing in Welsh and it was as though we had known each other for years. This is an occurrence that seems not to be Welsh in nature, but Celtic. When I once travelled through the Scottish Highlands, I came across a little café where the staff seemed to take an instant disliking to me. It was awkward and uncomfortable. However, the moment they heard me speaking Welsh to my travelling companions all tension melted away and the Scottish ladies running the café began discussing Wales and our similarities to Scotland merrily with me.

It is very much a feeling of: if you speak our language, know of our plight, or can discuss our land's stories and heritage, then you are one of us, and you are welcome.

Sacred Spaces and Places

Less than a five-minute drive from my childhood home, atop a cliff overlooking the sea, stood an ancient burial chamber known as *barclodiad y gawres*. Ever since I was a child, I heard tales of this magical place. Some said it was the home of fairies; after all, it is basically a hollow hill with a stone structure inside. Others said it was an ancient graveyard. Alternatively, I even once heard mention that the burial chamber was in fact the grave of a giantess. The name *Barclodiad y Gawres* after all translates to *the giantess's apronful*.[24] I spent many days of my youth playing here, exploring the chamber and the beach nearby. I wondered back then what ancient mysteries this space held. Whatever the truth behind this beautiful monument, even as a child one thing was certain: this place was sacred.

---

24. Cadw website, *Visit Barclodiad y gawres*, accessed March 17, 2021.

Wales is full of places just like *barclodiad y gawres*. In my local vicinity, it was only a short drive to a handful of burial chambers, standing stones, cairns, hut circles, and the ruins of ancient monuments. On top of these relics of Britain's ancient past Wales is also the country with the most castles per square mile in the world. With castles, standing stones, ruins, and burial chambers set against a backdrop of cliffs overlooking the sea, mountain ranges in the distance, and beautiful forests, it is no surprise that Wales is a land filled with sacred places and spaces.

Sacred space is a concept that is prominent to my practise. Having been immersed in a culture where you cannot throw a stone without hitting some ancient monument or sacred well, the concept has been ingrained into me from birth. Nevertheless, what exactly makes a space sacred? I often converse with my partner about the strange phenomena of graveyards. I am not sure if this is pertinent to everywhere in the world, but here in the UK graveyards are usually eerily still, silent, and heavy places. You could be in a very busy, loud city but the moment you step foot into a graveyard suddenly it is as though time has stopped. Everyone seems to be aware that a graveyard is very much a place of calm contemplation and reflection. As strange as it may sound, I adore walking through graveyards and old churchyards. They are liminal spaces, a place between life and death, the mundane and the holy. Regardless of what my mood is during the day, the moment I step foot into a graveyard my entire demeanour changes into a solemn, quiet one.

Burial chambers and ancient monuments in Wales evoke this same emotion. I have often wondered what exactly it is that causes this reaction among humans. This is how I decipher whether a space is collectively sacred. There are spaces that you make sacred for yourself, and then there are spaces that are simply inherently sacred. As though humanity has a hive mind that just seems to know when a place or space is one that requires a state of seriousness. Of reflection and solemnity. In addition, it is not just ancient monuments, graveyards, and places that are arguably holy and spiritual that hold this solemn and calm energy. Some woodland areas, banks of rivers, and cliffs that are otherwise rather mundane also hold this intense energy.

We can make a space sacred with our intentions. Most magical practitioners and Pagans today have altar spaces in their homes. My altar sits atop a very mundane cabinet in my living room. However, the altar itself and the immediate space surrounding it is undoubtedly sacred. Even though to most visitors who might not know me it seems like nothing more than a curiously decorated cabinet. I have made this space sacred to me personally. Places can also become sacred if we attach specific emotions and memories to them. There is a bench overlooking the sea on a cliff on the small island just off Ynys Môn called Caergybi that is exceptionally sacred to me. It is a place my partner and I would once escape to together. We have many fond memories there, and I remember so many deep conversations. We have made that place sacred to us, but to most, it is just a bench looking out toward the Irish Sea.

Sacred spaces and places can be very deeply personal areas. However, collectively sacred spaces and places are of utmost interest to me.

Sacred Lakes

Culturally speaking one of Wales' best examples of places that are deemed sacred are lakes. Lake in Welsh is *Llyn*. There are numerous folkloric tales and legends surrounding lakes. Purchase any collection of Welsh folk tales or fairy tales and you are bound to find copious stories pertaining to various lakes. They are almost never simply random lakes either; within the folklore the lakes are very much real lakes that still exist to this day.

Lakes have long been associated with Wales' fair family, the *Tylwyth Teg*, our version of the fae. Lakes tend to act as portals to the fairy world and therefore should be treated with the utmost respect and caution. One would never dream of offending the fae here in Wales; they are arguably more feared historically by the people of Wales than hideous wicked Witches of children's tales. A fine example of a tale that is of significant importance to anyone with an affinity for Welsh Celtic spirituality is the tale of the lady of *Llyn y fan fach*. The "lady of the lake" is a fairy woman who appears before a mortal man, and ultimately marries him.

The Witch goddess Cerridwen was said to have kept her mystical cauldron that brewed a potion of pure Awen on the shores of Llyn Tegid.[25]

Lakes would have been important to the people of ancient Wales. They would have brought their cattle to the lakes to drink, and they may have even used the lakes to wash their clothes and such in. Add in the factor that lakes had a history of being very much associated with the fae and there is no wonder that they are so very revered and loved.

Within my practise, I often took offerings to the spirit of my local lake, *Llyn Coron*. I sat at the shores of the lake and meditated as dragonflies and butterflies fluttered by me. If you have a lake local to you, perhaps consider taking an offering and spending some time connecting with the spirits of the water.

Wells and Their Magic

As well as traditions surrounding sacred lakes, wells are also an intrinsic element of Welsh folk traditions and practises. Wells were thought to be associated with numerous spirits, saints, or specific powers throughout Wales. People often undertook pilgrimages to certain wells around the country to receive a blessing or similar. Later in history, many wells became associated with healing. The concept of how one would receive a blessing from a healing well or sacred well is not dissimilar to the continuous occurrence of wishing wells. When one would approach the well one would offer the well a coin, usually a silver coin, which would not be tossed into the well but instead placed in a box. One would then approach the well and speak an incantation or prayer, setting the intention of what they would desire.

The tradition of offering something to the well to receive something in return was known in Wales as the tradition of *offrymu*.[26]

In the eighteenth century, suddenly wells became notorious not just for offering blessings and good fortune to those who offered coins to them, but also as cursing wells. People would travel from far and wide to give an offering to a cursing well, which in return would curse their enemies. This

25. From the tale *Hanes Taliesin*, a sixteenth-century account of the bard Taliesin, written by Elis Gruffydd.

26. Isaac, *Coelion Cymru*.

practise became so notorious and so feared that exceptionally well-known cursing wells, such as *Ffynnon Eilian*, were ultimately destroyed.[27]

Water seems to be a rather poignant element within Wales' culture, with both lakes and wells being seen as sacred. Many of the lakes across Wales are dark, deep, and murky; one can understand how they are believed to be portals to the realm of fairy.

As well as Wales' sacred bodies of water and wells, the Earth here is a remarkable sight. Looking out to the landscape with its outstanding, dramatic natural scenery, it is not difficult to feel a fond connection with the stable and nurturing element of Earth. Many modern Witches today connect to Earth in various methods, a favourite being to utilise crystals and stones. Wales is no stranger to native crystals. Beneath the Earth can be found numerous crystals that are often used within modern spiritual practises today. The Earth of Wales grows fluorite, azurite, pyrite, and quartz to name but a few. Growing up in Wales however, despite my affinity for Witchcraft I never truly felt drawn to buying copious amounts of crystals from metaphysical stores. Partly, because of a moral dilemma I had surrounding crystals in my teens. I believe many Witches are quick to forget that crystals are mined, dragged, and blasted from the Earth. The concept of "ethical" crystals is actually severely rare. Crystal mining causes devastation not only to the Earth, but also to animals and on occasion human communities. As a teenager I believe I must have been under the ignorant impression that the amethyst and smoky quartz I purchased from local stores must have been found washed up on a beach. That is rarely ever the case. I have met many Pagans and Witches who are adamantly against diamonds, yet most of our crystals come from the very same mines that precious gemstones stem from.

Early in my teen years, I spent much of my time finding new and alternative ways to connect with crystals. I would sit atop a cliff overlooking the sea and meditate, visualising the layers of dirt and soil, rock and stone beneath me. What geological wonders and secrets lay beneath my feet? I also chose, instead of purchasing crystals from stores that undoubtedly had originated from mines, to walk along the beach. As I walked along the beach, I found

---

27. Suggett, *A History of Magic and Witchcraft in Wales.*

numerous beauties washed up along the shoreline. Bloodstone, amber, beautifully coloured pebbles, quartz, and more. My altar is more likely to be decorated in pinecones and twigs found in the local forests, and shells and rocks found on the beach, rather than amethyst from Madagascar I bought from a store.

This is simply my opinion. In no way am I attempting to shame you if you adore crystals. If you feel an affinity to crystal collecting, I would never attempt to stop you from pursuing what you love. However, I believe that utilising what is available in our locale is a method of connecting on a much deeper level to the land and the sacred landscape. I am fickle when it comes to my altar tools and magical objects. I have a mixture of store-bought items, handmade items and items that I have simply found whilst out in nature. Some say that magical tools are far more potent when you have made them yourself. I am inclined to agree, that item will be imbued with your personal energy and, if using natural components, will also be imbued with the spirit force of the natural elements. The same can be said for crystals. A stone you find on the beach, or at the shores of a lake, or whilst hiking up a mountain will be far more powerful and useful than a stone you buy in store. This is for the simple reason that you have a deeper, stronger connection to that stone. You know where it originates; you know that it connects you to your land. It is something to reflect on and ponder. Witchcraft is a very personal endeavour. The more personal your tools, the more they connect to who you are, the stronger they and your Witchcraft will be.

A connection with the land that I call home is an integral part of my Witchcraft. I urge you, whether you live in Wales or far away somewhere else, do something today that helps you connect with the landscape surrounding you. Read the folklore of your people; go for a hike in the most beautiful locations around you. Take a walk through the city and notice the tiny plants growing through the cracks in the pavement, or the trees lining the streets. Learn the names of the native plants in your area. Watch the birds as they fly around your home. You are not separate from your landscape, and your landscape has a depth of magic, I assure you. Feel it, live it.

✹ EXERCISE ✹
A Meditation to Connect with
the Sacredness of the Landscape

As a modern Welsh Witch, a connection to the landscape is vitally import-ant to my practise. I connect to the spirit of my motherland, and value the sacredness of the natural wonders around. The purpose of this book is not to help you become a Welsh Witch, but rather to inform you of the rich cultural history of magic that permeates the land in which I was born. I suspect many reading this book will have Welsh ancestry, or will feel drawn to incorpo-rating Welsh folk magic and Celtic Paganism into their spiritual and magi-cal practise. A lesson I would adore that any reader of this book take away however, is how beneficial connecting to your local landscape can be to your magical workings. Modern Pagans today are often hypnotised by the intense beauty and potency found in traditions and magic of faraway cultures and lands. Many of the Pagans and Witches I know today who live in Wales and Britain call upon the gods of Egypt, Greece, and Rome among many oth-ers. However, as deeply interesting and powerful the spirits of lands far away from us can be, a Witch should, in my opinion, make every effort to con-nect with the land which they walk upon daily. The most powerful method of forging a connection with your sacred landscape is to first get to know it. Now, we can get to know the land by reading of its history, its folklore and its mythology. However, the easiest and most beneficial method of connecting to the spirit of land is by immersing yourself in it. To go for a long explora-tion out in nature, and fully embrace all that you sense and see around you.

This meditative exercise will help you to immerse yourself in the land and connect to the sacred spirit of the land.

Take yourself to a local place that you would consider sacred and close to your heart. This may be a local park, a woodland, a meadow or even just your garden. Ensure the place is quiet and devoid of too many mundane dis-tractions such as traffic noise, or clusters of people. Before you arrive at this place, plan a route that you wish to explore this area within. Plan it so that you can spend at least an hour in this place.

As you arrive at the beginning of your walk, stop and take a moment to close your eyes, and take a deep, calming breath. In through the nose, hold for a moment, and out through the mouth. With your eyes still closed, sense what you can around you. What do you hear? How do your feet feel against the ground? What is the weather like today? Is it cold? Warm? Do you feel comfortable? Take in any sounds you may hear. The purpose of this exercise is to fully immerse yourself in the land, and so do not ignore anything. Truly embrace all that you feel around you. When you have spent a good few minutes with your eyes closed, familiarising yourself to the scents, sounds, and sensations of this place, gently open your eyes and adjust your sight to what surrounds you. Take note on whether your perception of this place feels different now that you have spent a few moments allowing your other senses to familiarise themselves with it. Take a good look at what lies ahead, and when you are ready, begin your exploration.

As you explore this place, try not to mindlessly walk without taking in the surroundings. Continually look around you. Look at the ground; take note of any plants, flowers, or interesting things you see upon the ground. Do any stones call to you? What colour are the stones in this area, if there are any? Look at the sky. How do the clouds look today? Are there trees, mountains, or hills that frame your vision of the sky? What sights lie at eye level? Truly immerse yourself in this landscape.

Every so often as you explore, take a moment to touch things in your surrounding area. Intuitively decide what you should touch. Perhaps you feel drawn to feel the soil on the floor, to brush your hand against the trees as you walk by them, or to feel the texture of stones you pass by. If it is at all possible and safe to do so, perhaps you may choose to walk barefoot for a while. The aim here is to immerse yourself in the beauty of the land, exposing your senses to all aspects of that which surrounds you.

Whenever you feel drawn to do so, stop and breathe deeply, closing your eyes and repeating what you did at the beginning of your exploration. Do not rush this exploration; get to know the land thoroughly. Sit yourself down whenever possible to take in the sights. Breathe in the power of land, sea, and sky. Sense the sacred power of the land that you are slowly acquainting yourself with.

Spend as much time as required exploring the land. Repeat this meditative exploration at least once a month, if not more frequently. Take a notebook with you and attempt to identify any local foliage and wildlife. Collect natural items that you feel drawn to such as stones, sticks, and herbs that you may utilise in your magical practises. Keeping in mind a reverence and respect for the landscape, of course.

Chapter 4
Legends of the Land

I remember being twelve years old and sitting in a classroom during lunchtime on a school day years ago. I was the type of child who did not have many friends, especially as I ventured into the teenage years. Most of my school days during lunch and break times were spent alone with a good book, or a sketchpad. This particular day I happened to be reading a book all about world mythology. The book touched on practically all the main world mythologies, from Greek to Egyptian, Norse to Roman. Being somewhat of an outcast, I was also severely bullied. On this gloomy day, a group of boys decided they were too bored to entertain themselves and started mocking me for sitting and reading. The boys, noticing I was ignoring them, decided to grab the book out of my hands and throw it around the room. After some childish teasing and mocking, laughter and torture, I eventually got my hands back on the book. Funnily enough, it was not the bullies who upset me the most that day. It was another quiet girl who was sat on the opposite side of the classroom. She turned to me and said something along the lines of "Why do you bother reading mythology? It's not relevant to the real world." Even at that young age, my blood boiled at that phrase. The idea that myth was not relevant to the world in which we live. At that age, I did not possess the adequate knowledge to express why I felt she was incorrect.

Therefore, I went back to sitting in the corner, quietly reading. That comment stuck with me to this day.

What bearing does mythology have on our modern way of life? To the regular, mundane folk mythology is nothing but a collection of fanciful and complicated tall tales. Myths are practically packaged today as either being something for children to read and learn about, or as something that academics study intently. Many people believe they go about their daily lives with mythology playing no role whatsoever. This line of thinking is wrong. Mythology is embedded into our culture and identity. Regardless of where you live in the world, some form of mythology exists and informs your view of life and the world around you.

The mythology of our land is the remnant of ancient beliefs; the stories may have evolved and changed over time but their core principles speak of a way of life that predates our own. We live in a beautiful global community these days, where people from far-off countries are available for us to speak to at the click of a button. I could be communicating with someone from America and Australia at the same time using our modern technology. The mythology of our land however, harkens back to a time when this was not possible. When the world was a much smaller place for the majority of the common people. The myths remind us of how our ancestors made sense of their world, and what led them to becoming what we now know them to be. Mythology, though seemingly fanciful tales of magic and mayhem, is a window into the core values, beliefs, and stories of the long-lost people of this land. The people these stories originate from may be lost, but they survive through the tales. Mythology connects us to the very heart and soul of the land, a continued continuum of cultural beliefs and legacies that exist to this day.

For the Witch, mythology can offer much to our personal practises. When looking at it as a Welsh Witch, I see mythology as an initiator of divine inspiration. By reading the myths of my land, I am inspired to dive deeper into the legends, the characters, and the archetypes explored in them. I have also often found myself inspired to create art based on the mythical tales of the land, and I am certainly not alone in that regard. I believe it is a misconception among those who grow up outside of Wales that the mythology of this land is obscure, only known to scholars and Pagans. Many Celtic Pagans I know of in my personal life who are from America, England, and other countries across Europe seem almost shocked when I explain that I grew up being told these enchanting stories at home, and at school. I remember creating a large mural artwork of the scene of Bendigeidfran—a mythical giant king of Wales crossing the Irish Sea to retrieve his stolen and abused sister, Branwen—for my primary school. The story of Branwen was one that seemed to capture the imaginations of educators. With good reason too, for it is a tale of connections, of trauma, of battles, of giants, and of the spirit of Wales itself. In college at the age of sixteen, I took part in a theatrical production of the story. I vividly remember watching a puppet show that detailed the story of the prince of the kingdom of Dyfed Pwyll meeting the ethereal Rhiannon, who is revered today by various Pagans and Witches as a horse goddess. The mythology of Wales was interwoven into my education, my upbringing and inspired my imagination from a very young age. Therefore, these tales have obviously informed and influenced my Witchcraft.

I always feel as though mythology is part of something so much bigger than the mundane world. It helps me to delve into a sense of kinship and understanding of my land and my ancestors.

Of course, as a magical practitioner mythology also provides us an insight into powerful working allies of magic. Deities and prominent figures connected to this land can be found throughout the mythologies of Wales. Reading and exploring the mythology of Wales is the first step to understanding the deities and the archetypes interwoven into Welsh Celtic culture.

What Is Welsh Mythology?

The landscape of Wales is one packed to the brim with countless stories and legends. We are at heart a land of storytellers, of bards and poets. Our ancestors were no different. Each town, village and city across Wales boasts their own folk tales, legends, and myths. However, when I discuss Welsh mythology I usually am only referring to one particular collection of stories. That is, the four branches of the Mabinogi. This is not to say that I overlook folklore or fairy tales. Quite the contrary, I will discuss a little later why folklore and fairy tales of Wales tend to play a more prominent role in my personal practise as a Witch. The mythology of Wales as found in the Mabinogi, however, is a subject I approach with a calm and focused mind. Some of these tales are immensely complicated. I once explained to a friend that Welsh mythology is something you have to read once, then read again, then read backward, then read upside down, then re-read one more time and then, and only then, you will still be left a little confused. Of course, I was overexaggerating, yet it still rings true. At their face value, the myths of the Mabinogi seem like straightforward stories. Most include a hero, a challenge or obstacle, and a battle or ultimate ending. However, read between the lines and you will find an insight into pre-Christian Wales.

The Mabinogi are a collection of stories separated into four branches. Monks recorded the stories found within the Mabinogi in middle Welsh in the twelfth to thirteenth centuries. Although the oldest written manuscripts of these myths only date back approximately a thousand years ago, the stories themselves are far older. Harkening back to a period in Welsh history when the beliefs and important legends of the Welsh were not written, but passed on orally. If you were to purchase an English translation of the Mabinogi (which would most likely be sold as *the Mabinogion*) in a bookstore today, you might find yourself very confused by the overtly Christian language used throughout the tales. However, remember, the stories were collected and recorded into manuscripts by twelfth-century monks. Regardless of the Christianisation of the stories, the pre-Christian beliefs and archetypes are blatant and obvious. The Mabinogi are truly a feast for the imagination, with tales of magicians and kings, Witches and shape shifters, princesses and other worlds. I find it truly shocking that more literature and popular media do not pull on the themes found within Welsh mythology.

It is within the four branches of the Mabinogi we are introduced to deities that are exceptionally popular among modern Witches and Pagans such as Rhiannon, a goddess of sovereignty associated with horses; Cerridwen, the Celtic Witch goddess of transformation and inspiration; and Gwyn ap Nudd, the divine king of fairies. The very essence of the myths of Wales are transformative, initiatory, and intrinsically magical. Even the legendary King Arthur makes his first appearance in these myths.

A common theme I have found among those who are new to Welsh mythology is that they try desperately to compare it to other ancient myths. I have often come across people making fanciful connotations between certain Welsh deities and deities from the myths of Greece or Egypt. Whilst I am sure similarities can and do exist, I believe that attempting to compare mythologies will not aid anyone in attempting to gain a deeper and more profound connection with them. What make myths so fascinating is the fact that they are so specific to the land that they originate from. As I have already mentioned, mythology speaks of the very nature of the land, its inhabitants, and their ancestors. It harkens back to a time long before our own. It may feel beneficial to try to draw comparisons, but the best thing to do in my opinion is to see Welsh mythology as purely Welsh.

If you are a Witch with an inclination toward Wales and Welsh Celtic spirituality, I highly recommend reading, familiarising, and analysing the mythology of the land. Start by purchasing an English translation of the Mabinogi. Though it may sound childish and silly, I adore reading children's picture books of the various tales. It may not be as insightful or profound as the actual legends, but it is a great way of initially introducing yourself to them.

Annwfn: The Celtic Otherworld

When formulating this book I struggled with whether or not to discuss the Celtic underworld or otherworld, known as Annwfn. It is a realm that often baffles me, and I am continually studying the concept in order to gain a further understanding. However, mystery and uncertainty seems to be an intrinsic aspect of Annwfn. I believe it would be highly beneficial to touch upon the topic of Annwfn for the purposes of introducing it as best as I can.

Annwfn is a chthonic (underground) otherworldly realm that is one singular realm divided into various kingdoms. This is a clear reflection of historical Welsh society, as historically Wales was divided into various kingdoms ruled by various kings or princes. The concept of the Celtic otherworld is often oversimplified as we in this modern day and age will vehemently try to compare it to other underworld or otherworld systems apparent in various cultures and belief systems. It is very easy to attempt to compare Annwfn with concepts such as the Christian realms of Heaven and Hell, or the ancient Greek notion of Hades. Heaven, Hell, and to an extent, the Greek Hades are realms that are predominately inaccessible to mortals. These realms become accessible to us only by death, and often where you are able to reach in these realms depends on acts you have accomplished throughout your mortal life. The Celtic otherworld is a very different concept to this idea.

If we look at a few of the texts where Annwfn is described in great detail, we will notice that Annwfn is not an inaccessible realm existing in a completely different dimension to our own. In fact, tales of Annwfn often start with mortals stumbling upon it completely by accident. Being a chthonic realm, Annwfn is often said to be accessible via caves, lakes, or even by simply walking deeper into the woods.

Within the confines of Welsh mythology, we are initially introduced to the realm of Annwfn in the first branch of the Mabinogi, in the tale of Pwyll prince of the kingdom of Dyfed. Whilst out hunting in the woods he comes across a pack of strange, otherworldly-looking hounds who have just killed a deer. The hounds are completely covered in the purest white fur, aside from their ears that are the colour of crimson blood. He sends his own hunting dogs to feast on the newly killed deer carcass, a choice that eventually offends the owner of the strange unearthly white hounds. The owner of the white hunting hounds reveals that he is Arawn, the king of Annwfn, and as an apology for causing offense to him asks that Pwyll do him a great favour. Arawn explains that he has been in constant battle with another king of Annwfn named Hafgan. Arawn explains that whenever they battle, he wins each time, bringing Hafgan to near death; however, Hafgan always begs that Arawn strike him a killing blow and Arawn obliges, but this killing blow magically restores Hafgan to full health rather than killing him. Thus, the constant cycle of battling with Hafgan continues relentlessly. Arawn bestows upon Pwyll a glamour that will allow him to look like Arawn and live in his kingdom in Annwfn for the next year, after which he will meet with Hafgan and end the constant fighting. Pwyll, wanting to befriend the king of Annwfn and apologise for his disrespect, agrees to these terms and so Arawn escorts him to Annwfn.

There are two specific aspects to the tale of Pwyll that explain to us how Annwfn functions; first and foremost, is that Pwyll is able to access Annwfn by simply walking alongside Arawn. This showcases to us how accessible the realm of Annwfn is, and also how it is not a realm entirely different to our own. Walking to Annwfn seems to be no different to walking from one city to another today. No complex task or requirement is needed to access the otherworld as we would find in other belief systems surrounding the concept of an other/underworld. Secondly, we are introduced to the concept of Arawn being a king or overlord of Annwfn, with a troublesome other king of Annwfn fighting him for dominance over domain. Again, this is not an unfamiliar concept to medieval Welsh society. This proves to us that the Celtic otherworld was often understood via a reflection of the way the people of Wales lived. By making Annwfn seem familiar, working within the same confines as their day-to-day life, it makes the supernatural, the otherworldly accessible and easier to understand.

The entire court of Arawn in Annwfn is one filled with beautiful people, beautiful scenery, and bounties of food and drink. The way the text describes this strange otherworld is nothing like what one would imagine an underworld or hell to look. In fact, quite the opposite.

The story goes on and Pwyll, disguised as Arawn, lives a lovely life for the next year in the realm of Annwfn. He is taken on glorious hunting trips, basks in feasts of plenty on the regular and continues to have the most pleasing of conversations with the queen of Annwfn. The time finally comes for Pwyll, disguised as Arawn, to battle Hafgan—Pwyll follows Arawn's instructions to not strike Hafgan a second time once he is down, and ultimately leaves the battle victorious. When Arawn returns to the kingdom and goes to bed with his wife that night, his wife recoils in shock when he touches her in bed. She explains that for the past year, though he has been warm and friendly to her during the day, Arawn has not touched her in bed or been intimate at all. Arawn rejoices in the fact he has made a true friend in Pwyll, as he realises that Pwyll refused to sleep with his wife the entire time he was disguised as Arawn. This, like all stories within the Mabinogi, is a complicated tale to express briefly. I hope this brief introduction to the tale will inspire you to seek the tale in its entirety to read, explore, and study.

This tale helps us ascertain a vague understanding of the realm of Annwfn and how it operates. Much of how we understand the Celtic otherworld is based on assumptions that we can deduce by looking at the texts available to us. Again, it is very easy for us to fall into the trap of attempting to understand Annwfn via our understanding of the concept of an other/underworld as it relates to our understanding of the world today. However, the Celtic otherworld is not comparable to Hell, Heaven, nor concepts from other ancient civilisations such as the Greek Hades. If anything, Annwfn is but an extension of our world. A deepening of our realm. The name Annwfn translates to mean the very deep space or world after all. It is the realm from which Awen stems, a realm of depth and of course, mystery.[28]

The Cŵn Annwfn

Spectral hounds are abundant within folklore surrounding Witches, though they are usually large black hounds associated with demons and devils. These hounds are often ascribed an element of mystery and denote feelings of the unknown; it is no wonder that they are also heavily related to the otherworlds of various traditions and cultures. Tales of spectral dogs are abundant in Wales in the form of the gwyllgi, though these creatures are terribly frightful and not something one would wish to stumble upon whilst walking alone at night.

The cŵn Annwfn however, who have been unfairly demonised as being the Welsh equivalent of "hell hounds" by the Christian church for centuries, differ in one regard to most tales of otherworldly hounds. Rather than being pure black, the cŵn Annwfn are a pure and bright white in colour all over their bodies, aside from their ears. Their ears are a striking blood red. The cŵn Annwfn are the first symbols of the otherworld Pwyll stumbles upon when meeting the king of Annwfn. The dogs are otherworldly familiar spirits

---

28. Dr Gwilym Morus-Baird's YouTube video on the *Celtic Source* channel titled *"The Celtic 'Otherworld?'"* goes into more detail regarding the realm of Annwfn.

to the psychopomps that inhabit the liminal spaces between this world and the mysterious otherworld of Annwfn.

A Witch deals not only with the realm of mortality that we inhabit, but with the liminal energies that exist between all the realms. The *cŵn Annwfn* are exceptionally beneficial companion spirits for those of us that delve beyond the veil and into the realm of spirit. Gemma Gary discusses another form of spectral hounds, the Wisht hounds, in her book *The Devil's Dozen*:

"The various attributes and associations of the Otherworldly hound are exemplified in the creature's great significance to some traditions, streams and lineages of Witchcraft. The ancient concomitance of the hound with the mysteries of death and passage between the realms of the living and the dead, ally the creature to the Witches' vital dealings with the Otherworld and the spirits of the dead."[29]

Gary goes on to present a rite of calling unto the wisht hounds, which is powerful and poetic, enough to illuminate the spirit of any Witch. Inspired by her work I incorporated a similar rite into my magical practise, which draws upon the spirit of Celtic myth and instead of being a call unto the wisht hounds, it is a call unto the native *cŵn Annwfn* of Wales. I incorporate this rite into my circle conjuration when I am specifically hoping to work with the spirits of the dead, or with the symbolic nature of the otherworld and of liminality.

✹ EXERCISE ✹
To Call Upon the Cŵn Annwfn

This is to be done directly after hallowing the working space, but before conducting a rite you have planned for yourself. The addition of this element into a rite is better done when the whole rite is performed at a liminal space, at a liminal time.

Begin by walking into the centre of the circle which you have formed. Hold your arms down with your palms facing the earth. If you work with a wand, point the wand toward the earth itself. Take a deep breath and close your eyes. Visualise the *cŵn Annwfn* in their otherworldly beauty. How do

29. Gary, *The Devil's Dozen*, 81.

their white fur shine in the light? What shade of red do you visualise their striking ears to be? How do their howls, growls, and barks sound? Keep these visuals in mind. Allow your mind to enter a meditative state, intuitively visualising the *cŵn Annwfn*.

Once you feel ready to move forward, open your eyes and tilt your head skyward. Recite this petitionary chant:

Familiar spirits of the land of the deep,
I call to you in your arcane wisdom.
Creatures that hold the powers of the betwixt and between,
Walkers between life and death,
Cŵn Annwfn, spectral hounds of the deep realms below,
Join me in my magical workings,
Aid me in my rite.

Then, repeat this chant three times:

Cŵn Annwfn, with fur so pale and bright,
Gather here upon this night,
Empower and embolden my Witch's rite.

Visualise the hounds of the otherworld running around you. There are countless legends and tales of the *cŵn Annwfn* howling in the skies; perhaps if you listen intently you will hear the howls approach you. It is said within the lore of the *cŵn Annwfn* that their howls are louder the further away they are. Listen from the depths of your spirit as they approach. Allow them to wander the boundaries of your working circle. Once they are there, treat them with the respect that liminal entities of the otherworld should receive.

When the rite is complete, thank the spirits of the *cŵn Annwfn* for their aid in your rite. Use this chant whilst walking in widdershins around your circle:

Hounds of the otherworld,
Spirits of the land of the deep.
I thank you for your presence.
This rite is now complete.
Cŵn Annwfn with ears of crimson red,

The work is done, the words have been said.
Return once more to your land betwixt and below,
Know that I respect and thank you as you go.
Cŵn Annwfn, I bid you good night,
A thousand blessings, and thanks for joining my rite.

Once you feel their presence has left your circle, continue with closing the rest of your working ground.

The Realm of the King of Fairy

In the mythical texts of Wales, we are introduced to numerous kings, including three specific kings of the realm of Annwfn. In the first branch of the Mabinogi, we meet Arawn and his foe Hafgan, two kings who consistently battle in the Welsh otherworld. Kristoffer Hughes states in *The Book of Celtic Magic* that there is enough evidence to point toward the notion that Arawn and Hafgan are in fact two counterparts of the same being, the same king. I can certainly see this while reading the original myth; a consistent and unbeatable enemy does seem like the perfect metaphor for battling your own inner demons or shadow self. Arawn and Hafgan are certainly interesting figures in the Welsh mythos; however, it is the next king of Annwfn that truly piques my interest.

The next king of Annwfn we are introduced to comes in much later in the texts. In the fourth branch of the Mabinogi, in a very early Arthurian legend, we are introduced to the entrancing figure that is Gwyn ap Nudd. When his name first appears in the Mabinogi, you would be forgiven for overlooking it entirely. He is originally simply listed as one of the legendary King Arthur's men. He plays a prominent role in the tale of the abduction of Creiddylad. Creiddylad is the daughter of a Welsh king, and is considered a minor character in the Mabinogi. Gwyn ap Nudd, along with another of Arthur's men Gwythr, is deeply in love with Creiddylad and ultimately both kidnap her. Within the original mentions of him in the Mabinogi, Gwyn proclaims that he vows to go into battle with Gwythyr every year on *Calan Mai*, or May Day, for Creiddylad's hand. This is a battle that rages year by year, without fail, until the end of time.[30]

---

30. From the fourth branch of the Mabinogi.

The concept of an annual divine battle being raged by two prominent figures of myth and legend is one that would not be unfamiliar to most modern Pagans. I remember being taught the tale of the Holly and the Oak kings when I was a teenager, a tale that is repeated by many Witches and Pagans today. The tale of the Holly and Oak kings is a rather modern invention, one to help us understand the turning of the cycle of the year. The Oak king fights to preserve the warmer, lighter days of the year, but is vanquished by the Holly king who brings forth the darker, colder half of the year and vice versa throughout the cycle of the year.[31] It is very much possible that Gwyn and Gwythyr's battle is the archetype upon which the tale of the Holly and Oak kings is based. It still astounds me to this day how much of Welsh mythology is often overlooked, and yet seems to have played a prominent role in formulating many beliefs, stories, and practises found in modern Paganism and Witchcraft. As a Welsh Witch, uncovering these things certainly grants me a sense of pride and joy.

Despite the introduction of Gwyn ap Nudd in the original texts being very much mundane on the surface level, Gwyn is revered today by many practitioners of magic as a rugged, liminal god, king of the otherworld of Annwfn and leader of the wild hunt. These versions of Gwyn ap Nudd stem from later folkloric interpretations of this god, such as in the tale of Collen and the king of fairy. To me he is the god of the wild, untamed wilderness, the liminal entity who acts as a psychopomp chaperoning souls from this realm to the next, and he is the figurative embodiment of the bridge that connects our realm to the otherworldly realms of the spirits of nature, and the fairies. I forge my understanding of Gwyn ap Nudd from a fusion of how he is presented in both the original mentions of him in the Mabinogi, and his presence within Welsh folklore as King of fairy. He is a deity I often turn to when working during liminal periods of time, or when I am within a transitional period of my life. Beyond being a Witch and a Welsh woman, I am also transgender, and Gwyn being a god of liminality and transition drew me

---

31. The Tale of the Holly and the Oak king: A commonly repeated modern folk tale among modern Pagans and Witches.

to call upon him in my rites and workings when I was first coming to terms with my identity. Within meditative journeys and spiritual quests around the time I made the choice to live my life authentically, Gwyn often appeared to me in visions and dreams; he would push me to strive for authenticity and change. His presence initially scared me; he is after all a rugged and masculine figure. I have never particularly had positive experiences with those who exude intense masculine energy. However, Gwyn's masculinity is one that in my experience is almost devoid of toxicity and harmful beliefs. Having never had a supportive masculine figure in my life, it was lovely to feel the accepting embrace of a deity who is very much the embodiment of rugged, untamed masculinity.

Gwyn as a deity of the Welsh traditions can help us, as mere mortals, glimpse into the realms of immortal otherworldly entities. He can aid us in both connecting with the rugged, untamed wilds of the woods that surround us as well as connecting with the otherworldly magic of the fairies, the gods, and even the dead. He opens our eyes to the vastness of the many realities, and aids us in seeing beyond our shrouded mortal perceptions. As a liminal deity, he provides us with the knowledge of connectivity: how all the realms are vastly different from one another yet also intimately and intricately connected on a deep, important level.

Where to Go Next

Now that I have offered an insight into what mythology means to me as a Welsh Witch, and explained the various myths one could dive into as part of their spiritual and magical practise, I thought it would be best to offer a vague guide as to where to go next.

Exploring the mythology of Wales, in my opinion, is something that is best done firsthand. When I have in the past attempted to force myself to learn about the mythology of my land, the information did not stick, and my interpretations and understandings of the myths were shaky at best. I do not believe you have to read the Mabinogi in a linear order to grasp an understanding of Welsh myth. My first piece of advice is to dive into the myths that your heart draws you to. Which deities, figures, or characters intrigue you the most? Perhaps your heart has always fluttered at the sound of Rhi-annon's name, and so the best course of action for you would be to read a myth that features Rhiannon. On the other hand, perhaps you are intrigued by the cauldron in Celtic myth and lore, in which case perhaps the story of Branwen, or that of Cerridwen and her divine son born of Awen, Taliesin, is the best tale for you to venture down next. I do not believe we feel drawn to things at random. Our heart and soul know what they need, and so rather than forcing yourself to sit down and read all four branches of the Mabinogi in order, choose which stories light your soul on fire and delve into them on a deeper level of exploration. Get to know the characters, the landscape which the story is set in, the archetypes present in the tale, the metaphors and sym-bolism within them, and the recurring elements found in them. This, in my opinion is the best way to familiarise yourself with the myths.

There are numerous translations of the Mabinogi available; however, I personally choose to go with Sioned Davies' translation. It is a wonderful translation of the tales that is not only accurate, but easy to follow and a joy to read. Beyond that, as I mentioned earlier in this chapter, I thoroughly enjoy reading children's books which feature these tales as a supplementary method of familiarising myself with them. Even better if they are written by Welsh authors and are illustrated. I also highly recommend the works of Kristoffer Hughes, another native Welsh speaker and Pagan who resides on the Isle of Anglesey. His works have heavily inspired my practise, and con-tinue to do so to this day.

If it is at all possible then visit Wales, visit the land in which these myths were formulated and have existed for thousands of years in some form or other. I adore visiting the areas where some myths are set, as it provides a deeper insight into the tale for me. When I stand on the shores of *Llyn Tegid*, I can visualise the cauldron of Cerridwen brewing the potion of Awen, smoke swirling through the air, the smell of herbs burning and boiling as the mountain air brushes my face. If it is not possible to visit Wales, then watch videos online of drones flying over the landscape and then meditate on these visuals, placing yourself into the areas and exploring them spiritually rather than physically. The myths of Wales are heavily connected and intertwined with the land.

Overall, have fun. Delving into ancient myths, which connect us to times of old, can seem like an awfully serious thing, and it certainly is. However, as serious as a spiritual pursuit of this nature might be, we must also allow our inner whimsical nature and creative power to run wild. Dive into the spirit of Celtica, a spirit that is ripe with artistic expression and childlike wonder.

Chapter 5

Beyond Human:
Divinities of the Land

My first encounter with what I believe to be a deity happened when I was a mere twelve years old. I was leaving the comforts and security of childhood and entering a much bigger world. At this age, I was beginning to come to terms with my sexuality, my individuality, and my identity. It scared me that I felt like some broken, misunderstood freak of nature. I felt as though I had no one in my life I could truly turn to. On this day in particular, I had been targeted by a group of older boys, and bullied to the point of breaking down. I arrived home off the school bus and instantly isolated myself in my bedroom. I drew the curtains, locked the door, turned off the lights, and threw myself into bed. I began crying, having those hopeless self-deprecating thoughts: *Why am I such a freak? Why can't they all just leave me alone? What have I ever done to deserve all this torment?* I cried and I cried, until I had no more tears. My head ached and pounded, my nose felt clogged and disgusting. I drifted to sleep, exhausted at the thought of continuing to live like this.

The dream began; I was walking through a meadow filled with the most vibrant wild flowers. The sky was a beautiful crimson colour, as the sun set before me. There was a smell of lavender in the air, as well as wood smoke. Tiny glowing insects flitted around me, little fireflies. I continued walking until I came to a small river or stream cutting through the meadow. I glanced at my dim reflection in the water below me. Listened to the water as it gurgled against the rocks. Then, suddenly, I felt a presence. As though I was being watched. I looked up, and there she was. A woman, sitting on the opposite side of the river to me, her feet bathing in the clear running water. She wore what looked like a long, white nightgown. Her long, waist-length, auburn hair tied in a messy, yet elegant braid that fell down her right side. She was beautiful. There was an innocence to her, though she looked like an adult. She had a childlike wonder that made me feel at complete ease. She smiled, and I smiled back at her. She held out her palm and gestured for me to copy her actions. I cupped my hands, palms facing my face. She dunked her hands into the water of the river and allowed the stream to gently wash over them. I followed suit, feeling the cold yet comfortable embrace of the river. She then raised her cupped hands and washed her face with the water, and as she did so did I. We sat there together, washing our faces. No words were exchanged, only gentle smiles. I woke up to my mother telling me that food was ready. The emotions that had plagued me before my nap were no longer weighing so heavily on my shoulders. I felt renewed, refreshed.

I can still visualise that dream with perfect clarity to this day. Whenever I conjure an image of a goddess in my mind, that auburn-haired river lady always comes to mind. I do not think that just because it was a dream it was a simple conjuration of my imagination. She came to me when I needed her, and I have felt her embrace countless times since. She was a goddess, this I know. Who exactly she was I still wonder. Was she Braint? In her healing, gentle power, possibly. Braint is the goddess of spring and of healing. Braint is the divinity that I associate the most with this divine lady that came to me. However, she may well be another spirit associated with my locale, her name lost to the mists of time.

Working with Deities as a Witch

A Witches' relationship with deity is an exceptionally personal and individualistic endeavour. Even two Witches, who believe in, work with, or worship the same deity, will have two completely different experiences. The way we perceive the deities, work with them, and see them will differ completely. It is this personal, unique relationship that makes writing about deities extremely difficult; however, it is also what makes it an experience worth doing.

I cannot with a clear conscious attempt to write about deities as some expert in the field; in fact my personal relationship with deities is chaotic and filled with more questions than answers. I still struggle with how exactly I believe in deities, whether I see them as personifications of natural events and places, or whether I view them as cosmic entities who watch us from above, or a mixture of both. I have even toyed with the idea that deities do not literally exist, and are instead just projections of our own human psyche tapping into something bigger than just ourselves. My job is not to tell you what a deity is, or how they function; that is for you to explore and delve into in your own spiritual endeavour. In fact, it is also absolutely possible to explore Witchcraft and magic without including deities into your practise. However, despite my chaotic and confusing relationship with the concept of deity, they do play a prominent role in my practise. I felt it was important to touch upon deity as we have deities that are specific to Wales and Welsh Celtic practises. Welsh mythology is littered with prominent divine entities who can offer an insight into our complex world, and be highly useful and informative allies in magic and spirituality.

As I have already mentioned, working with deities is not a requirement for exploring magic or Witchcraft. However, understanding and acknowledging the existence of these deities in the myths and cultural continuum of Wales can offer us a depth of understanding of the land, the people, and the culture of Wales as well as the magic found in the Welsh Celtic cultural continuum. Whether your hope is to explore Welsh deities in order to find a deity to work with on your path, or your hope is to explore deities simply as a means of understanding the spirit of Celtica and the magic of the people of Wales, you are entirely valid and justified in your exploration.

Within the Witching communities, especially in modern online groups and forums, you will find mentions of patron, or chosen, deities. There is much confusion among those who are new to the path of Witchcraft or Paganism regarding how one finds "their deity." The idea of each of us having a deity we are meant to specifically work with is an ideology that is common among modern practitioners, and one I deeply disagree with. The truth of the matter is that you can choose to work with a deity regardless of whether that deity specifically chooses you. You can and should in my opinion, if you so choose to work with deity at all, work with and turn to a number of deities. Can it sometimes seem as though a specific deity is choosing directly to work with you? Absolutely. Often we will find ourselves dreaming, and feeling intensely drawn to specific deities. Certain deities can also appear to you seemingly out of nowhere not long after you have read about them or heard of them. Almost as though by giving them the tiniest bit of attention, they are popping up to see if you are willing to work with them in a more personal context. However, being drawn to one or two deities specifically does not, under any circumstances, mean that you must devote your entire spiritual practise to them and them alone.

Some view deities not as divine entities but as archetypes of universal concepts and patterns. I once toyed with this idea in my practice, especially as it became a buzz-topic in Pagan spaces for some time. The way in which some Pagans and Witches discussed the idea of deities being archetypes made it sound scientific, grounded, and realistic. The idea was attractive, but after some time and consideration, I do not truly believe deities are simply archetypes. An archetype is an idea, and ideas do not have their own agency and forms of influence. I believe the gods are real divine beings, capable of taking on their own forms and influencing the world in which we live in. Through experience and practice, I understand the gods as sentient, emotive entities with their own personalities and influence. They do not merely exist within my mind as a construct.

Deities are powerful spiritual allies for the Witch, though our relationship with them need not be merely transactional in nature. Throughout history, across various cultures, people have called to the gods to help them with numerous facets of their lives. We may turn to a god such a Gwyn ap Nudd, a psychopomp whose power is directly related to liminality and transition, when dealing with the death of a loved one. However, the very foundation of a relationship with the gods should be, in my humble opinion, built upon love and appreciation. The gods challenge us, love us, and aid us in connecting with the world around us in profound and magical ways. Beyond being a Witch, I am also a Celtic polytheist. I hold a reverence and love for the many gods of my regional landscape. Allow me to introduce you to them as best as I can.

The Deities of Wales

The majority of the most commonly known deities of Wales stem from the Mabinogi, the collection of Welsh myths and legends. By exploring the various tales and legends in the Mabinogi, we are made familiar with a variety of important and powerful characters. However, beyond the mythologies and texts there are also entities and deities specific to various locations throughout Wales. Rivers, locations, and even certain towns and cities not only in Wales but also across the world have region specific deities rarely found in much recorded mythology, yet still commonly found in folkloric legend and belief. One goddess of this regional variety is Aerfen, a goddess often associated with the River Dee. Living a short walk from the banks of the river Dee currently, I have become accustomed to hearing about Aerfen despite the fact that when I lived on Ynys Môn, I had not heard of her at all. Finding reputable sources regarding Aerfen as a goddess is difficult. Many claim that Aerfen is associated with war, battle, and sacrifice. I have not dived into a more scholarly study of Aerfen; instead, I have simply built a connection with the spirit of the river over the years of living near its banks. Rivers run through many towns, cities, and villages in Wales and across the world today. Once upon a time, these stretches of water would have been the beating heart of these regions, either being a primary source of water or being where boats and ships brought food and items to the people. It is easy to see how these rivers gained identities of their own, and those identities are an insight into the connection deities have with the land and the local people.

The deities found throughout Welsh mythology are fickle entities. Whilst discussing Welsh deities with a non-Pagan friend of mine who was also born and raised in Wales and is familiar with Welsh mythology, she became completely confused at my description of Cerridwen as a goddess.

"But Cerridwen isn't a goddess," she said to me. "She's just a Witch, just an ordinary Witch. The story doesn't mention she's a goddess ever."

This is the tricky thing with Welsh mythology; much of the deities we as Pagans and Witches turn to from the Welsh texts are presented in their stories as being ordinary mortals. However, read between the lines and you will notice qualities that these entities hold which make them obviously more than human, and denote a divine existence. Cerridwen is a Witch with transformative abilities who manages to brew a potion of pure Awen, a feat I am not sure many a Witch today could accomplish. If Cerridwen was not a goddess during her original tale, then she should certainly be considered deified today. The tale of Cerridwen brewing her potion of Awen in the Mabinogi may appear to present her as completely human on the surface, and yet certain components of the story certainly imply she transcends mortality. The same can be said for many of the prominent Welsh deities.

Within the next few pages, I will outline some of the key deities I have worked with, and continue to work with in my personal practise. This is by no means an exhaustive list of Welsh deities; far from it, in fact. I heartily recommend that you look beyond this book to find information on other Celtic deities. These are deities specific to my magical practise, and my personal spiritual beliefs. The majority of the deities mentioned here stem from Welsh mythology, with one deviant being the Witches' devil, who whilst not specifically Welsh I believed was important to include here as the Devil in his many guises plays a prominent role in the historiography of Witchcraft in Wales. You will notice that I will mention goddesses a bit more frequently than I will mention gods. This is not intentional; this is merely a peak into my personal practise, and it just so happens that at this current moment in time whilst writing this, I have had much more experiences with goddesses than gods. This might be to do with the fact that I am a young woman who is still learning to accept and embrace my own divine femininity. As I mentioned before, each individual's experience with the divine will be unique.

There are various other deities from the Welsh Celtic cultural continuum that the Celtic Witch may choose to involve in their practises. Again, this is far from a comprehensive guide. Some may be screaming that I left out any detailed insight into deities such as the celestial goddess Aranrhod (often spelt Arianrhod), Mabon the divine son, and various other Welsh divinities such as Pwyll, Rhiannon's consort and a prince of the kingdom of Dyfed, the glorious Bran from the story of Branwen and the dark, shadowy Efnisien. However, those deities have not played a poignant role in my personal practise as of yet and that is why I felt I was not of authority to speak much of their nature. I heartily suggest that those with a drawing to working with deities should continue their research far beyond the constraints of this book. Delve into the mythology of the land, read of the experiences of other Pagans, Witches, and magical practitioners with a Celtic practise and forge your own connections and experiences.

Modron: The Great Mother

I would argue that it is difficult to find a Witch today who does not have a deep spiritual connection to our bountiful Mother Earth. The archetypes surrounding the great Mother Earth goddess are highly revered in various streams and traditions of modern Witchcraft. The great goddess is a central and pivotal aspect of many a Witches' practise, and so it should not be a surprise that as a Welsh Witch I feel a reverence and devotion to Modron, the Welsh great mother goddess. Modron is the one constant goddess who plays an active role in my daily practises. Throughout the year, throughout the ever-changing seasons she is relevant and important to me and my magic. I keep a seasonal altar, and this altar changes throughout the year with the changing of the seasons. Whenever I decide it is time to change the altar I feel that it is Modron who initiates the desire for change. She speaks to me through various methods, and I instantly know it is time for the change to occur.

Modron is akin to various great mother goddesses found globally in various traditions, cultures, and religions. However, within my personal spiritual explorations and practises I have found that she simply is the very spirit of our planet, our home. She represents all that it means to be a mother; she is nourishing, maternal, protective, and wise and yet beyond her delicate, healing nature she is not afraid to teach you the tough, hard lessons of life. Many find it easier to create a human-like image in their mind of their deities, and I do indeed do this with many of the deities I work with; however, Modron is one I find it difficult to do this with. When I visualise Modron as a human woman I disconnect with her and feel deeply uncomfortable. To me, Modron is a feeling; I feel her constant presence in the gentle breezes of spring, the heavy heat of summer, the stinging cold of winter, and the powerful storms of autumn. She is the only deity that has no face in my mind's eye, and yet she is easily recognisable to me.

Those who practise modern Witchcraft from a Wiccan or Neopagan perspective should be adequately familiar with the concept of the goddess and her consort who also happens to be her child. Modron is most notably associated with her divine son, Mabon, he who is imprisoned and kept from his mother only to later be released. The story of the great mother and her divine child is ripe within modern Neopagans traditions, and may be associated with various Celtic deities including Modron and her son, Mabon. I will not be diving too deeply into who Mabon is as an entity in this section, as instead I would like to focus on Modron as a Welsh equivalent to the standard image of the goddess who is central to many Witch traditions. However, if you are familiar with the modern telling of the tales of the goddess and her consort then you are familiar with the very spirit of Modron and Mabon's place in Welsh mythology. Tales of the goddess' child or consort being taken from her, only for the Earth to wither and die in his absence. Once he is reborn or released, the Earth flourishes once again. Modron and Mabon are the very deities who aid the magical practitioner in studying, learning, and knowing of the secrets of the changing of the seasons.

Within a Welsh tradition of Witchcraft and magic, we have various goddesses, which we can look to as allies in our magical practise and our spiritual journey. Each Welsh goddess, from Cerridwen and Aranrhod through to Rhiannon, hold qualities associated with Modron. That of the divine mother. However, Modron is the goddess whom I feel the deeply maternal presence of in all aspects of my life. She is our mother, our home, our land, and our constant guide.

✪ EXERCISE ✪
Breathe with Modron

This exercise is a meditation that draws upon the transformative nature of Modron throughout the seasons. Modron represents the changing landscape, our Earthly home that undergoes change on a regular basis. As the seasons change, as summer becomes autumn and autumn becomes spring and so forth, we can hone in on and recognise the changing nature of the mother goddess herself. Who she is throughout the cycle and how she may influence our spiritual and magical practise.

Begin this exercise by finding a quiet, comfortable space that you will not be disturbed in for the duration of your meditation. Make the space your own, light candles and incense to your desire. If possible, perhaps find a place from which you can look at the outside world from. This could mean a room where you can look out the window into a garden or natural space, or perhaps you feel drawn to conduct this exercise outdoors surrounded by nature. Whatever works best for you.

Make yourself comfortable; sit down or lie down. Take three deep breaths, in through the nose and out through the mouth. Allow your diaphragm, or stomach region to expand with each inhale and release completely with each exhale. Once you have taken three deep breaths, close your eyes.

Focus in on your breathing to aid you in letting go of any mundane, outside worries and fears you may have carried with you throughout the day. With each inhale focus on those worries, and with each exhale let them go, disperse them into the universe and out of your body. Allow yourself to fully relax, noticing any tense muscles and focusing on relaxing those tensions. For a moment, simply focus in on your body and your breath, not allowing any outside world influences or mundane worldly concerns to flood your mind. You are here to connect with the great mother, an element of which exists within you.

Once you are fully relaxed and feel ready to continue, begin by pondering over the season of spring. What does spring mean to you? What imagery does spring evoke in your mind's eye? Perhaps spring makes you think of potentiality, new beginnings and birth. Perhaps spring to you evokes imagery of the stirring of the Earth, after a cold, dark, harsh winter, new life is breaking through the soil and clearing the way for brighter, warmer days ahead. Truly delve into this exploration of spring, ponder over any memories you have from the past springs you have experienced. What does the spring truly mean to you? As you ponder over these things, begin to visualise the great mother goddess in your mind. How does she look in her spring guise to you? For most Pagans and Witches who work closely with the goddess, during the spring time she appears to us as a young girl, a maiden, a young, spritely goddess bursting with the spirit and magic of potentiality. How does she appear to you? Embrace any imagery that emerge from your subconscious.

Continue to breathe deeply, allowing any potent imagery to store away in your mind for the final part of this exercise. When you feel as though you have spent enough time pondering over the spring elements of the Mother, begin to shift into the season of summer.

Once again, focus on what imagery and emotions the season of summer evokes within you. In a traditional sense, the goddess is within her guise as a mother, a bearer of new life and potent fertility during the summer months. The summer months bring us a spirit of independence, of blossoming experiences, and of pure warmth. Connect this tradition imagery associated with the goddess with your personal experiences of summer. Ponder over what happens to the Earth, to your local natural areas during summer. Allow those images to flood your mind.

Once you have spent enough time pondering over summer, it is time to move on to the crisp, transformative, liminal season that is the autumn, or fall.

What does autumn look like in your part of the world? Do the leaves turn crimson and gold? Does the air grow colder and crisp? Do the rains fall heavily? Ponder over these things. As you consider what the autumn months mean to you, ponder also over the spiritual symbolism found in the season. The autumn is a time of transformation, of liminality. Things are dying, yet not quite dead. It gets colder, but not quite cold. It is a time of letting go, of releasing any energies that no longer serve us. The goddess grows older, wiser. It is a time to harvest all that we have sown over the warmer months that have passed. We prepare for what we intuitively know is coming next. Breathe deeply as you visualise the goddess in her autumnal guise. Who is she to you? How does she appear to you? Take one deep breath before changing the seasons in your mind's eye one final time.

Now we come to the season of winter. The liminal, crimson days of autumn have come to an end. Creatures are now hibernating, trees have shed their leaves, and the air is sharp and cold. This is a time of death, of darkness, and of delving into our shadow elements. It is a time when the goddess is now old, ancient, and reaching her end. Of course, the end is but the beginning. For the Celtic Pagan, death is not an ending or a purely negative thing. Darkness is but another light that offers us a new, deeper perspective on life. Death is transformative, powerful, and necessary. Therefore, we honour the goddess at this time of year in her guise as the ancient crone, but also as the bearer of new beginnings. Soon the Earth will be born anew, but for now, we must dwell in that uncomfortable environment of shadow. What lessons can this time of year teach us? Visualise how the goddess in her winter guise appears to you.

Take another deep, cleansing breath. This time breathe deeply into your diaphragm on a count of four, and hold your breath for four counts, before finally releasing a powerful sigh from your gut on another count of four. Ponder over all you have visualised and considered throughout this meditation.

Open your eyes once you are comfortable, and shake out your body to wake it up. Grab a notebook and a pen and journal all that you experienced within your meditation. Carry these experiences with you out into the world. As the seasons change in your local area, consider the goddess, our great mother. She guides us and carries us throughout the cycle, offering us an insight into what the seasons may bring.

Rhiannon: The Goddess of Sovereignty

Arguably the most popular Welsh deity, Rhiannon is a goddess many Witches worldwide feel drawn to work with. As a teenager, I felt heavily drawn to Rhiannon, and for a time even referred to her as my patron deity. Nowadays I do not work as closely with her; however, I still hold a deep reverence and respect for this enigmatic goddess.

Rhiannon is first introduced to us in the first branch of the Mabinogi. In the tale Pwyll, prince of Dyfed, hears whispers that upon a hill named *Gorsedd Arberth* if one was to sit there for a while, one of two things may happen to them: they would either go insane or they would see something absolutely miraculous. Pwyll, deciding he had no fear, went to the hill to seek the miraculous thing that might happen to him. Lo and behold, as he sat upon the hill he came to notice a beautiful maiden riding on a graceful white mare. Pwyll, besotted by this ethereal maiden, went chasing after her. By some mischief and magic, he found that neither he nor his men could catch up to this lady as she rode on her horse, despite the fact that she never seemed to go any faster than a gentle trot. Eventually, after chasing for a while Pwyll called out to her and asked her to stop so that he may speak to her. She did stop, and said to him that he need only ask and she would have slowed down much earlier.

Rhiannon is an ethereal lady, originating from the Celtic otherworld. Eventually she marries Pwyll. Her later tales are exceptionally sorrowful. Later in the Mabinogi, she is falsely accused of murdering her own child, and is punished by having to carry people upon her back whilst reciting her apparent crimes to them.

With her associations with mystical white mares and her punishment being to carry people on her back like a horse, Rhiannon is quite obviously associated with horses. The Welsh goddess of horses, as well as being the powerful deity of sovereignty, grief, and even as a liminal entity who can aid the magical practitioner in connecting with the realms beyond our own. I find Rhiannon to be a very accessible and comforting deity to connect with, and I can clearly understand why so many Witches today are drawn to her healing and nurturing nature. Rhiannon can aid us in healing from intense grief and trauma, as she is very much aware of what it feels like to go through such things. She also teaches us how to stand tall and proud in our own lived truth. We live in a world where people make nasty and judgemental assumptions about us and our lives without having heard the full truth. Rhiannon is a deity I often turn to when I struggle with insecurity and doubt propelled by the perception of me others hold in their hearts.

✸ EXERCISE ✸
Rhiannon's Embrace Charm Bag

The goddess Rhiannon is a nurturing, maternal figure who can aid in helping us heal from our traumas and insecurities. She relates to any pain you may be feeling, and if you forge a connection with her, she will take you on a visceral, emotional journey into healing and self-betterment. Through experience, she has always been the goddess I turn to when at my lowest points, when I needed a gentle, loving spirit to hold me in her embrace and give me a slight nudge toward what I needed.

This *Swyn* or charm spell is practical, and can be utilised with ease. Taking inspiration from traditional Welsh charmers and their petitionary prayers to help heal ailments and other issues, this spell is primarily a petitionary prayer to the goddess Rhiannon. It can be used daily, especially if you struggle with social anxieties and deep insecurities.

What you will need:

- A piece of paper
- A pen
- Dried lavender
- A small pouch or bag

On a piece of paper, write out the following prayer. You can write it in either Welsh or English; I personally choose to write it in Welsh in order to honour Rhiannon's mother tongue.

Cyfarchaf ti O Rhiannon, cariad mamwys y tir hon,
Cymortha fi heddiw i fod yn hyderus, nerthus a hapus,
Rho dy gymorth i mi ddyru my mhryder,
Rho dy gymorth i mi ddyru amheuaeth,
Rhiannon, sofraniaeth y tir,
Gofynai i ti fy annog i fod y gore y gallai fod heddiw.
Cyfarchaf ti O Rhiannon, fy arglwyddes, fy Nuwies.

Translation:
I call to you, O Rhiannon, maternal spirit of this land,
Support me today to be confident, strong, and happy,
Give unto me your support to aid me in banishing anxiety,
Give unto me your support to aid me in banishing doubt,
Rhiannon, sovereign of the land,
I ask you to aid me in being the best version of myself,
I call to you Rhiannon, my lady, my goddess.

Once you have written the prayer down on the piece of paper, take a deep breath and recite it aloud. It may be beneficial if you choose to utilise this as a daily prayer to familiarise yourself with the words and learn them by heart. Next, roll the piece of paper up and place it into the small bag or pouch. Take your dried lavender and sprinkle it into the bag with the paper. Fill the bag to your desire with the dried herb. Close the bag once done, and ensure its contents are completely secure.

You now have a charm bag. Carry this charm bag with you on days that you are feeling less than great. Remember that the charm bag is with you, carrying your petitionary prayer to the goddess Rhiannon. Allow her nurturing spirit to be with you, and provide you with strength for the duration of the day. When you are feeling entirely low, recite the prayer aloud again, truly embracing each word, allowing the goddess' spirit to fuel you, fill you, and guide you.

You may also choose to hide the charm bag in your home, or at your workplace. Keep it somewhere that you will be reminded of it on a regular basis, and allow its potent magical energies to empower you and strengthen you.

Llŷr: The Divine Power of the Sea

Despite my partiality toward goddesses, one god has played a prominent and powerful role not only in my spiritual and magical practise, but also in my personal life since I was born. That god is Llŷr, the very god of the sea itself. I have always held a deep kinship and reverence with the sea, having grown up on an island, it surrounded me. Not only was I raised on an island, but also I was specifically raised in a seaside village. My village home boasts some of the most beautiful and diverse coastal paths and beaches that I have ever seen in my life. A five-minute walk from my childhood home led you to the river Ffraw; follow the river due southwest and you would come to the mouth of the river and the glorious sea, which overlooks the Snowdon mountain range. The sea has always been a prominent part of my life; I spent many of my childhood days either feeling the salty sea air against my skin as I walked the coastal paths or swimming in the waves with friends and family.

Within the Welsh mythology Llŷr is the divine father of various other prominent figures, such as the great king Bran, and the tortured, mistreated Branwen.

To me, Llŷr is a beneficial ally to aid in understanding the intricacies of connectivity. The sea and the vastness of the ocean stretches across our blue planet. By tapping into the energies of Llŷr, we see beyond what separates us and makes us different to one another, instead focusing on how we are similar. Evolutionarily speaking the sea is every single human's ancestral home. We are all the accumulation of creatures who at one point chose to crawl onto land from the depths of the sea. Llŷr can also help remind us that life is still full of mystery and wonder. In this modern day and age, it is easy to assume that we humans know all we could ever need to know about the world in which we live. Yet, our Earth's oceans is still largely unexplored. Approximately eighty percent of the world's oceans are a complete unknown for us. This is an alarming and important insight into the notion that there is always so much to learn. I often turn to Llŷr when I wish to reignite my desire and passion for learning. He reminds me of how much I still do not know, he humbles me and sparks my desire to question everything.

If you live near the sea, you could tap into the spirit of Llŷr by visiting the nearest beach or coastal areas and practicing this simple meditative ritual.

✪ EXERCISE ✪
Visualising Llŷr

Take yourself to the sea, and stand watching the waves as they lap against the shore. Whether the sea is calm and gentle, or rough and stormy, it holds a potent strength. Watch the waters for a while, envisioning what might dwell beneath the ripples and waves you see upon the surface. As you watch the waters, focus on how the surface of the water looks. Notice any differences in colour, any tidal movements and currents. Truly familiarise yourself with how the sea looks before you.

Close your eyes and take a deep breath with the sea, smelling the salty sea air and embracing its healing qualities. With eyes still closed, listen to the sounds surrounding you. Hear the waves, hear the winds, and hear the creatures that surround the sea. For a moment just be. You alone with the sea.

When you feel ready to do so, open your eyes and find the horizon. Focus on the horizon ahead; what lies beyond the boundary of what our eyes can see? Whilst focusing on the horizon, take deep breaths and ponder over how the sea connects us all. Every continent on Earth touches the sea. It is also our evolutionary home; all life originated from the waters of this Earth. Just breathe, and consider these facts. Consider also how the sea was once exceptionally important for the many Celtic nations. Before roads and transportation vehicles on land were commonplace, many folk travelled by sea to and from important places. Many communities relied on the sea to help nourish and feed them.

Visualise Llŷr in your mind, the mighty Celtic sea god. How does he appear to you? Can you visualise him as a physical manifestation? A personification of the strength of the sea? Take note of how he appears to you in your mind's eye. With one deep breath again, exit your meditative state. Take notes in your journal about your experiences breathing with the sea, for these simple meditative tasks are a form of communing with Llŷr and the spirits of the sea.

Braint: Fiery Goddess of Spring and Healing

As the clutches of winter slowly release to give way to the warmth and potential of spring, we feel the gentle embrace and stirrings of this wonderfully healing spirit. The goddess whom I celebrate most often in the spring within my practise is Braint. She is worshipped throughout Britain as well as the rest of the world under the guise of Brighid among various other names. Braint is specifically special to me as a deity considering that I grew up on Ynys Môn, the isle of Anglesey, where the *Afon Braint* runs through the island. This sacred river was one I passed on my daily travels. A river steeped in rich lore of being said to be bestowed with potent healing qualities.

Kristoffer Hughes in *The Book of Celtic Magic* delves into Braint as a goddess, her history, and lore in a far deeper manner than I will here. He mentions that Afon Braint was originally a river named after the goddess Briganta and that over time Briganta became Braint. She is a goddess with many names, many facets; the popular Brighid, Brigid, Brig, Brigit, Brigatona, and even the Welsh Saint Ffraid all have their origins in the same divine entity.

She is among the more nurturing, caring deities I have ever worked with. Braint makes me feel at home, at one with myself. In February I usually clear a space and create a little altar near my primary home altar specifically dedicated to Braint. On this altar, I place an abundance of candles, as well as some freshly picked daffodils in a vase and sometimes a bottle or jar filled with water collected from *Afon Braint*.

For the Witch, Braint is a beneficial ally in healing magic. Her gentle warmth soothes the soul and assists in promoting good health. As someone who has dealt with and still occasionally deals with mental health issues, Braint is a go-to deity of mine to invoke in petitionary spells for mental well-being and calm.

⊛ EXERCISE ⊛
A Simple Candle Spell for Distance Healing

Braint is a goddess of spring, of the fertile stirrings of the Earth, but she is also a goddess of healing. Though she is a specifically potent ally in promoting self-healing, she can also help us to send healing manifestations unto those we hold near and dear. This simple candle spell can be utilised to send distant healing to those we feel need it. This could mean healing of a spiritual, mental nature for those who are struggling with mental traumas and concerns, but can also be used as an additional healing spell to aid the healing of physical ailments too.

Begin with a pure white candle; it can be in any shape you desire. This spell requires you to burn the candle down completely; therefore, I suggest using a candle with a short burn time to err on the safe side of things. Using a knife or other carving tool, carve the name of the individual you wish to send healing to onto the candle. Next, allow the candle to soften and melt slightly. There are many ways you could accomplish this: you could leave the candle in front of a fire or heat source for a while, or perhaps leave it out in the sunshine for a while if you live somewhere warm and sunny. The idea is to try to get the candle tacky and soft, so that things can stick to it easily. When the candle is soft enough for things to stick onto it, grind some healing herbs and rub them onto it. Use whatever herbs you feel would work best; research herbal magical knowledge and decipher which would be best to use. I suggest using ginger, utilising its revitalising and healing qualities. You could also rub seeds onto the candle as a symbol of the goddess Braint and her sacred season, the spring.

Once the candle is covered in herbs and ready to use, sit with it for a while and meditate on that which you wish to accomplish. Visualise the individual you wish to send healing to, and imagine them being engulfed by a gentle, healing embrace.

Hold your hands above the candle and recite this chant, or construct your own chant.

Gentle Braint, goddess of spring,
Hear my words and hear my spell,
Send healing energies to (name) this day,
Know I only wish them well.

Take a moment to breathe deeply, focusing your intent on your desires. When you are ready, light the candle. Take a few moments to watch the flame, considering the intention behind this spell and the individual you wish to send healing to. Visualise the glow of the candlelight emanating out into the universe and reaching the target of this spell. As the light touches them, Braint's healing embrace surrounds them. Giving to them the strength they require to heal from whatever might be troubling them as of late. Allow the candle to burn down completely. Repeat this spell as and when necessary.

Gwydion: The Magician

Through the various texts, tales, and legends scattered throughout Wales, we find various spiritual and magical allies that can accompany the Witch along the crooked, mystical path. Among the various deities and entities already mentioned, and those not mentioned, one of the most beneficial and helpful entities to work alongside for the Celtic magical practitioner is probably Gwydion. Gwydion is an undoubtedly powerful magician, and his legacy is known throughout Wales today. He, alongside his sorcerous uncle Math, are probably the most recognisable of Celtic wizards or magicians from lore and legend.

Gwydion, as a prominent entity to walk alongside in your magical workings, will enlighten you to the importance of embracing your intrinsic whimsical nature, whilst also remaining scrupulous and consistent in your aim to become a competent and knowledgeable worker of magic.

Within the Welsh mythos he pops up quite consistently, though a personal favourite tale of mine is how he conjured a woman made entirely of flowers. The tale of Blodeuedd is one most individuals who grew up in Wales are familiar with. I remember the story being read to death in primary school, and I attended various theatrical performances of the tale throughout my youth.

The tale begins as a woman named Aranrhod, who is revered today as a Celtic goddess associated with the moon, the stars, fertility, and more. Aranrhod is having her virginity tested. The way in which her virginity is tested in the tale is by having her step over the semi-divine sorcerer and king Math's magic wand. As she does so it is made clear that she is not a virgin from the fact that she instantly gives birth to two children, one of which is a child of the sea and instantly crawls his way into the waves, vanishing into the realms of water. The magician Gwydion, however, conceals the other child. Gwydion vows to raise this child as his own, but there is one prominent problem. Aranrhod in her fury places a vicious set of curses on the child. The three curses she chooses to place on him are that he will never have a name, he will never bear arms, and he will never have a wife that is of this mortal realm. By his magical competency and wit, Gwydion manages to break each curse, allowing the child to be named as Lleu Laaw Gyffes. All is well and good, until Lleu begins pining for a wife. Aranrhod's final curse, that a mortal wife shall never love him, cuts deep and saddens the lad. Seeing his plight, Gwydion alongside his uncle Math construct a plan to conjure a wife for Lleu who is made entirely of plants and flowers.

By broom, meadowsweet, and oak flowers Gwydion and Math wave their wands, working transformative magic so that the ethereal and beautiful Blodeuedd can be born. With that, all three of Aranrhod's curses on Lleu are lifted.

There is more to this story, as heartache and magical chaos ensues. Delve into the fourth branch of the Mabinogi to explore this tale in more depth.

Though often foolhardy and childlike of spirit, Gwydion's magical prowess is a thing to be admired. By drawing on the tales of Gwydion and his nature as the very magician archetype, he can aid the practitioner and student of magic in furthering their studies and enhancing their magical competency.

Beyond this, he also aids us in connecting with the natural world around us, appreciating the connective energies of magic that flow throughout nature. In the *Kat Godeu* or *The Battle of the Trees,* a poem by the bard Taliesin, Gwydion is portrayed as being a caller or summoner of trees. This, alongside his ability to transform plants into people assigns him to being a useful ally in aiding us in connecting with trees and plants.

✪ EXERCISE ✪
Finding Your Wand

For many modern practitioners the concept of waving a magical wand within serious magical workings may feel silly and childish. When we think of magic wands today, they evoke imagery of fantasy, and fairy tale whimsy. However, wands are powerful tools when utilised by the Celtic practitioner of magic. Within Welsh myth and legend, wands are among the very few tools or magical paraphernalia ever explicitly mentioned to be used by magical practitioners of the past. Alongside the cauldron, the wand is a primary tool for the Welsh Witch if one chooses to use any tools at all.

Gwydion, as well as various other magicians throughout Welsh legend and lore, is known for using a wand when performing his magical talents. It seems that transformation and transformative energies are a core aspect of Celtic magic, as both the cauldron and the wand are symbols and useful tools in harnessing and casting transformative, creative magical workings.

Today wands are easily accessible. One can easily walk into a local metaphysical store and purchase a ready-made wand. Some carved beautifully from wood, others made from crystal and other materials. However, there is something deeply personal and effective about constructing your own wand. For the student of Celtic magic who wishes to include a wand into their practise, it is best suggested that they construct their own wand from wood that is native to their locale. This enhances a connection with the land and local spirits of place. There is no right or wrong way to forge a wand. Your wand should be unique to you, an extension of who you are as a person. Research the native trees in your area; consider which you are drawn to the most and which correspond with your personality the best. Some magical practitioners prefer to use readily fallen twigs and branches to make their wands; others ask the tree if it is acceptable for them to cut a fresh branch. Within a traditional sense, it is most commonly agreed upon that it is far more potent to utilise wood cut directly from the tree in order to construct any magical tool. This ensures that the tool will be imbued with the potent energetic spirit force of that tree. Many traditional Witches consider fallen twigs and branches to be "dead," and therefore not of magical value.

Here is an outline of how to construct your own wand to use in magical workings. The same method can be applied to construct a staff, walking stick, stang, or broom handle.

Step 1: Study and Preparation

Upon deciding to embark upon the endeavour of constructing your very own wand, the first step is study and preparation. Begin by thinking what it is you will use this wand for. Do you need it for a specific purpose? Or are you merely drawn to creating a wand in general?

If the latter suits you better, then you may benefit from merely wandering out into the woods and seeing what trees you are intuitively drawn to. Remember, however, research must be conducted to ensure the wood you construct your wand from is safe. You do not want to end up with a skin reaction or poisoning due to lack of knowledge.

However, if you have a specific purpose in mind for your wand, such as you wish to utilise it in healing workings, or for baneful magic, then it will benefit you to first delve into the virtues of trees and decipher which wood might best suit your desire. A guide to the virtues of most woods that wands and other tools can be constructed from will be found in a later chapter of this book.

Do not rush this process. Study what woods would best suit your desires, and what folklore surrounds that tree. Are there any specific times or dates that would be best to collect the wood during? Compile your research, put the work in, and keep in mind that the more effort you put into a magical endeavour, the more potent the outcome will be.

Step 2: Connecting with the Source

Once study has been completed and you are ready to gather your material, it is time to venture into the woods and begin searching for your tree. Once you have found the tree you feel most drawn to pull material from for your wand, spend some time connecting with the tree. Sit with it, meditate with it, speak to it. When you feel ready, ask the tree for permission to take of it what you need. Witches often ask me, "How do you know if the tree says no?" My personal method of deciphering whether the tree agrees with my taking a branch from it is a mixture of intuition and there being no obvious signs of protest. You will know if the answer is no, for the natural world will send omens your way or you will intuitively feel that something is deeply wrong. Some practitioners I know prefer to give the tree time and will ask the tree for permission and then leave it for a few days or weeks. If the branch has fallen or any dreams enter the practitioner's mind steering them away, they see this as a sign that it is not meant to be.

Step 3: Cutting the Branch

The next step is to cut the branch. Ensure that you cut cleanly with appropriate tools, never snapping a branch off the tree in a vulgar, violent manner. Once it has been cut, do not allow it to fall to the ground, preserving the virtues of the branch and the streaming spirit force of the tree as much as possible. When carrying it home, you may choose to carry it in your hand as a method of connecting to your soon-to-be tool, or you may place it in a bag or pouch made of natural fibres. Leave the branch in a dry, warm place until it is completely dry.

Step 4: Personalisation

Once the branch is dry, it is time to personalise it to your desires. Carve out the wood, smooth it out, and apply paints, oils, ribbons, strings, or anything you feel drawn to add. This is the time to get creative. Ensure your wand is personalised in a practical manner; however, there is no use in a wand that is uncomfortable to hold.

Step 5: Dedication

The next step is to dedicate your wand to your working practise. Spend some time running the wand through incense smoke, such as incense made from dried elderflower, a plant of magical empowerment. You may choose to rub certain oils onto your wand also. This step must be personal: dedicate the wand to your magic, to the deities and familiar spirits that you work with, and solidify it as a tool that will serve you and your Witchery well.

The wand, acting as a road of power, utilised to direct energetic flow, and even as a tool for blasting, can also be used to draw out the magical circle, as well as any symbols the practitioner may wish to carve into the ground during their workings. The wood used to construct a wand would depend on the intrinsic qualities the Witch may wish for the wand to harness. Some wands, however, were traditionally said to be made with a bone handle. This was common for the traditional *consuriwr* or conjuror, whose ars magna was to conjure spirits, or work necromantic rites. Bone is a useful tool for spectral conjuration and communication, as bone speaks to bone. Therefore, a wand constructed of bone would be beneficial for necromantic and spirit-focused practise.

Chapter 6

Cerridwen: The Archetype of the Welsh Witch

Up to this point, I have merely offered you, the reader, a quick glimpse into the array of Celtic deities accessible to the Celtic Witch. However, I felt it necessary in a book exploring the Witchcraft and magical practises of Wales to devote a larger body of exploration into the Witch goddess herself. Cerridwen, the Welsh goddess of inspiration, transformation, and of course magic. A Witch wandering down the path of the Celtic practitioner should certainly familiarise themself with this enigmatic and powerful figure who exudes empowerment and a desire to delve deeper into the never-ending questions surrounding life.

Many authors, some far more learned and qualified than I, have undertaken an exploration of our revered Witch goddess. In approaching the writing of this chapter of the book, I will admit that I held a lot of fear. I was anxious of merely repeating the information I have read in the past, or of offending those who have a close bond with Cerridwen. Cerridwen herself however, would scrunch up her face in utter disgust at my cowardice had I chosen to abandon this chapter out of nothing but silly, self-induced fears and anxieties. I felt her presence shaking her head at me, and giving me a stern telling off to get to work, before she then placed her maternal hand on my shoulder and offered me gentle words of encouragement. I hope that this displays the kind of goddess Cerridwen is. She is a fierce, take-no-prisoners sorceress, and yet also a nurturing and caring motherly figure.

Cerridwen is the very archetype of the Welsh Witch. Keeper of the cauldron, she who guides us through the mysteries and points us in the right direction. Her image is that of a wild, magical woman that stands on the shores of her sacred lake stirring her powerful cauldron. All Witches who wish to explore the very nature of magic and mystery should strive to forge a lasting connection with the initiator of spiritual and magical competency. She may be a daunting figure to approach at first, yet keep it in your mind, that though Cerridwen may be assertive and domineering she is not cruel, nor sinister. Like many women who simply know who they are and stand proudly in their own power, Cerridwen is a figure who challenges our deeply ingrained prejudices and insecurities. We should be able to look at Cerridwen's fierce assertive tendencies and feel inspired, empowered and driven by them, not belittled. The first step in connecting with Cerridwen is to familiarise and educate yourself with her history, her power, and her legacy.

Earlier in this book, I mentioned that I do not believe deities to be archetypes. It may be confusing then that this chapter speaks of Cerridwen as the archetype of the Welsh Witch. I am not saying that Cerridwen herself is an archetype, but rather that she influenced the very archetypal image of a Witch within the Welsh cultural context. As we established earlier in this book, the image of the Witch as a pawn of Satan was not well-established in Wales as it was in Englasnd and Scotland. Cerridwen helps us define what a Witch is in a purely Welsh way.

Cerridwen is well known within the Welsh texts to be highly skilled and learned in the three magical arts. Those are the art of sorcery, of conjuration, and of divination. For the Witch or magical practitioner who yearns to be more competent in these areas of magical practise, Cerridwen is the perfect ally and guide.

Where does Cerridwen's legacy stem from, however? What myths, legends, and stories are there in Celtic Wales that speak of this powerful and enigmatic Witch goddess? There are mentions of Cerridwen littered throughout the notable Welsh bard Taliesin's poetry. In these poems, she is described as the very initiator of inspiration for artists, the divine keeper of the cauldron. However, her most notable and most prominent legend is probably that which is ultimately the tale of Taliesin's creation and birth. This tale goes by many names; however, I know it best as *Hanes Taliesin*, or the history of Taliesin. It is a tale that in my youth absolutely captivated me, and now in my adult years I am once again being drawn to the array of spiritual and magical symbolism found within the words of this story. Allow me to briefly summarise the tale. I would like to note that I highly suggest you seek alternative texts to aid in exploring this legend in depth.

Hanes Taliesin: The Tale of Taliesin

On the shores of a beautiful lake near the town of Bala in North Wales, lived a great and powerful Witch who went by the name of Cerridwen. Cerridwen was an enigmatic and powerful woman; the people who lived in the region held great respect for her, and a touch of fear. Cerridwen was learned in the three magical arts and was undoubtedly wise and knowledgeable.

Cerridwen, with her husband, the nobleman Tegid Foel, had the most beautiful daughter. They named her Creirfyw, which was apt as that name meant "the finest." Indeed, she was undoubtedly the finest, most beautiful woman in all the land. However, despite Creirfyw being blessed with ethereal beauty, Cerridwen and Tegid Foel's son seemed to have been cursed with utter wretchedness. The very sight of him was enough to render anyone absolutely disgusted. He was ugly, and so he was named Afagddu, "utter darkness."

Cerridwen was the only one who looked past Afagddu's hideousness. She loved him with maternal ferocity and yearned for him to be accepted by society. She knew he was capable of greatness, but the curse of his appearance would forever hinder him. Being a wise and powerful Witch, Cerridwen began to wonder if her magical knowledge could help her release Afagddu of the shackles of his ugliness. She ventured on a quest that could make her son loved by the people. Within an ancient grimoire, she discovered a potion that would give to he who ingested it the knowledge of all the mysteries of the universe. She decided that if Afagddu held superior intellect and wisdom, people would find it easy to look beyond his appearance. This potion was not an easy concoction to make; it took a long time to brew, a year and a day specifically. Regardless, Cerridwen loved her son so intensely that she was willing to do anything.

Cerridwen had a cauldron crafted for her, a large vessel made of cast iron. This cauldron would hold the potion that brewed a concoction of pure inspiration. She employed two individuals to care for the cauldron, the first being a blind man named Morda to watch the fire that boiled the mixture within, the other being a local farm boy named Gwion Bach to continually stir the potion. As time went by, the ingredients for this potent magical mixture were collected and the cauldron bubbled away. A year and a day went by without a single issue.

However, when the fateful day arrived Cerridwen was absent from the cauldron as something terrible happened. The potion was finally ready, when suddenly three drops of the potion leaped out of the cauldron and landed on Gwion Bach's thumb. Instinctively the poor farm boy rushed his burning thumb into his mouth to try to soothe the pain, ingesting the three sacred drops. Without realising it, Gwion Bach had taken the mystical concoction of inspiration. The rest of the potion was rendered useless, turning into a horrendous poison. Gwion was now the keeper of all the secrets of the universe.

Cerridwen arrived at the cauldron and intuitively knew what had happened the moment she laid eyes on Gwion. Gwion, now being supremely wise, knew that Cerridwen would be furious that her long act of labour had gone to waste. He instantly began to run away from the Witch. Now being bestowed with the wisdom of the Awen, he found that he had the magical ability to shapeshift and so took it upon himself to become a hare in order to outrun Cerridwen. Cerridwen in her fury chased after him, changing her shape to that of a sleek and quick greyhound. They chased each other over the realms of the land, the hills, and mountains until eventually Gwion came to a river. Gwion dove into the river and transformed himself into a salmon. Cerridwen was relentless and followed him into the icy waters, transforming herself into an otter bitch. The chase continued through the realms of water, as they followed the currents. Gwion, fearful that Cerridwen might catch him, leaped from the waters and into the skies, changing this time into a wren. He flew up into the clouds. Cerridwen's anger propelled her into the sky too, as she changed to become a hawk and continued to pursue her victim. She desperately wanted to kill him for spoiling her magical potion that would save her son. Gwion flew over a farm and concluded that Cerridwen would never find him if he were to transform himself into a single grain of wheat. He flew himself into the wheat heap and transformed instantly. He must have underestimated the depths of Cerridwen's anger, as she transformed herself magically into a black tufted hen and pecked at the grains of wheat. She pecked and pecked until none were left: Gwion Bach as a grain of wheat had been consumed.

By the magic within him, and the power of the Awen, Gwion would not die however. The grain transformed into a baby growing in Cerridwen's womb. As months went by, she began to feel the kicks of the baby within her body. Cerridwen decided that she would destroy the baby after she gave birth to him. However, when the day arrived that the child was born she could not bring herself to do it. The child was blessed with such beauty, and the ethereal power of the Awen that swelled within him was obvious. She decided the child would live, but not with her. She placed the child into a leather coracle and set it out to sea, allowing the spirits of the realm of sea to do with him as they saw fit.

The baby remained a baby for forty years, floating in the seas of Wales. Until one fateful night, a man by the name of Elffin found it. As he unwrapped the child from the coracle a light shone on the child's brow and so, he was aptly named Taliesin, he with the radiant brow. That is how the great bard Taliesin came to be.

The End.[32]

Read this tale and digest the main elements. It is a tale of transformation, of magic, but most notably, it is a tale of initiation. Unwillingly, Cerridwen initiated the mundane farm boy into the secrets and mysteries of the universe. Gwion Bach began as but a simple boy, employed to stir a grand cauldron for a wise Witch, and ultimately he is reborn as a wise and powerful

---

32. This is my retelling of *Hanes Taliesin*, inspired greatly by the explorations found in Kristoffer Hughes' *From the Cauldron Born*.

character. He would become a powerful prophet and bard. As a magical ally, a goddess to be revered within your practise, Cerridwen can offer an insight into the same mysteries for you. Work alongside her and bestow upon her the respect a powerful and enchanting goddess deserves, and she will lead you down the crooked path.

The Witch's Cauldron

One of the most enigmatic and captivating components of the tale of Cerridwen and the birth of Taliesin is her magical cauldron within which she brewed a potion of Awen. This mystical artefact aided in producing a concoction that held the entire wealth of knowledge and wisdom found in the known and unknown universe. The cauldron itself is a symbol of transformation, inspiration, and the mysteries of magic. This is why I believe the cauldron to be one of, if not the, most important tools utilised by the Celtic Witch.

It must be remembered that tools are but mundane objects until imbued with power, which we give to them. A Witch's power comes not from their collection of artefacts, items, and oddities but from within. The cauldron is a potent, powerful tool to utilise in magical practise and serves many practical functions, too. However, I am not saying that one must rush out to their nearest metaphysical store to purchase the grandest of cauldrons they can get their hands on in order to be able to perform magic adequately. A tool is only as powerful as the practitioner that utilises it. My first-ever cauldron was nothing more than a simple old cooking pot. Over time, my cauldrons have evolved with my practise. I have owned cauldrons made of stainless steel, brass, clay-based materials such as ceramic pots, and of course cast iron. Nowadays I use a decent-sized cast iron cauldron for numerous magical workings. Your cauldron, much like most aspects of your practise, should be unique to you. Some of the best Witches I have ever met are crafty and are blessed with creative ingenuity, which allows them to think outside of the box. If you are drawn to use an old cooking pot, a plant pot or even a small teacup as a cauldron, there is no shame in that at all. In fact, there is something to admire about a Witch who utilises what they have at hand. The only advice I would give is to be cautious of material depending on what you wish to do with the cauldron. A plastic Halloween cauldron might be perfect for mixing cold liquid ingredients; however, it would not be very suitable or safe to burn herbs or place flaming pieces of parchment into it.

⊛ EXERCISE ⊛
Finding Your Cauldron

If you are searching for your new working cauldron, this is the spell to utilise. This spell will help guide you to the perfect item to use as a cauldron. It is a very simple petitionary chant, no complicated ingredients or tools necessary. This chant could also be altered to help you in finding other useful working tools too! Simply switch the word "cauldron" with whatever it is you are searching for.

Step 1

Think about the item you would like to find. If, for example, you want a cauldron that looks like the traditional cauldron associated with Witches, then visualise that image in your mind. If it aids you in visualising better, draw the item on a piece of paper. Keep this image in your mind for an entire day and then at sunset, go outside to a place that is special to you and write this chant on a piece of paper:

By power of land, sky, and sea,
Tool of magic, come to me.
I long to find a cauldron that will serve me well,
Hear my chant, hear my spell.
Cerridwen, keeper of the cauldron's might,
Allow my cauldron to enter my sight.

Fold up the piece of paper and place it in your pocket, or perhaps in a bag that you carry with you often.

Step 2

Plan to go somewhere that you are likely to find a cauldron. If you do not have any local metaphysical stores that stock cauldrons, I suggest venturing to second-hand stores or car-boot sales (flea markets, yard sales, etc.). Antique stores would also be an adequate place to look.

Once you are in a place where you might find your cauldron, find a quiet space to recite the chant you wrote down three times over.

This spell, if successful, will draw you toward the perfect working tool. It will very much be a "you"ll know it when you see it" moment. Trust in your own intuitive abilities to seek out the best tool for you.

————

I remember once discussing cauldrons at a local moot when one of the individuals attending said that they believed cauldrons were "redundant" within modern Witchcraft. They went on to say that cauldrons were only useful as decoration, symbolic tools, rather than as practical tools. I whole-heartedly disagree with that frame of mind. As a Celtic Witch, cauldrons are incorporated into the majority of my magical rites. They are usually in a central position of the working ground, and act as the grounding item that aids me in focusing on what it is exactly I intend on doing. They work beautifully as symbols, representing magical potentiality, the potent spirit of transformative energy and the inspiration found within the tales and legends of the land. However, their functionality extends far beyond being symbolic or aesthetic tools.

The first and most obvious modern usage for a cauldron is to burn herbs as incense. Many modern-day Witches have useful, compact cast iron caul-drons within which they burn loose herbs or resins on charcoal discs for a variety of reasons. This is a very effective way to cleanse a space as well. Simply light a charcoal disc, place it into the cauldron, and throw a hand-ful of a loose, cleansing herb into the pot. Allow the herbs to simmer and burn on the disc, filling the room with smoke. Do not forget to open the windows of your space to allow fresh air to flow, as well as allow any stagnant or residual, harmful negative energies to escape. The herbs I choose to utilise for cleansing purposes are usually lavender, juniper, or even dried nettles for an extra protective kick. If you don't want to turn to charcoal discs and loose herbal incense, you could also simply place incense cones into the cauldron.

When working outdoors with my larger cauldron, I am able to place an abundance of charcoal discs into the pot as well as larger quantities of herbs. My rule for working outdoors is to try to incorporate as many local herbs and plants as possible, rather than inflicting the space to the scent of foreign herbs burning. By burning local herbs and plants in the cauldron, I allow myself to imbue the magical workings with the potency and powers of the native spirits of place.

As mentioned earlier, ensure your cauldron is suitable for holding heat before burning anything within it. You do not want the heartbreak of a melted or smashed pot, nor the devastation that playing with fire and heat can cause. Just as with candles, never leave a burning cauldron unsupervised—though they are somewhat safer than candles as there is no open flame, if the charcoal discs or burning herbs manage to make their way onto flammable objects it can bring about unforeseen dangers. A wise Witch is one who is scrupulous with taking considerations for the safety of themselves as well as the safety of the surrounding environment. The local spirits of place will not take too kindly to a Witch who accidentally causes a forest fire, after all.

However, what use does a cauldron have beyond being utilised as an aesthetically pleasing incense burner? That is precisely what we will now explore.

The conventional image of a Witch and their cauldron that the general population would concoct in their mind is that of a bubbling, liquid substance being stirred by a cackling Witch. This imagery harkens back to the times when cauldrons were primarily used for cooking broths, stews, and soups as well as being used to wash clothes, and boil water for drinking. The cauldron, once upon a time in human history, was the beating heart of the home, much like the dishwasher, the washing machine, and the cooking pot are today. Its uses were multifunctional and necessary. Nowadays most of us barely have a fireplace yet alone a hearth with a large, practical cooking pot hovering on a hook over the fires. Today we have machines and gadgets to do all the work for us, and so it is easy to dismiss the cauldron as being entirely impractical. However, for the practising Witch the cauldron can be utilised for a variety of purposes.

As well as burning herbs and incenses in the pot, we can also use the pot to cast within. Pouring in useful herbs, oils, and various ingredients that correspond with our magical workings is a useful way of casting a spell. We can even utilise the cauldron to mix and make magical oils within. The cauldron can also act as a practical item for transporting other objects and tools to the ritual space, if big enough. My largest cast iron cauldron is often utilised as a carrier for my candles, herbs, and other ritual items when travelling from home to my favoured places to conduct magical workings and rites.

One of my favourite uses of the cauldron is as a divinatory tool. Cerridwen herself was said to be learned in the art of divination. We can call upon the very essence of Cerridwen's magical competency and utilise our cauldrons as effective, compact, and transportable scrying pools.

What Is Scrying?

Scrying is the act of searching for spiritual, ethereal messages and symbols in reflective surfaces or scrying tools such as crystal balls. It is peering into something with the aim of evoking powerful energetic imagery in your mind's eye. People who are bestowed with clairvoyant abilities may claim to literally see images, figures, messages, and symbols in scrying tools and reflective surfaces. However, for the majority of us we do not literally see something whilst scrying. Instead we search for patterns and markings as well as movements that our eyes are drawn to and making correlations and messages from those things. Some may believe that spirits, entities, or deities show the messages and the things that we view whilst scrying. Others instead believe that it is our own subconscious making correlations and coming up with messages and meanings to what would otherwise be mundane reflections and imagery. Either belief is valid, and both beliefs hold great power. Messages from our subconscious mind can be very powerful and useful messages to decipher. Just as with dream interpretation, a glimpse into our subconscious can tell us a lot about what is going on with our own mind and reality. Let us now dive into how to utilise the cauldron as a scrying tool.

⊛ EXERCISE ⊛
The Cauldron as a Lens into the Realm of Spirit

In order to use the cauldron as a scrying pool, it must first be entirely clean. It is better to use a black cauldron for this working, such as one made of cast iron. Size does not matter for this; however, I have found that it is easier to scry in a larger body of water. Take yourself to a dark room, lit only by candlelight if possible, or at the very least extremely dim lighting. Darkness can aid in opening up our intuitive senses, allowing us to divine with greater ease.

The cauldron should be filled with water. You may find it useful to use a water that is sacred to you, perhaps collected rainwater or water collected from a nearby lake or river. If you worry about using tap water, simply boil the water first. You could also use newly boiled water with herbs scattered into it, allowing the aromas of the herbs to aid in the divining, and the patterns the herbs float into to aid in the scrying process.

Fill the cauldron with water and stir in a clockwise motion, allowing the water to spiral and whirl. Whilst stirring, if you feel drawn to, you may chant something of this nature:

Vessel of transformative power stir,
Aid me to see, help me be sure,
I divine in you by power of Witch light,
Show me what must be seen, give me the sight
Whirl and swirl, or bubble and boil,
Show me what must be seen, whether joy or toil.

Now cease your stirring, and gaze into the cauldron as the waters begin to calm. Search for any imagery, visions, or symbols the water might hold. Continue gazing, and make note of anything that comes to mind. Do not worry too much about deciphering the meanings of the messages yet; simply take them all in and note them down to decipher once you have finished divining.

If you struggle to see much of anything at all in the water or in your mind's eye, try adding something into the water. A few pinches of dried mugwort stirred into the water could help. Allow the loose herbs to swirl around the cauldron and watch to see if they float into any particular patterns or symbols. Again, take note of anything that comes to mind.

Once you feel ready, come away from the cauldron and give yourself a moment to breathe and reflect. Come back to the notes you have made on what you might have seen or divined in the cauldron's water. Now is the time to decipher that which you have seen. This is a process of analysing the symbols, imagery, and visions brought to your mind and relating them to your current reality. Delving into these messages may unlock any current blocks, issues, and ailments bothering you, or alternatively may offer an insight into something you have been questioning as of late. Utilise the ability to scry in your cauldron whenever you feel necessary. The eve of Calan Gaeaf, or Samhain the 31st of October, may be a highly beneficial time to scry in your cauldron. Liminal times such as sunset, midnight, or at the changing of the seasons are highly useful times to work divinatory magic and workings. Consider Cerridwen and her mystical cauldron throughout the process of divining in your cauldron, drawing upon her arcane wisdom and power.

We have deduced by now that the cauldron has very many uses, and is a practical tool for the Celtic Witch to incorporate into their practises. The cauldron is a potent and powerful symbolic tool representing transformative energies and the power of potentiality. It is also a practical tool aiding in divination, cleansing the home or sacred space, and burning useful corresponding ingredients for magical workings.

A respect and reverence for our multi-purpose, practical cauldrons is one way to honour the Witch goddess in her might and wisdom. How else, though, could Cerridwen influence and inform a modern-day Witch's practise? Being the goddess of inspiration, transformation, and an entity heavily associated with initiation, she is a powerful and potent magical ally.

Cerridwen acts as a disciplined, stern, and powerful teacher. She teaches us the beauty and power that can be found in learning to be patient, remaining disciplined and secure in our plans. Cerridwen collected ingredients and hired two individuals to watch over a magical concoction of hers that would take a year and a day to complete. If it was not for her disciplined nature and fierce maternal passion to help her son be accepted and recognised as more than his appearance, she may have failed in creating the powerful potion that she successfully brewed. Within our modern world of instant gratification, it is becoming ever more difficult to truly appreciate the need for a disciplined, focused mind. Cerridwen can aid the student of magic to focus their intention toward their studies and magical workings. A Witch who knows how to remain disciplined and focused is a Witch that can remain scrupulous and competent in their magical prowess.

As an initiator, Cerridwen lifts the veil on the mysteries of life, stoking the flames of our desire to learn more, to challenge what is conventionally accepted, and to strive for a deeper understanding of our magical, beautiful world. She sends us on difficult yet meaningful quests to challenge our deeply rooted prejudices and fears, and opens our eyes to the limitless potentiality of our unbound spirit. Just as Gwion Bach was transformed from a mundane, simple farm boy into a keeper of arcane magical wisdom and powerful sorcerous skill, Cerridwen can aid us in reaching our fullest potential, but only if we are ready to undertake the tumultuous and difficult process of initiation. As modern-day Witches, we have likely grown accustomed to hearing the word *initiation* only in connection to covens and secretive organisations and groups. However, we all embark on our own unique initiatory journey. The fact that you decided to pick up this book and read this chapter is an indication that you are journeying on your initiatory quest. You are opening your eyes to the potential knowledge accessible to you, willing to learn and grow as an individual. Cerridwen can act as a beneficial guide in initiating you to the secrets and mysteries of the known and unknown realms.

On the mundane side of life, Cerridwen can also inspire our creative aspects. She is a Witch who successfully brewed a potion of Awen. She is a goddess of inspiration as well as of the magical and mysterious, and it is not just magic that inspires us as Witches. We are well-rounded individuals with interests and passions that dwell beyond the magical and the occult. I often call to Cerridwen to aid in pushing me out of my comfort zone when creating art or embarking on a quest to learn a new skill. I call to her divine help in sparking my inspiration; she can be both my guide and my muse. Whether your creative tendencies are unleashed through art, or cooking, writing, or dancing, Cerridwen is a supportive and inspirational ally.

Beyond all of this, the mighty Witch goddess Cerridwen inspires us to fiercely embrace that which sets our soul afire. Just as she fiercely sought out to help her son, no matter the cost or challenge ahead, she insists that we do not approach anything within the realms of our passions with less than full devotion and power. With the Witch goddess as your guide, she will empower you to reach your full potential, to approach the sacred potentiality of your spirit, and to lean into your passions with fierce determination.

Chapter 7
Fairy Tales of Wales

Fairy tales are special things. They are usually our introduction to storytelling, to the legends and myths of our land. We all have a favourite fairy tale if we dig deep and truly ponder over it. Whether that favourite fairy tale happens to be the story of the beautiful princess with long flowing hair who was locked away all her life, or it is the tale of the humble shoemaker who was blessed by a group of little elves. These tales speak to the spirit of what it means to be human. What is truly exciting however is learning that beyond the classic fairy tales we all grew to love as children, collected and written by the likes of the brothers Grimm and Hans Christian Andersen, there are also regional fairy tales specific to almost every region in the world. Practically every village, town, or kingdom worldwide have their own collections of tales. Some may be preserved and remembered to this day, whereas others have long been forgotten. However, the truth of the matter is, wherever you are sat at this very moment whilst reading these words, I can guarantee you that there are stories and fables that originate from where you currently are.

What is the difference between a myth and a fairy tale or folk legend? Is there much of a difference at all? Some would say no, that they are all simply fantastical tales that teach us something or dive into an element of what it means to be human. For me personally, I view it like this: myths are old legends that speak of the heart of the land, the beliefs that have long prevailed in that land, and the remnants of ancient civilisations and their practises. Whereas fairy tales are old stories that speak of the heart of the people, the core principles the people of the land live by, and the remnants of old customs and traditions that the people partook in. It is a very subtle difference in my mind, which many would disagree with. Many would argue that myth is far more important than simple folksy fables, because myths speak of gods and faith whereas fairy tales are often presented as simply being educational flights of fancy to help children learn and to warn them of the dangers of the world. Nevertheless, fairy tales are so much more important than that, and deserve to be treated with respect and the same level of ponderous meditation that myths are granted.

In my personal experience, most Witches and Pagans are deeply intrigued by and interested in fairy tales; however, not very many Witches and Pagans view them as anything more than stories. Magical practitioners are more likely to turn to the deities, figures, and characters presented in the more conventionally studied myths than they are to attempt to forge a connection with an entity found within a fairy tale. However, it must be remembered that many scholars do in fact believe that the majority of fairy tales and folklore are the remnants, the relics of older mythologies.[33] The princesses, queens, and fairies found in fairy tales might indeed be the echoes of what were once divine entities, goddesses, and the kings, princes, and warriors relics of gods. Beyond all this, fairy tales speak of the heart of the people and their customs and traditions in specific regions. Delving into and studying the old folkloric tales littered throughout the land is an insightful and meaningful method of deepening one's connection to the land and their ancestors. It is time we stop viewing fairy tales as being simply entertaining but otherwise meaningless stories for children. That is precisely why I decided to devote an entire chapter of this book to the fairy tales of my land, the stories and fables found in Wales. Many of the tales I will present in this chapter offer an insight into folkloric practises that can inform a magical practitioner's practise and aid one in connecting with the land itself. They are tales and stories that I grew

---

33. Sikes, *British Goblins*, 251.

up hearing, either at school or at home. Fairy tales and folklore are exceptionally important elements of what informs my Witchcraft, and therefore I would like to share them with you.

My Personal Exploration of Fairy Tales in Wales

My personal exploration into fairy tales began at a very young age. Even as a child I seemed to relish the fantastical stories and fables we learnt at school more so than any of my peers. I spent much of my childhood reading books that presented the *"chwedlau"* (tales) of Wales. I was always aware of the powerful and enigmatic myths of the Mabinogi. However, the legends found within that body of work did not quite stir my spirit as much as stories such as that of *Cantre'r Gwaelod*, a story often dubbed as "the Welsh Atlantis" about a city that is submerged under the sea. Or the tale of the Witches of Llanddona, about a family of Witches who turn up at a village in Anglesey only to cause rampant mischief and chaos. As a teenager, I purchased countless books that were collections of Welsh fairy tales, folklore, and regional legends. As I grew older, I began delving into the various other well-known fairy tales of the world, such as those collected by the brothers Grimm. Despite my brief deviation toward the fairy tales of the world however, I always found myself returning to the rich folkloric tales and *chwedlau* of my own ancestral land. This land is littered with stories, and many of them give an insight into the very magic of the people and the culture of Wales. I am not a folklorist, nor do I hold any qualifications in terms of the study of fairy tale and legend. I am but a hobbyist who is deeply passionate about these fantastic stories of magic and mystery. This chapter will serve as both a means to present the rich fairy tales of Wales to an audience which I'm certain has an interest in them, as well as being a personal gnosis into how fairy tales can aid in informing magical practise.

The select tales I mention here are those I have grown up with, or fallen in love with over the years. I will present my own retelling of some of the tales, as well as a personal exploration of what they mean to modern Wales, and how fairy tale and legend can aid in informing a Witch's practise, as they have done my own. For the most part, my primary goal with including these tales here is not only to aid in informing your Witchcraft, but also to introduce these captivating and enchanting tales to a new audience. These tales are but a handful of a multitude of tales available to delve into.

The Tale of the Red Dragon of Wales

The flag of Wales is a curious thing. Upon a background of green and white stands a mighty, detailed red dragon. Many know of the dragon on the Welsh flag; however, fewer know the true tale of magic and royalty that caused this mighty dragon to become the emblem of Wales. Sit back and relax as I tell you a tale of a king, a boy, and a dragon or two.

Long ago, in the time of warriors and wizards, there lived a mighty king named King Vortigern. This king was a Celtic king who was in constant battle with the invading Saxon armies. Fearing an attack from the Saxon barbarians, King Vortigern approached his council of wise men and asked them what he should do next. They instructed him that he must travel to seek a location to build a mighty castle, one that will spawn a new city where he can easily defend himself from barbaric invaders. The king rejoiced in this wonderful idea, and set out to find a suitable location immediately. Eventually, whilst travelling through the mountains of Eryri the king came across a place that was named *Dinas Ffaraon*. It was decided, this is where his new castle and city would be.

The king gathered his men and asked they collect all the materials, and find all the skilful folk they could find to help him construct his mighty castle. As time went by the materials were successfully collected and the building began. All seemed to be going exceptionally well, that is until one morning the skilled labourers who were in charge of building the castle awoke to find that the entire castle had been utterly destroyed overnight. The king was frustrated by this setback, but demanded everyone get back to work to continue building the castle. However, this became a daily occurrence. Every day the labourers would build and build, only to find the fruits of their labours utterly destroyed overnight. There was no rational explanation for what was occurring, and so the king approached his council of wise men again. Being a time of superstition and magic, the wise men deduced that the king must perform an elaborate sacrificial ritual in order to prevent his new castle from falling once more. They advised the king to seek out a fatherless boy, to sacrifice him and to sprinkle his blood upon the ground that he wished to build his castle. This would solve his problems, they reassured him.

Following the advice of his well-renowned, wise council, the king sent his men to seek out a fatherless boy immediately. They eventually found one and brought him before the king ready to be sacrificed. The boy proved to be confident and strong of spirit, for before the king he asked enthusiastically "Good sir, what do you intend to do to me?"

"We will sacrifice you and sprinkle your blood on this soil, so that my castle can be built," the king replied.

"Sir," the boy responded, "with all due respect, who advised you to do such a thing?"

The king, taken aback by the boy's fortitude, explained that it was his wise men that had advised him to do so. The boy laughed and asked the king if his so-called "wise men" had told him what was going on beneath the ground where he wished to plant his castle. The king shook his head in disbelief and asked the boy to explain. With the aid of the king's men, the boy showed the king that beneath the ground upon which they were attempting to build the castle lay a large, underground lake. Beneath the lake, the boy explained, were two mighty dragons resting. Each night the dragons would emerge from the lake to battle one another. It was the quakes from this awesome battle that were causing the king's castle to collapse night after night. That night the king, his council of wise men, his guards, and the boy watched as the dragons battled. One dragon was pure white in colour, and it was intensely ferocious. The other was blood red, and appeared weaker. Yet, despite appearing weaker, the red dragon consistently managed to fight off the ferocious white dragon.

The young boy said to the king that there is an omen to be found in the imagery of the red and white dragon. He explained that the red dragon represented king Vortigern and his Celtic men. The white represented invaders attempting to claim their land. Though the invaders would consistently and constantly attempt to squash those of this land, they would always fail in the end. The boy also explained to the king that perhaps he should be rid of his so-called "wise" men, before they convince him to kill another innocent boy. This boy was rumoured to grow up to become the infamous Myrddin, or more conventionally known today as Merlin. Despite the dragons, King Vortigern successfully built his city eventually and named it *Dinas Emrys,* meaning Emrys' City. Emrys is an old, alternative Welsh name for Merlin. That is how the red dragon became the emblem of Wales.

The End.[34]

The emblem of the Welsh dragon as we know it today has been in existence among various peoples of Britain since at least the fourth century.[35] However, it was not officially recognised as the Welsh flag until approximately the late thirteenth century. It is exceptionally interesting how there is a Welsh folk legend associated with this mighty emblem, though not surprising at all. The tale certainly speaks of the spirit of the Welsh; even today, the concept of our culture, language, and heritage being erased is met with a battle cry. Countless songs and stories exist to give the Welsh a sense of pride in our survival, despite constant attempts to wipe us out. The red dragon is very much a symbol of pride and the legacy of the Welsh culture and language today. For the magical practitioner it is a powerful symbol to utilise within spells of self-empowerment, protection, and confidence. A version of the red dragon is on the cover of my private grimoire; the image aids in empowering my magical workings and connects me to my land and my language. It is difficult to speak of national pride today without raising eyebrows, due to the abundance of ignorant fools masking their hatred and intolerance as simply being patriotic pride. However, being proud of being Welsh has nothing to do with superiority nor with race. Welsh pride stems from a place of survival, and a desire to see our language, our culture, and our traditions preserved and embraced.

This tale, as well as the emblem of the dragon itself empowers my magical practise. It reminds me of the richness of my land, and Merlin is a character any student of magic can admire. The council of wise men, who turned out to be not so wise after all, are symbolic of the various people in power who

---

34. My retelling of this tale, based on the story found on the *Visit Wales* website, and Thomas' *The Welsh Fairy Book.*

35. For more information, find the *Visit Wales* website, specifically the page titled: The *Welsh dragon and the Welsh flag*, https://www.visitwales.com/info/history-heritage-and -traditions/dragon-spirit-legend-welsh-dragon.

use their sway and power for their own twisted, warped ideologies. Within occult and magical circles, you will meet folk who match this archetype quite often. They are usually folk who promise they can open your eyes to the mysteries of the world, and heal your pain and traumas. For a price, of course. When encountering people of this nature, we must remain true to our intuitive feelings. We must remain confident and calm, and stand our ground just as Merlin did before the King.

The Perils of the Fairy Harp

Once upon a time, in a sleepy Welsh village that lay near Eryri, there lived a man named Morgan. One wet, stormy evening Morgan was warming himself at his hearth when he heard a faint knock at the door. Without hesitation, Morgan yelled at whomever it was at the door to let themselves in. From the stormy outdoors walked in three tired-looking travellers. They begged Morgan for a moment of rest by his fire, and some food and drink. Being a kind man, Morgan allowed them into his home and gave them some of his finest bread and cheese as they warmed themselves up. After they ate together, the three travellers rose to their feet and looked at Morgan.

"Thank you for your generosity," they said. "We must admit, we are no ordinary travellers."

Morgan's eyes lit up in disbelief as the travellers revealed to him that they were in fact fairies. They told him that due to his act of great kindness they would bestow a blessing on him, and grant him one wish. Morgan spent a moment pondering over what he might wish for. He had always wanted to be a musician, but had never had enough money to buy himself an instrument. Turning to the three fairies in his home, he asked them if they could gift him a harp. The three fairies ushered themselves into a corner of Morgan's home, and whispered among themselves. The whispers came to a halt and they approached Morgan again.

"Yes," said one of the fairies. "We will grant your wish. Now please close your eyes until you hear us leave, and upon opening your eyes the wish will have been granted."

Morgan closed his eyes and stood anxiously. He heard his front door open and close, and with its closing, he opened his eyes once more. There it stood. The most glamorous, ethereal-looking harp Morgan had ever laid eyes upon. Morgan was delighted to own such a magnificent instrument. Suddenly his mind filled with dread as he remembered that he had no idea how to play the harp. He reached out to touch the harp, when suddenly by some intuitive power he began playing the harp perfectly. Not only had he been gifted the world's most beautiful harp, but he was also gifted the power to play it. The music that emanated from the harp was so delightful and otherworldly. Morgan was filled with joy to have been blessed with such a wondrous gift.

Morgan's wife, who had been visiting a few of her friends, arrived home later that night with two of her friends alongside her. Morgan was delighted to share the fantastical story with his wife and her friends, and asked them if they would like to see the beautiful, ethereal harp he now possessed. Morgan's wife and her friends all unanimously agreed they would love to see this harp. Morgan sat to play on his new fairy instrument for his small audience. As he began to play, the women began to dance uncontrollably, as if hypnotised by the music. Morgan laughed and laughed as they danced to his melodies. After some time had passed and Morgan still had not stopped playing, his wife began to beg him to stop as she was becoming excruciatingly tired but had no control over her body. Morgan merely laughed, as if he was not quite himself. He had not a care in the world that his wife and her friends were suffering, and found the whole ordeal rather amusing. He eventually stopped, and his wife and her friends were rightly furious with him for putting them through such stress.

Months went by and Morgan continued to cause absolute chaos with his magical fairy harp. He played it around the village. The farmers in their fields stopped tending to their sheep in order to dance, causing their sheep to run far away. The elderly who had various ailments shot up out of their seats to dance to the hypnotic music; despite their insufferable pain they could not stop. Every soul in the village begged Morgan to stop, but he did not. One fateful morning, Morgan awoke to find his precious harp had vanished in the night. No trace of it was ever found. Morgan's wife told him that it was the fairy travellers who had taken their gift back, angered and disgruntled by how much chaos Morgan caused his neighbours and friends. Morgan believed his wife, but who knows? Perhaps it was not the fairies who took back their gift. Perhaps the villagers in their frustrations took it upon themselves to rid the region of that horrid harp.

The End.[36]

This is a particularly interesting old fairy story, as it not only gives us an insight into Welsh fairy lore but also the perils of the mischief of the fae. It displays quite clearly that fairies, when met with kindness and generosity, can bestow blessings of good fortune onto mortals. Morgan wished more than anything to be a musician, and that wish was met. However, fairies live by a completely different set of laws and morals than us mortals. Perhaps to the fae a harp that fuels people to dance nonstop is a good, brilliant thing. However, in our mortal world it causes nothing but wanton chaos. For any magical practitioner, the desire to work with elemental forces and otherworldly beings is often strong. However, we must remind ourselves that their blessings are to be taken with an air of caution. Everything is not always as it seems when contemplating on the realm of fairy. Blessings can easily become curses. I adore this story and the insight it delivers of the rich lore associated with fairies in this Celtic land.

The Tale of the Cat Witches and the Conjurer

Many moons ago, there lived a highly respected conjurer who went by the name of Huw Llwyd. He was the seventh son of a family of magical practitioners and conjurers, and his potent skills were known throughout the land. He was a highly learned man of magic, having gained much of his skills by reading old grimoires and studying the intricacies of baneful magic. In order to make money and food, Huw used his magical knowledge and skills to help people find lost objects, to cure ailments caused by curses and magic, and most notably to solve crimes and mysteries.

At an inn near what is known today as Betws-y-Coed, people were waking up after spending the night to find they were robbed in their sleep. This became a highly common occurrence, and it frustrated regular travellers in the area greatly. No trace of any robber was found at the scene of the crimes.

---

36. My retelling, based on the tale named *The Fairy Harp* in: Thomas, *The Welsh Fairy Book*, 96.

Eventually the conjurer Huw Llwyd was consulted to solve the mystery. He agreed to solve the mystery by his specific set of skills. He booked a room at the inn, and began his investigation. He told the owners of the inn, two sisters, that he was merely an ordinary traveller on his way to Ireland. The sisters gladly set him up in a room. The sisters and Huw spent the night together, Huw spinning tall tales about his supposed travels, keeping his identity a secret. As it became late, Huw made the decision to retire to his room for the night. Preparing for a robbery, Huw lit an array of candles in his room and set a sword beside his bed as a form of protection from any who might enter the room and wish him harm. Hours went by, and there was no sign of any robbers.

Deep into the night, around the Witching hour, a stirring came from the fireplace on the opposite side of Huw's room. He tucked himself into bed and pretended to be asleep, but kept one eye slightly open. Soot fell down the chimney, and then, quietly, a pair of black cats tumbled down into the room. They shook themselves of the chimney's soot and began exploring the room. The cats ran around the room, and climbed on top of Huw, but he did not move an inch, keeping up appearances that he was fast asleep. He wanted to watch the cats and see what mischief they would get up to. Eventually, deducing that Huw was asleep, the cats began pawing at his possessions. Huw remained calm; that is, until they reached for his wallet and all his money. Huw rose from his bed and slashed at one of the cats' paws with his sword. In a panic both cats rushed back up the chimney and out of sight. Huw was certain the cats were the thieves, but he had a striking suspicion that something of the magical nature was also occurring in this inn.

The next morning only one of the sisters came downstairs to serve Huw his breakfast. Huw inquired as to where the other sister was, and he was told that unfortunately she had fallen ill overnight and could not come down to bid him farewell. After finishing his breakfast, Huw insisted that he say goodbye to both sisters, and thank them individually for being such kind and entertaining hosts. The one sister eventually reluctantly agreed to take him up to her ill sister's bed to bid her farewell. When he entered the room, he offered the poor, sick woman any help that he might be able to offer. She insisted there was nothing he could do, and that she merely needed bed rest. Huw said farewell to her and offered his hand out to shake hers. As she reached her hand out, Huw noticed that her hand was bandaged and bleeding. Aha! He thought, as he finished the puzzle in his mind. The two sisters were the thieving cats he had seen the night before. They were Witches, who by some transformative power had turned themselves into cats to commit the crimes. Being a conjurer, Huw knew that by drawing her blood he had now rendered her unable to perform any more magic for baneful purposes. He pulled a letter opener from his pocket and sliced the other sister's palm in order to ensure she also could not commit crimes via her magic any longer. No one was ever robbed at that inn again, but the sisters remained as its owners, now living honest and good lives as ordinary women. Huw had solved yet another mystery.

The End.[37]

A tale of conjurers, of Witchcraft, of thievery, of transfiguration, and of mystery. What an insight into the beliefs surrounding magic and Witchcraft this tale offers us. It is interesting to note that two streams of magical practise exist in this tale. Our hero, Huw, is a conjurer who is highly learned and skilled in magic, yet he is not seen as evil. Likewise, the sisters' practises as Witches is not what is seen as the most vile aspect of this story, rather the fact that they were robbing unsuspecting, innocent travellers. This tale may be more modern than most, delving into the practises of conjurers and cunning men, which were rampant throughout the British Isles between the eighteenth and nineteenth centuries. However, it is still an interesting portrayal of magic and Witchcraft at work in Wales. It speaks of the very belief found in Wales that magic itself is not inherently evil but that evil comes instead from the heart of the individual practising it. A stark contrast to beliefs found in England and across Europe that Witchcraft and magic are purely the work of the devil. Huw Llwyd matches the concept of the old Welsh *Consuriwr* (conjurer) or *Swynwr* (male magical practitioner) perfectly. It is also refreshing that the sister Witches were not put to death, nor cast out of society after

---

37. My retelling, based on the story found in Owen, *Welsh Folk-Lore*.

their magical crimes. Instead, they are simply stripped of their ability to use magic for baneful purposes.

Living the Legends

I hope that this insight into the richness of Welsh folk tales and fairy tales leads you to further an investigation into the longheld traditions of story-telling. The stories of the land that have been repeated for hundreds of years are a window into the very practises and beliefs of the people, reflecting the depth of storytelling found worldwide. Many streams of traditional Witchcraft specifically turn to folklore and folk beliefs of the past to aid in informing their practises, and the practise of the Welsh Witch should be no different. The land tingles with these fantastical, captivating tales. Beyond anything, these tales help us to feel a deeper connection to our ancestors and the spirits of the land itself. The very fact that these tales and legends have been passed down for centuries upon centuries, constantly evolving and changing yet remaining more or less the same, is magic. The fact these tales live on to this day is also proof that they still speak to us, to our spirit, and have relevance even in our modern day life. I feel personally honoured to have the opportunity to share even a fragment of Wales' history of stories. Seek out the folk tales and fairy tales of Wales; they are useful, captivating insights into the very heart of the land. In turn, by reading these tales we may also find useful tidbits of information that we can incorporate into our personal practises as Witches today.

Chapter 8
Welsh Fairies

D
o you believe in fairies? Have you ever wandered through the meadows and hills late at night, and heard the strumming of ethereal harps, or the melodies of spectral flutes in the air? Or perhaps you have come across mystical lights floating near marshes and bogs, only to follow them and find yourself dancing, drinking, and being merry with a group of miniature people who do not look altogether human. These are the traits commonly found throughout various Welsh folk tales; the fairies are apparently in abundance throughout this magical Celtic land. Regardless of whether you believe in fairies or not, it is no doubt that people throughout Wales' history certainly have.

We have become accustomed today to fairies being depicted as tiny young women, clad in dresses made of leaves and flowers and with beautiful lace-like wings extending from their backs. The fairies of the Celtic lands however, were not described as angelic and beautiful as this. The true fairies of our myth, legend and folklore are mysterious beings, who are not very easily classified and understood by our mortal standards. They are beings who are not altogether governed by the same laws of nature, science, or even morality as us. As humans, we adore pinning things down, labelling them, and understanding them to the best of our ability. When it comes to fairies however, it is not always possible to fully understand their nature. Perhaps we never will understand them completely, and should not either. However, I believe any magical practitioner hoping to feel a oneness with their land and culture should get to know the mysterious and intriguing beings from the folkloric tales as much as humanly possible.

Fairies have been an integral part of my practise and craft. I would even be so bold as to claim that without fairies, I probably would not be a Witch today. My initial infatuation with magic and Witchcraft began with my intense love for fairies and fairy lore. I grew up on the lore of the fair folk in my beautiful country; they continue to inspire my creativity, connectivity, and magical practise. Some form of fairies can be beneficial allies to the Celtic Witch, whilst others should be avoided at all costs. Connecting with the spritely folk of the forests, streams, meadows, and marshes is useful for any Witch who yearns for a deeper connection to the land surrounding them. Many Witches today understand fairies to be the spirit or souls of nature and trees, but fairies from Celtic lore and legend are far more complicated than that.

The Ellylldan and Me

The village in which I grew up was a tiny, rural place. My childhood playground was the fields, meadows, and farmland extending behind my home, or the cliffs and beaches down by the coast. I remember my first experience, which I would label as "magical" to this day. I was very young, probably somewhere around the age of seven or eight. It was during the height of summer, when the days were warm and long. I was playing with my friends in the field, which was directly behind the estate in which I lived. My friends were all called in to go home. It was getting late but it was hard to tell it was in those summer days; the sun barely set until quite late into the evening. Trees lined the back of the field, and in these trees as children, we would build dens for ourselves. I was sat in one of these dens when it suddenly came upon my heart to get up and walk toward the church, which was not very far from the field at all. It was as though I was being pulled by some ethereal force. As I approached the old churchyard gate, I peeked in at the gravestones. Beside the churchyard gate was a beautiful tombstone carved into the shape of an angel. This angel was an icon of our village; it was said that on Halloween night she came to life! I was somewhat fearful of her at that age. She was missing a hand, and her face always looked sorrowful to me.

That is when I saw it from the corner of my eye. There in the churchyard, was a ball of spectral light. It was around the size of an adult's fist. It hovered over the tombstones, lighting up the churchyard at dusk. It shined with an orange light. It was strange; though it was orange and looked very much like fire, it moved and flowed as if it was water. Slow, calm, and completely ethereal. You would think as a child I would have been full of fright at this spectral encounter, but I was not. I was hypnotised by the light. I stood at the gate, frozen. Suddenly a loud truck drove past distracting me and freeing me from my hypnotic state. When I turned to look back at the ball of light, it had vanished.

I still wonder to this day what that light was. When I told my family or friends, they thought I was playing make-believe. I was, after all, a child who was obsessed with fairy tales, fantastical creatures and magic. For years, I called this spectral ball of light a "fairy light." It was only after delving into Welsh fairy lore that I began calling it my encounter with the *Ellylldan*, or "elf fire." The *Ellylldan* are the Welsh equivalent of the well-known spectral lights known as "Will-o"-wisp." In folklore and legend, they are known to lead wanderers toward marshy grounds, or to where the fairies might be dancing.

Many people might have written this experience off as a ghostly encounter; however, something deep inside me refuses to accept that it was a ghost encounter. I am certain this was an encounter with fae.

Fairies of Wales

I separate the fairies of Wales into two main varieties. There are the corporeal, humanoid variety such as the *Plant Annwfn* (the children of Annwfn) and the well-known *Tylwyth Teg*. This variety of fairy is mysterious, otherworldly, and entrancing to the human imagination. Then there are the ethereal, goblin like variety. This variety tends to be closer to what most would associate as "fairy" today; it covers the *ellyllon*, or elves, as well as varieties of goblins and household fairies.

The Tylwyth Teg

In modern Wales, the term *Y Tylwyth Teg* has become the blanket term for all fairies. In school, we are taught that *Tylwyth Teg* is simply the Welsh translation of the English "Fairy"; however, this is not quite true. The literal translation of "*Y Tylwyth Teg*" is "the fair family" or "the fair folk."[38] Contrary to what most may believe, these fairies are not small, insect-sized beings with ethereal wings. The Tylwyth Teg are said to be a race of beings who are tall, graceful, fair, and beautiful. They reside in an entirely different realm to us, though of course they visit our realm to interact with humans occasionally. There are various tales of Tylwyth Teg visiting markets and occasionally bestowing blessings unto mortals of their choice.

The Tylwyth Teg come from a realm far different to ours. Some legends and tales speak of the "Green islands of Enchantment" or in Welsh: *Gwerddonau Llion*. These enchanted islands are said to be where the Tylwyth Teg call home, mystical islands residing somewhere in the Irish Sea. They are liminal paradises, lush and warm at all times of year. Existing in a realm not quite our own, yet not quite the otherworld either. The concept of *Gwerddonau Llion* is not vastly dissimilar to the Irish *Tir na nÓg*. The islands are said to move, or become invisible and are very difficult to find for mortals. However, occasionally mortals stumble upon the islands by accident, often completely unaware of where they are.[39] The Tylwyth Teg of the green isles of enchantment were frequent visitors to the markets at Aberdaugleddau and Talacharn.[40]

Bendith Y Mamau

The next variety of fairy who fit into the first category of seemingly corporeal, humanoid entities are the *Bendith y Mamau* ("the mother's blessing") also known as *Plant Annwfn* ("the children of Annwfn"). These beings are often found near lakes, rivers, and caves that are said to be portals to the Celtic otherworld. The majority of tales surrounding these types of beings

---

38. Bevan, *Geiriadur Prifysgol Cymru*, 3673.

39. Cooper, *The Element Encyclopedia of Fairies*.

40. Sikes, *British Goblins*, 4–5.

are those that focus on the *Gwragedd Annwfn* (literally: "wives of the lower world"). The *Gwragedd Annwfn* are fairy women not too dissimilar to the fabled lady of the lake from popular Arthurian legend. Almost goddess-like, they haunt the shores of desolate lakes high upon the mountains and are often said to entrance and seduce mortal men. Though they are known as lake fairies, dismiss any ideas of them being at all similar to mermaids; they do not possess any fishy qualities such as scales or fish tales. In fact they are very much human in appearance.

What makes the Bendith y Mamau different to the Tylwyth Teg seems to be their ability to integrate perfectly into mortal human society. Legends speak of Bendith y Mamau not only marrying or falling in love with mortal men, but also mating with them.[41] There are also whispers throughout Wales that people may exist in modern day Wales, or among those with Welsh ancestry, who have "fairy blood" within them: descendants of those men who mingled with fairy women in times long ago.

The Gwyllion

Though I claimed that I separate fairies of Wales into two categories, there is one Welsh fairy that baffles me. They seem to be neither corporeal nor ethereal, neither goblin-like nor entirely human in appearance—a mixture of both. These are the *Gwyllion*. At first glance, one would find it difficult to understand how the *Gwyllion* differ from the *Gwragedd Annwfn*; they are after all fairy women who haunt the mountain trails of Wales. However, these beings are much more spectral, having the ability to teleport themselves from one space to another in the blink of an eye. Acting almost like a vengeful ghost, shrieking and wailing at nighttime travellers in an attempt to make them stray off the path and become lost in the dark mountains.

These mountain fairies are said to be frightful to look at, and are very similar to what one might think of when visualising the stereotypical fairy tale imagery of a Witch. Hag-like and fear-inducing, wild and untamed. They are the spirits of the untamed wilds of the Welsh mountainous regions.

---

41. One example of this would be in the tale of the lady of *Llyn y fan fach*.

The shrieking nature of the *Gwyllion* has caused many people to compare them to the Irish Banshee. The *Gwyllion* however, is not quite an omen of death, more so an omen that you are to certainly lose your way. Travellers walking the mountains late at night who heard the cries of the *Gwyllion* were certain to find themselves lost in no time. The *Gwyllion* are a sub-group of Welsh fairy that I am rather glad I have never had the pleasure of experiencing, and a part of me hopes I never stumble upon them.

Ellyllon

When we think of fairies today our modern mind-set is likely to make us think of one of two visuals: either the sweet and innocent butterfly-winged girls from Victorian flights of fancy, or goblin-like spirits of nature with their animalistic features such as pointed ears, hands baring only three fingers, or long warty noses. The latter would be described as being the closest concept to the Welsh *ellyllon*, our second grouping of fairies in Wales. Ethereal, somewhat spectral entities who are commonly found among the natural areas of Wales: in bogs and marshes, meadows and streams, woodlands and valleys. These beings are often described as being short in stature, goblin-like, and merry.

It is a common folk belief in Wales that the English word for "elf" might have originated from the Welsh *ellyll*, especially considering a Welsh word for spirit is *el*, with the Welsh word for element being "elf."[42] However, etymologically speaking the word "elf" is not recognised as being derived from Welsh at all; yet still an interesting thing to note. Modern magical practitioners today often refer to the ellyll as elemental beings. Folklore describes them as being pigmy elf creatures, not dissimilar to what one might envision when thinking of Santa Clause's elves. However, they are beings that have the ability to change their shape, and seem to be the somewhat physical embodiment of the spirits of nature.

They are very much the spirits of place, representing the playful yet destructive spirit of nature. Ellyllon are known for playing wildly, overpowered by their obsessions with the childlike joys of life: singing, dancing,

---

42. Sikes, *British Goblins*, 13.

drinking, and laughing. Alternatively, they are causing wild, rampant mischief and chaos.

Being the spirits of place the *ellyll* can be found everywhere. One would expect to find them in meadows and fields, dancing in a fairy ring under an oak tree. However, they can also be found in our homes. As household fairies we understand them to be known as *bwbachod*. The household fairies reward those with tidy homes who offer them suitable offerings with good deeds. However, the *bwbachod* can be just as full of mischief and terror as any of their elven counterparts. They can turn from being a helpful household spirit to a terrible and menacing ghoul if you do not take care of the home, speak ill of them, or take life too seriously and piously.

No *ellyll* seems to be very fond of priests or churchmen. There are countless tales of *bwbachod* and *ellyll* terrorising men of the church. Similarly, men of the church are also not very fond of *ellyll*, referring to them as evil and ungodly creatures. The *ellyll* take a disliking to priests and men of the church due to the fact that they prefer people who drink alcohol, who are merry, and who prefer to enjoy the comforts of life in front of their warm fires at home. With priests being pious men who prefer to sit at home reading the bible to enjoying a good merry drunken singalong before their warm hearth, the *bwbachod* take great offense and are quick to fling mischief their way.

As well as the *ellyll* of the natural areas and the *bwbachod* of the household, we also have the *coblynau*. The *coblynau* are the fairies of mines, quarries and underground regions. In a mining country like Wales, it is no wonder that people would encounter the spirits of the underground regions. *Coblynau* are again short, pigmy beings who are probably the original inspiration for goblins. They remind me of the dwarves from Walt Disney's Snow White and the seven dwarves—they are known to carry tiny hammers, shovels, and lanterns. They spend all their time digging in the mines, and helping miners to find rich ores. The presence of the *coblynau* in the mines is a sign of great fortune, and miners would be foolish to ever offend these benevolent mining fairies. In some streams of lore the *coblynau* are completely invisible beings.[43]

43. Isaac, *Coelion Cymru*.

Music and dancing are strong components heavily associated with the *ellyll* of the natural world. Tales and legends tell us of fairies dancing vigorously around fairy rings or under oak trees. They use their ethereal music to enchant and seduce mortals into their merry dance, causing them to stray from the path and causing them to lose sight of their responsibilities as they dance without a care in the world.

Fairy rings are a sight found throughout the Welsh countryside, and various legends and folklore surround them. In Wales, fairy rings are not a circle of mushrooms, as one would see in a children's book of fairy tales. Welsh fairy rings are discoloured circles of grass among otherwise entirely ordinary coloured grass in fields, in meadows, and upon hills. Some believe that stepping into a fairy ring will transport you into a pocket dimension, where you become invisible to the outside world. Others believe that fairy rings are simply remnants of where the fairies did dance at some point in the past. Regardless of which you believe the consensus seems to be clear that for your own safety and sanity you should never step into a fairy ring of your own volition.

The fairies' sacred day is supposedly Friday. At the very least, Fridays seem to be the day of the week where you would be most likely to see the fairies dancing in the evening.[44] They could be found near female oak trees, as the female oak is sacred to them—to cut down a female oak tree in a fair, dry place is to bring misfortune upon yourself at the hands of the fairies. If you are intent on seeing fairies, your best bet is to find a fairy ring under an oak tree and camp out there on a Friday evening. Who knows, you may hear the enchanting melodies of the fairy music and find yourself dancing hypnotically with whimsical, elven beings. But, perhaps to keep on the safe side you should try to avoid seeking the fairies. As beautiful and ethereal as they might be, the fairies are known for causing all manners of mischief and misfortune, even occasionally causing death.

---

44. Daimler, *A New Dictionary of Fairies*, 88.

Changelings

Were you an unruly child? When you were born, were you sweet, calm, and quiet then suddenly your personality seemed to change drastically, and you became a wild infant uncontrolled by anything? If so, in old Wales you might have been considered a *plentyn-newid*. The concept of *plentyn-newid* (changed child) is rather well known throughout popular culture today. Countless novels, comics, and television series speak of changelings today. Changelings were a rather poignant, and at times dangerous, aspect of the fairy faith in Wales.

The concept of the changeling is a very peculiar one. Fairies are apparently exceptionally drawn to beautiful things, and that includes babies. The fairies would seek out beautiful and calm infants and would swap them with an impertinent, "monstrous" creature. At first, the creature left in a baby's place would look identical to the human child but over time they would develop hideous features and become unruly, a complete terror for the parents. Unfortunately, surrounding the belief in changelings are rather barbaric "tests" to attempt to decipher whether a child was indeed a changeling or not. These tests were not dissimilar to the trials put unto accused Witches across England and Europe: that is, deadly. These tests aimed to see if the infants had unearthly abilities, and included being bathed in a solution of poisonous foxglove or even being placed on a shovel and held above a roaring fire.

In my opinion and in the opinion of many people I have discussed changelings with, the concept of changelings could easily be explained away by little-understood disabilities and illnesses. Of course, it is also entirely possible that fairies did indeed switch children or perhaps it is a mixture of both explanations. However, we must remain educated on the fact that much of the lore surrounding changelings most likely descended from a place of ignorance and intolerance.

Allies, Foes, or Both?

It is a debate I see often among modern Witches today: are the fairies useful, powerful allies in magic which we should seek to make a connection with, or are they terrifying entities we can never fully understand, and therefore should avoid at all costs? The answer might be less binary in nature than we might think. Fairies are fickle creatures. Many people insist we should stay well away from them, describing them as arcane entities who exist outside of the laws of nature and human morality. Whilst others take them as being whimsical creatures of pure folly and fancy, taking them lightly and treating them as cute and quirky spiritual guides. In our modern day and age, it can be tricky and difficult to expel the childlike fairies of our fantasies from books and media. Numerous tales throughout Welsh folklore warn of the perils of fairy.

The *ellyll*, that is all the various types of spirits of place, are beings Witches can and do connect with and work with as magical allies. It would be hard to understand how one could find a sense of connectivity to their land, their home, or the regions surrounding their home without respecting and honouring the fairies of those areas. However, they can be tricky beings and one would never wish to be on their bad side.

The important thing to remember about fairies is that they are not Tinkerbell, and they are not governed by the same laws of morality as we are. What may simply be a comical joke to the fairies could be a deadly situation for us. Regardless of whether you choose to actively work with the fairies, which I would not suggest you do until you are exceptionally experienced in practicing Witchcraft and have a strong understanding of Welsh fairy lore, a reverence and respect for the fairies is something I wholeheartedly suggest you obtain.

Ways to Connect with the Spirit of Your Home

If you wish to approach the idea of working with the fae, I would first and foremost recommend honouring, respecting, acknowledging, and reaching out to the household fairies that most likely reside within your home. Household fairies, or in Welsh the *bwbachod*, are the spirit of the heart of your home. They are the epitome of what one might consider "home." Comfort is the main intrinsic element of the *bwbachod*; they do not like being burdened by things such as messes, folk who take life too seriously and don't enjoy the small joys, and those who speak unkindly of their home. To speak ill of your home is in a way a form of speaking ill of the *bwbach*.

Do You Have a Bwbach?

When I discuss household fairies with Witches and those who believe in fairies, a common question I get asked is how one might go about finding out whether you even have a household spirit. There are numerous whispers found within folklore surrounding the concept of how *bwbachod* operate. Some folk beliefs state that *bwbachod* are specific to families and that once the family who originally owned the home moves out then the *bwbach* also leaves that home. This was even considered a method of ridding yourself of pesky, mischievous *bwbachod*—simply move out and into a new home and you will be free of their nuisance. However, my personal beliefs and experiences do not align with this method of thinking.

It is my belief that the *bwbachod* are literally the spirit of homeliness. So long as you feel at home in your house, and you treat the home with respect and value then a household spirit will be found there. I often connect with the household fairy of my childhood home, despite the fact that my childhood home is a council estate house, which does not date back much further than the 1980's. The age of the home has no bearing on whether the household fairy resides there; the main element of a home being viable for the presence of a household fairy is simply that it is a space one considers and treats as home.

My current living situation at the time of writing this book is a very peculiar one. I live in a small one-bedroom apartment in the middle of a busy city centre. Regardless of how urban and lacking in spirit that may sound, this place is actually packed to the brim with spiritual energy. The apartment is within a building which dates back to the early nineteenth century, is right next door to a seventeenth-century building and situated right above twelfth-century crypt chambers. The history of this place is not lacking, and so the ghosts of the past frequent this area often. I spent many months upon first moving here feeling a sense of emptiness, as though the place was lacking in a house spirit or fairy. What I quickly realised was what was truly lacking was my perception of this place being a home. It is only recently that I have truly began to see this place as my home, and now I feel the presence of the household fairy on the daily. Delving into the history of your place of residence is the first step toward connecting with your household spirits. If your residence is a fairly new build, perhaps delve into the history of what was situated on the land before your home.

It was a common tradition among Welsh households to ritualistically clean the home in order to keep the household fairies happy.[45] Keeping the household spirits happy was imperative; if they were happy they would aid you in keeping the house clean and secure, and able to conduct your daily tasks with ease. Upset the household spirits however, and only chaos would ensue.

✸ EXERCISE ✸
Connecting with the Spirit of Your Home

Here is a very easy rite created by me, with modern living kept in mind, to honour and respect the household fairy.

Step 1: Clean the Home

Witches are often looking for effective methods of cleansing the house of any negative and unwanted energies. The most effective and easy method of cleansing a home, however, is not to burn any herbs or conduct any complicated rites; it is simply to clean the house. Spend some time vigorously cleaning the house, ensuring to clean the most important areas including the oven, the hobs, the fireplace if you have one, and the food cupboards. By cleaning the home, it sends a message to your *bwbach* that you truly care for them and respect them.

Step 2: Be Considerate of the Household Fairy

In times of old, Welsh maids would leave their fires on through the night to keep the house warm for the *bwbach*. Nowadays not everyone has a fireplace to burn a fire through the night in; however, most of us have a heating system or a method of keeping the house nice and toasty. It may be difficult considering keeping pesky things such as bills at bay to keep the home continually warm, and we must consider our impact on the environment as well, but the main element of this process is to try to promote a considerate environment

---

45. Sikes, *British Goblins*, 130.

for your household fairy. Keep the home clean, well maintained, and well cared for, and then you have done very well.

Step 3: An Offering to the Household Fairy

The fairies of Wales tend to be incredibly fond of dairy products. A glass of milk, a bowl of fresh cream, a block of cheese. These are all perfect items to give to the household fairies. It is important to note that fairy lore is very much clear that fairies are not fond of meat. Alcohol however, they very much enjoy. Choose an offering wisely; I tend to provide the household fairy with a bowl of fresh cream as well as a small shot glass of rum.

Once you have chosen your offering, place it either on the stovetop or somewhere in the kitchen, and if you wish, recite this petitionary chant:

I gift to you this offering of food,
So that our bond can remain calm and good,
Bwbachod of the household,
Brethren of home and hearth,
Know that I respect you and value your worth,
I ask for nothing in return, I only wish to honour you,
Spirit of this household, know my words to be true

In the morning, once the offering has served its purpose, dispose of it in a way that is kind to your home and the environment surrounding it. Do not worry about throwing away an offering the next day; its purpose is to show respect, and once it has served its purpose you have no need to keep it around.

It is always best to stay on the good side of the fairies; this is a simpler task than one might think. Connecting with nature and respecting the land surrounding you are some of the most important aspects of ensuring you stay in the fairy's good books. Especially take great care of oak trees; they are a sacred and important tree to the fairy. One might also take care to treat animals with respect, especially those animals that are important to the fair folk.

Goats are among some of the animals sacred to Welsh fairies. Goats are considered cunning creatures who are the keepers of arcane wisdom and occult knowledge. The fairies are incredibly fond of goats. Folk legends state that the fairies, on their sacred day, Friday, often spend the day with goats grooming their luscious beards and whispering all the secrets of the world to them. The goat has become an important symbol in my personal practise, and it is fitting that goats have associations with both fairies and Witches alike.

Fairy cattle feature prominently in various folk tales from around Wales. These pure white cows produce the finest of milk, and anyone who is lucky enough to be gifted one from the *Bendith y Mamau* or *Gwragedd Annwfn* will find themselves in great abundance for years to come. However, treat these cattle with disrespect and the fairy folk will call them back into their otherworldly home.

Remember that words hold a very potent power, especially it seems in Wales. Speaking ill of the fairies is considered a sign of utmost disrespect, one that will leave you a target of the fairies' terrible mischief and mayhem. On the other hand, speaking kindly of the fair folk is always seen as a beneficial act to do. Fairies are especially kind to those who speak well of them and treat them with sincere respect. Who knows, perhaps by speaking kindly you could become the next to be gifted some fairy money or a pure white cow.

What is one to do if they are targeted by the fairies' mischief and mayhem? It is said that fairies have an aversion to iron. Whether or not this is true is unknown, as their aversion to iron might be more a symbolic and poetic method of saying that the fairies do not think highly of humans in our new industrialised, metal world. Our modern way of living surrounded by machinery and technology is a thing of wonder, and yet it has done nothing but send us further away from connecting to the natural beauty of our land and the magic of our Earth. With most fairies being highly connected to the natural world it would only make sense that they would not approve of our way of life today.

Welsh lore specifically states that a bush of prickly furze surrounding your home will protect you from fairies. Whether this works as a protective measure against mischievous household fairies is not clear. The *Gwyllion* are supposedly easily sent away by the pulling of a knife, though I do not personally suggest you carry a knife with you if you plan on going on any late-night mountain hikes.

At the end of the day however, if you find yourself a victim of fairy mischief it is very likely you have done something to cause great offense and rightly deserve it.

The spirits of place, fairies of the wilds, the households, and the underground regions can be wonderful allies to a magical practitioner if approached with caution and consideration. Regardless of whether you plan on working with fairies, or whether you even believe in fairies at all, learning about the rich legend and lore surrounding fairies is very important. These legends and old beliefs speak not only of fantastical creatures, but also of the heart of rural Wales and the persistence of beliefs that seem to predate, or at the very least contradict Christianity. The fairies represent a spirit of rustic wildness, which is the very nature of the Welsh countryside. Hearing the stories of the fair folk in all their varieties and forms creates a sense of oneness with my land for me. These legends, customs, and beliefs existed long before I did, and will persist to be told and possibly believed for centuries to come.

Whether you believe in fairies or not, this Welsh Witch certainly does.

Chapter 9

Practical Welsh Witchery

Witchcraft at its heart is a wholly practical endeavour. Some utilise Witchcraft within their religious worship, however, Witchcraft is not intrinsically a religious or wholly spiritual endeavour. Witchcraft is simply finding a means to an end; bringing about the change that you wish to see in the world. It is utilising your magical knowledge, your knowledge of correspondences, and your knowledge of how the world works in order to influence an outcome, usually to your advantage. Being a Witch means standing in one's own power, and rather than whining or worrying when things do not go your way, the Witch's solution is to make things go your way as much as possible.

This section of the book will focus on the practical elements of Witchcraft. We will explore methods of utilising magic, how to cast effective spells, and the morality behind curses and baneful magic.

This is an insight into my personal *Llyfr Cyfrin*, or magical journal, the practises that I delve into on the daily. As a Welsh Witch, I draw inspiration from Welsh folklore, folk magic, and mythology as well as local superstition into my practise. It is important to note that I do not claim these practises are the practises of ancient Welsh Witches, steeped in antiquity. Quite the contrary, these practises are wholly my own inventions; they are inspired and informed by older traditions, practises, and beliefs native to my Celtic land, but are formulated and created by me, a modern Welsh Witch. My craft is only as ancient as I am, and I would never claim a false sense of antiquity.

The methods in which I practise my Witchcraft may differ from those which you have read about in other books, depending on your personal preference. The Witchcraft I outline here will not be as familiar as most books on Wicca or more eclectic forms of modern Witchcraft; however, if you are familiar with modern traditional Witchcraft then some aspects outlined here will be familiar to you. I am not Wiccan, and I do not believe in the three-fold law, nor in the need for a duality of a goddess and god in my workings. Though I do prefer to work within a consecrated circle for the majority of my more formal rites, the methods in which I create a working ground may feel alien. Have no fear, whatever your personal method of approaching magic, you will be able to incorporate aspects of these practises and methods into your own.

As I previously noted, none of these rites have any specific ancient antiquity behind them; they are purely my creations. However, the way in which I created these rites was by utilising what knowledge I had of the history of beliefs surrounding Witchcraft and magic in Wales. I also fused that knowledge with folk practises and traditions as well as some more modern Druidic elements. Many of the incantations, charms, spells, and curses I utilise are adapted versions of those few spells which have been recorded from the late medieval to early modern period. I was also heavily inspired by the magical workings of the Cornish, and many of my rites have been adapted from the rites of traditional Witchcraft from our close Celtic cousins in Cornwall.

My hope is not that those reading this book will adapt my methods of practicing magic word for word; in fact, I hope the exact opposite. Witchcraft is an art, which I firmly believe should be unique to each individual practitioner. I hope that by reading my method of practicing magic you will be inspired to use it as a leaping board to formulate and concoct your own individualistic methods of practicing. The very basis of my practise is about a connection to the landscape within which I dwell. However, these practises that we will delve into in the following pages are not limited to those who currently reside in Wales. Those who are drawn to a magical practise informed and inspired by the Celtic landscape of Wales may be drawn to it for a variety of reasons; ancestry, cultural ties, or indeed simply a deep reverence and pull toward this beautiful continuum of magic, these are all valid. I humbly offer you here an insight into my personal magical journals, my studies. I also invite you, as the reader, to use what I have provided here as a springboard to develop your own practise inspired and informed by the continuum of Welsh magical practise that stretches back through history. Allow the following pages to awaken your inner Welsh Witch, and allow the Awen to flow as you consider how these practises may or may not be incorporated into your own authentic, individualistic brand of Witchcraft.

The Spoken Word and Magic as an Art

The spoken word is a powerful tool when utilised for magical purposes. Modern Witches today tend to lean one way or the other, either embracing the spoken word within their spell work or completely dismissing the need for words at all. I have known Witches who enjoy creating intricate and poetic verses, which they interweave perfectly into their ritualistic work, or spontaneous spells. However, I have also known Witches who turn up their nose and cringe at the idea of memorising and reciting a string of words to project their magic through. I have found through experience that magic and Witchcraft are not entirely a science; we can discuss the scientific ideologies behind magic all day long. However, the truth of the matter is that at its heart a magical practise is one fuelled by an artistic expression of your personal identity and connection to the world around you. There is no use attempting to force yourself into something that will not serve you well. If the notion of reciting spells, charms, and incantations aloud fills one with dread or discomfort then, by all means, a Witch of that nature should not pursue the spoken word. However, I prefer to utilise the spoken word in my practical magical practises and in doing so I feel a connection with the continuum of Welsh Celtic magicians and folk magical Welsh traditions that predate me by very many centuries. Wales is a land of art, and the spoken word is just as much an art as any other medium might be. In this Celtic land, we have strong traditions of bardic influences on the culture. Poets and singers are often revered in the land of the red dragon; even within our national anthem, we proudly relate the land to singers and bards *"gwlad beirdd a chantorion enwogion o fri,"* which means: "a land of bards and singers of great renown." Woven into our land's mythology, the Mabinogi are what we would call *englynion,* which are best translated to be: song spells. Verses and rhymes with deeply magical tendencies. Throughout the history of Wales, people have utilised the spoken word to bless, heal, curse, and enchant others. Therefore, it is no wonder that my personal practise, which is inspired greatly by the land, its history, and its folklore, is laced with the spoken word. I write my own spells, and I recite my own chants and incantations. I often utilise the Welsh language when speaking a spell, as it simply comes naturally, but also because the Welsh language is one that feels intrinsically magical to speak. Ancient and arcane, yet blissfully modern and comfortable. However, for the purposes of this book and for accessibility I have attempted to include mostly English incantations and spells.

I would urge anyone with a poetic tendency and a preference toward Celtic magical practises to fuse the two interests as frequently as possible. You are a unique, powerful, and artistic soul; your magical practise should not lack any of your artistic expression. A magical practise based purely on logic and reason is a magical practise that sorely lacks heart and soul. Beyond being a Witch I am also an artist, a dancer, a poet, and a singer; these things are not mutually exclusive from one another. Tapping into the continuum of Celtic magic and utilising my artistic expression allows me to feel at one with the land, my ancestors, and the gods of Celtica. It fuels my spell work, heightens my ritual practises, and lends a power to my magic that I cannot fully explain.

The Working Circle

Mentioning drawing the circle causes many practitioners to turn up their nose, as the working circle has become synonymous with the workings of twentieth-century forms of Witchcraft, such as Wicca. However, the utilisation of the working circle long predates Wicca and stretches back throughout ceremonial magical practises. The circle is used within ceremonial magic and in many streams of modern, Neopagan Witchcraft as a method of protecting the practitioner. For the Welsh Witch however, working within a circle has very little to do with protection and much more to do with constructing a powerful atmosphere to work in, a place where the Witch forges their own sacred area of liminality and magic. Within the circle, the boundaries that exist between the realm of spirit and mortal are brushed aside. Here within the working circle, the Witch may enter into contact or compact with allied forces.

An Example of a Modern Welsh Folk Magic Ritual

Here I will outline my personal method of creating a hallowed or consecrated working space or circle. My method is completely self-constructed, pulling inspiration from many sources including but not limited to: Welsh Witchcraft lore and history, folkloric traditions of Wales, the utilisation of the compass in modern traditional Witchcraft, and modern Welsh Druidic ritual.

Step 1: Preparation

The first step of any magical rite would be to prepare oneself for what is to come. The first thing I tend to do is begin to note down either mentally or in a notepad what exactly the goal of the rite will be: what do I wish to achieve? This will then lead me to the question of, what will I need for the rite? Will any specific herbs, incenses, oils, flowers, tools, or garments be required? Take time preparing the rite thoughtfully and carefully.

Where is best for a Witches' rite? I know many Witches today who prefer to work within the comfort of their own home. Many older Pagans and Witches I know tend to refer to these Witches as "carpet Witches," as the majority of their rites are performed on their carpeted floors. I do not believe there is anything particularly wrong with performing rites from the comfort of your own home; it is where we usually feel our most comfortable and our most free. If performing a rite at home is what suits you best, then by all means do just that. There are certain areas in the home that will hold more potent energies. I personally prefer to practise my magic by my fireplace if working indoors. If you have a garden that might be a good option too, even better if it is concealed. Witchcraft should be, and very much is, accessible to all. You do not need to venture deep into a dense forest or find a rural crossroads to perform your rite; however, you may prefer to. Historically magical practitioners would have preferred to venture away from the interruptions of the modern world; but in our modern, urban lives not all of us will have access to rural, untouched places where we can remain safe. The rite I detail here in this section is specifically created to be done outdoors; therefore, take that into consideration and ponder over any alterations if you choose to do this indoors.

My rites are usually performed in liminal spaces, or in concealed and hidden spaces in nature. I made good use of my rural countryside back in the village I was raised. My rites would often be conducted on cliffs overlooking the sea, far from any homes or peering eyes. Now that I live in a city, I tend to walk a mile or two to the nearest woodland area in order to conduct any rites. I enjoy old churchyards or graveyards, a place where the living and the dead converge. Graveyards have an energy that is calming, soothing, and sacred. Graveyards and churchyards here in Britain are more or less no different to parks and woodland areas with their abundance of trees, hills, and greenery. It may seem strange for a Witch to work her rites so close to the church; nevertheless, these spaces are energetically unique and immensely powerful. Beyond churchyards, graveyards, beaches, cliffs, and dense woods. I also enjoy seeking out ancient monuments; ancient monuments are in abundance across Wales, especially on the Isle of Anglesey. Cairns, standing stones, chambered tombs, circles of stones, and more are a common sight and the perfect spaces for a late night rite.

Wherever you choose to perform your rite, it must follow these simple rules:

1. Is the space safe, and do you have permission to be there?

2. Will any rite you perform in this space cause any discomfort to the environment, or the local people to that area? If yes, find a new space.

3. Will you feel comfortable working your magic in this space?

If you can follow those simple rules, you will easily find your working space.

These are the basics of preparation. You may add other steps as needed, such as cleansing your body by having a ritual bath. Alternatively, perhaps you would like to meditate on the rite ahead before moving forward.

Now that you have planned your rite, and found the perfect location, it is time to move on to the next step.

Step 2: The Journey

The next step of your rite is the journey to the rite itself. Many of the Pagans I know today consider the consecration of the working circle to be the "beginning" of their rite. To me, the beginning is the preparation, but the part of my rites that always feels like the true beginning are the journeys toward the rite. I prefer to walk to wherever it is I plan to conduct my rite, regardless of whether that means walking for miles. I use the walk itself as a meditative task, a time to clear my mind, and enter the mind-set of magic. Every step I take I visualise that I am connecting with the Earth. I take in the sights surrounding me, making note of any animals, insects, or signs I may see on my way. Sometimes I will hum or sing a song as I walk, anything that aids me in entering the magical mind-set.

This is the time to think about what is to come, what you wish to achieve, and why you are conducting this rite. The planning process should already be done by now, and this time should be spent solemnly preparing one's mind and energy.

Step 3: Empowering the Working Space

Once you have arrived at the space in which you plan to conduct your rite, and have your tools at the ready, take a moment to assess the area. Clean it of any debris, rubbish, or pollution. Try not to alter any natural landscapes; however, do your best to clean up any human-made messes left by those who came before you. This acts as a devotional practise to the local spirits of place, and also clears the space of any items which may hinder the rite at hand.

Place your tools in a safe, secure place and begin by burning fragrant herbs that correspond with the working in your cauldron. This activates the virtues of the herbs being utilised, dispersing of those virtues and qualities into the air. However, it may also act as a method of cleansing the space of any unwanted, malignant entities whilst simultaneously inviting the allied spirit forces to your working. The cauldron should sit in a place where the smoke from within it can permeate throughout the working space. My cauldron usually resides in the centre of what will eventually become my working circle.

The next stage of forging your ritual space will be to raise the energies adequately. There are countless methods of raising the energies, and the process has already begun with the utilisation of the burning herbs. Sound is a powerful force to utilise in raising energy. Drumming, singing, incanting, and clapping are all worthwhile methods of raising the energies. Choosing your own personal method of raising the energies of a space, awakening the vital spirit force in the area, is a crucial aspect of your work and may require adaptation depending on the context of the rite at hand. If avoiding drawing attention is an issue, you might choose to empower the space by simply lighting candles, or meditating and allowing yourself to connect deeply with the environment around you by listening to all the sounds, taking in all the sensations of the space.

Once the energies are raised, the herbs are burning, and the time has arrived to begin the rite, the next step will be to draw the circle.

The traditional method of drawing the circle is to literally draw the circle physically into the ground with the wand, stave, or stang. This method was commonly recorded as being utilised by folk magical practitioners, conjurers, and cunning men of Wales. Take heed of which direction to draw the circle, and with which hand. The connotation I have established is that drawing a circle clockwise with the right hand is best suited for magical workings that hope to encourage growth and increase as well as any work requiring the summoning of spiritual entities. Whereas, drawing the circle anti-clockwise with the left hand may benefit workings of a banishing nature, decreasing, and curses or spells of a more baneful or vengeful nature. Once the circle has been drawn, then the practitioner shall begin to call forth the energies and spirits that will be invited as allied forces to the workings. This would usually begin with an incantation.

Many traditional magical specialists in Wales were known to spew elaborate incantations in Latin or archaic languages, most likely drawn from various grimoires. The modern practitioner could continue this methodology and draw a spirit invocation from an older text. However, for the sake of regional specific entities and spirits it may be beneficial to instead begin with an incantation in the Welsh language. Here is an example of the incantation I use to begin any magical working, in order to draw forth allied forces to work alongside me to aid in achieving my desires. This incantation is actually merely a verse of the national anthem of Wales, with an added sentence beforehand calling upon the spirits of the land. Some may find it strange that I begin my magical workings by reciting the national anthem. However, these are words of power. What is a national anthem, other than a devotional offering for the land itself? As a Witch, I view it as a devotional to the spirits of the land and those who have lived and died on these shores. The aim of reciting this incantation is to stir up your own spirit, as well as the spirit of the place itself.

> *Cyfarchaf i'r tir, cyfarchaf i ellyll ac ysbrydion y lle hon,*
> *clywch fy ngeiriau...*
> *Hen Gymru fynyddig, paradwys y bardd, Pob dyffryn, pob*
> *clogwyn, i'm golwg sydd hardd; Trwy deimlad gwladgarol, môr*
> *swynol yw si, Ei nentydd, afonydd, i fi.*

Or, in English:

> *I call to the spirits of the land, the ellyll and spirits that reside in*
> *this space, hear my words...*
> *Land of the Bard, Oh mountainout place,*
> *My devotion to this landscape is brought forth to this space,*
> *I listen to the whispers of each mountain and stream,*
> *And these whispers set the whole landscape agleam*

This would then be followed by the following incantation, in either Welsh or English. This incantation is of my own creation, unlike the above opening incantation which derived predominately from the Welsh national anthem:

> *Cyfarchaf a swynaf chi, O ysbrydion y tir hon,*
> *Cyfarchaf a swynaf pwer y bodau anweledig yn y lle hon.*
> *Dewch! Ysbrydion fy hynafiaeth, hynafiaeth o gwaed ag asgwrn.*
> *Ysbrydion y tir, ysbrydion y dŵr, ysbrydion y tân, ac ysbrydion yr aer.*

Fel y fydd hi yn y teyrnas uwch ben, felly fydd hi yn yr teyrnas islaw.
Dewch! Rhowch aed i mi yn fy swyngyfaredd, fy chonsurio ar yr awr hon.
Yn enw yr sarphes goch ben llydan, ac yr hen ysbrydion y tir, byddwch
yma. Dewch!

(I summon and conjure thee, spirits of this land; I summon and conjure the
powers of those invisible forces present here. Arise! Spirits of my ancestors, ances-
tors of blood and of bone. Spirits of land, spirits of water, spirits of fire, and spir-
its of air. As it shall be in the realms above, so it shall be in the realms below.
Come! Aid me in my magical rite, my conjuration upon this hour. In the name
of the broad-headed red serpent, and the old spirits of this land, be here. Arise!)

It would be my recommendation to recite these words in the language you are most competent and confident in. The power behind the words stems from a depth of understanding them; therefore it would be of no use to stumble through the Welsh version if you are not adept at speaking the Welsh language. Words can be powerful and useful magical tools when utilised correctly and with dedication and power behind them; however, without a decent level of understanding the language the potency of the words may be rendered empty and useless. The English translation of my incantation is just as potent and powerful as the Welsh so long as the intention and dedication behind it stems from the right place. The Welsh occult systems have developed primarily from the Bardic traditions and thus many of the methods of invoking and summoning that one might attempt to do in English in other occult systems of practise will not translate perfectly adequately into the Welsh. The conjurers and practitioners of Wales' history would have more likely invoked in English or Latin, pulling from the grimoire traditions and streams of Western occultism. So though I make every effort to incorporate my native Welsh language into my practise, oftentimes the best route for magical working is in the English. Unless, of course, you feel more drawn to the Bardic influence on Welsh occult practises. I present my personal incantations here as an example, and happily invite you to either use mine word for word, or construct your own using mine as either a leaping board for inspiration, or as a base.

Step 4: The Rite Itself

The desired magical working would then be performed within the confines of the circle. When completed, offerings to the spirits of space and the allied forces would be given. Following in the tradition that the spirits of nature in Wales are fond of good drink, the offering would usually consist of a locally brewed alcoholic beverage or spirit. The drink would be scattered around the space, or would be taken into the mouth and spat around the circle, allowing the practitioner to taste it first. Alternatively, freshly baked bread, cheese, and fresh cream are opportune offerings.

Leave the space as though you were never there in the first place. Beyond leaving offerings, attempt to leave no trace of you being there. The offering being either drink or perishable goods is perfect for this style of working, as it will either perish into the soil or serve as nourishment for the creatures that dwell in the space.

The Witch Light

Fire is an elemental force of pure transformation and creation. Without the rays of the sun, our world would not thrive and survive, and similarly without the fires of our souls we would not have inspirational and creative forces in this world to keep us entertained and happy. It is no wonder that, historically speaking, Witches have always been associated with strange lights, mystical flames, and an ethereal glow. Many historical accounts of Witches in Wales mention strange lights, and a distant glow emanating from the woods or a nearby grove was usually seen as a sign that Witches were at work in that direction. Illumination is a word I often associate with Witchcraft. Delving into the mysteries and magic of our world is an act of illumination for the soul; Witches are illuminated by their drive to learn and to grow as powerful weavers of magic, knowledge, and wisdom.

This is what I refer to as the Witch light. The illuminated spiritual glow within the heart of each Witch. You can feel your Witch light grow within you when you learn something new, or when you are conducting a rite or performing a heavily empowered spell. I visualise my Witch light as looking very similar to the glow of candlelight. A steady flame, strong and bright. Your Witch light is inextinguishable.

When I say that I am invoking my Witch light, what that means is that I am emboldening and empowering myself to feel at my best, my most confident. The rite of invocation of the Witch light is one of self-empowerment, and self-love. It may sound like fluffy spiritual rhetoric, but I firmly believe that the more confident you are in yourself, the more powerful and potent your magic and effect will be to this world. The more confidence and power you feel within yourself, the brighter your Witch light will grow.

This is an outline of a rite I perform every so often as an act of self-care and love. It is an invocation of my Witch light; drawing on the element of fire and the creative forces which fire exudes.

This rite can be performed anywhere, though somewhere you can safely light as many candles as possible is best. Ensure that wherever you are performing this rite is mostly dark or dimly lit.

⊗ EXERCISE ⊗
The Invocation of Witch Light

Set up a table or flat surface with as many candles as you can find. The colour and type of candle does not matter; the idea is to fill a space with as many candles as safely possible.

Comfortably place yourself before the candles; you can be stood or sat for this rite, whatever feels most comfortable to you. Take a deep breath in and close your eyes, breathing in for at least four counts. Breathe out for five counts. Continue this rhythm of breathing, deep inhales of four counts followed by five counts of exhaling. With your eyes still closed, recite aloud:

I am Witch,
It is wisdom I seek,
I am Witch,
Hidden knowledge I keep.

Repeat as many times as necessary to raise the energies of the space.

When you are ready, open your eyes and focus on the candles before you. Light each candle one by one, and for each candle you light say one positive affirmation about yourself, such as:

I am intelligent
I am beautiful
I am worthy of respect

Continue lighting the candles and speaking aloud the positive affirmations until each and every candle is lit. Once every candle is lit, bask in the warmth and glow of the candlelight. Feel the light extend around the space. Take a few moments to watch the flames; watch as some may flicker or grow while others might dim. Study the movements of the flames and watch how the light bounces off of the walls or the ceiling.

After you have spent a while watching the candlelight, close your eyes once more and visualise that you are glowing from the inside out. Ask yourself these questions, internally:

- Where does your glow emanate from?
- How does the glow feel?
- How do you visualise your glow to look like?
- How strong is the light?

Focus and meditate on this glow for a while. Then once you feel ready, open your eyes.

Extend your arms skyward and recite the following chant:

Through darkest night, my light shall shine,
Intense and potent power is always mine,
Like a fire that glows and cannot be put out,
I shall feel the light glow from the inside out.
This Witch light is mine,
The wisdom it holds,
Reminds me of Witches from times of old.
Gods and goddesses live within me,
My inner power I now unleash.

Focus on the flames before you and continue to say aloud;

I call upon the healing qualities of the sacred goddess Braint.
Be here with me now in this time and place,
Surround me with your gentle healing embrace.

Close your eyes for a moment and visualise the nurturing embrace of the goddess Braint, the resilient spirit of spring and healing. Allow her spirit to hold you tightly, warmly. Then, once you feel Braint has graced you with her healing take a deep breath and blow out all the candles.

Close your eyes again, and focus on that inner light within. Feel it grow stronger and brighter. This is your Witch light, the power within you. Do not ever deny yourself this power, this strength that dwells from within ever again. Recite aloud, as confidently as you can;

My Witch light is strong.
And so am I.

This rite is an effective method of raising confidence, and nourishing yourself with the healing embrace of the goddess of spring. I often perform this rite when I am feeling dishevelled and low on confidence. Some may turn their nose up at it, or call it fluffy, but self-love and spiritual healing are important and integral parts of any spiritual practise. You must love and appreciate yourself in order to feel the presence of the strong power within. Let this rite embolden any of your magical workings and endeavours.

Swynwyr

A common motif adored by many modern Witches is that of the local wise woman, the village healer who offers remedies and services to the local folk. There is a lot of romanticism surrounding the wise woman image in modern Witchcraft; many Witches consider themselves to be the modern equivalent of being a wise woman. Of course, in this day and age it is much easier to pop down to the local pharmacy or supermarket and buy a pack of painkillers than go to a quirky and eccentric neighbour for an herbal tea remedy when feeling unwell. Still, the imagery of being the wise old woman who lives on the outskirts of town, harvesting her herbs and coming to the aid of the common folk is one filled with magic and romance.

In medieval Wales the wise folk who attended to the sick and to those in need were referred to as *Swynwyr* or, in English: charmers. The charmers of rural Wales were not incredibly learned folk who studied magic or the occult immensely; rather they were simply regular folk who happened to have a good understanding of healing *Swynion* (charms) as well as a knowledge of herbal remedies. Most charmers were women, and they often had ordinary jobs. Charming was a side skill that they usually practised to help people. Many charmers would not take money in return for their services; instead, it would be a fair-trade system. If a charmer helped heal your sick child or wife, perhaps you would offer them a loaf of bread, a stick of cheese, or a pint of milk in return.

The *Swynwyr* were approached much more often than conventional physicians in rural, medieval Wales. Most likely because they would be a more affordable choice for poorer communities, but also because they were familiar faces and local characters, and so it was easy for the common folk to place their trust in them.

Swynion, or charms, were at their core prayers. Contrary to what many might believe, the charmers of medieval Wales were not practicing some ancient, surviving Pagan magical tradition. I have heard some say that the more traditional charms might have pre-Christian roots, but all recorded charms known today feature God, Jesus, and the presence of saints. For a modern Witch who leans away from Christianity and more toward Paganism, it might be uncomfortable to read these charms aloud. However, I believe these charms are imbued with powerful energies that could easily be utilised by modern practitioners of magic.

The following charm is the English translation of a charm that Gwen ferch Ellis, the first woman to be executed on accusations of Witchcraft, provided to the bishop who interrogated her.

> *In the name of God the father, the son, and the holy spirit of God,*
> *And the three Marys, and the three consecrated altars,*
> *And the blessed son of grace,*
> *And by the stones, and by the herbs,*
> *To which the son of grace bestowed their virtues*

In order that they should defend thee, the sinner who suffered adversity,
As Christ defended.
In the name of the Father, the Son, and the Holy Spirit,
Against adversity above wind, against adversity below wind,
Against adversity above ground and below ground,
Against adversity of the middle of the world,
And against adversity in any place of the world,
God keep you and preserve you from a wolf of a man,
From the evil thing of hell,
I take thee to be a child of God,
And a follower of Christ and an heir to the kingdom of heaven.[46]

Reading this charm, it is difficult for us, as modern people, to understand how one might have ever considered this to be satanic Witchcraft. The abundance of mentions of biblical figures makes it clear to us as some form of folk prayer. However, this was the common structure of most charms throughout Wales as well as other parts of Britain.

I find it interesting to note that there are aspects of this prayer that baffle even historians today; why the mention of three consecrated altars? What might the meaning behind that be? What are the references to the elemental force of wind, "wolf of a man," and the "middle of the world"? This charm, at first glance, may seem like a simple common prayer to the Christian God, but perhaps there is more to it than meets the eye. Charms were usually passed down throughout the generations, so it would not be unreasonable to think that perhaps some charms are exceptionally old, and though probably altered to suit modern sensibilities and beliefs, perhaps harken back to older beliefs.

The question I found myself asking when originally stumbling upon the charms of the *Swynwyr* was: can they be utilised by a modern, Celtic Pagan Witch? And the answer I found was a resounding yes. Whether you simply recite the charms word for word, God and all, or whether you alter them to suit your own beliefs and practises. The primary basis of the charm remains the same: a petitionary, protective charm. I have always found myself fascinated by

---

46. Suggett, *A History of Magic and Witchcraft in Wales.*

the above charm in particular as recited by the notable, self-identified *Swyn-wraig* Gwen ferch Ellis. And so I took it upon myself to re-write the charm with a more Celtic, verging on Druidic expression.

A Swyn (Charm) for Protection against Adversity

This charm can either be recited aloud before the person you wish to bless, or can be written on a piece of paper and kept somewhere safe. Buried in your walls, hidden beneath floorboards, or tucked beneath the bed would be a suitable place for a written charm. I have included here the words of a personal charm, which I utilise often, as inspired by the charm of Gwen ferch Ellis.

> *By the power of the sacred triskelion, the three realms of existence,*
> *By the three realms, the land, sea, and sky,*
> *And by the divine child,*
> *By the powers of standing stones and chambered tombs,*
> *Within which the power of our ancestors lie,*
> *May you be protected, shielded, and kept safe from all peril,*
> *As Taliesin was protected at sea by Cerridwen's coracle.*
>
> *By the power of land, sea, and sky,*
> *Against adversity from nature's rage,*
> *Against adversity from the worlds beyond,*
> *Against adversity from trickster spirits, and mischievous fae,*
> *May the gods of the land keep you and preserve you from harm.*
> *I take thee to be a child touched of the Awen,*
> *May the transformative cauldron of creation nurture you,*
> *May you be safe and protected.*

Utilise this charm as you see fit, or feel free to alter and change it to suit your beliefs and desires.

Constructing Your Own Charms

One aspect of modern Witchcraft I adore is the abundance of creativity that can be tapped into by practitioners. The spirit of *Awen* is something that is often utilised by most modern Witches. Tradition and history is important, but we must remember that we are modern Witches with our own individualistic path, and forging our own new traditions is a sacred act.

Charms in their traditional formats are at their simplest forms petitionary prayers. Charms would have been utilised for protection, for healing, and even occasionally for harm. Charms could be recited aloud with power and confidence, or they might have been written onto a piece of paper and kept somewhere near the individual whom the charm was meant for. Constructing your own charms is a fairly simple process. I prefer to construct my charms in the Welsh language, being a native Welsh speaker. When I do construct charms in Welsh I add a poetic element and attempt to add a rhythm and a rhyme to them. These rhymes do not always translate perfectly into English; however, if English is your first language there is nothing to stop you from making your charms rhyme. Constructing a charm is no different to constructing a poem, verse, or song. You simply choose the theme of your charm and write a few lines surrounding that topic. For example, a charm for healing may be as simple as:

Gods of the land, hear my desire,
Grant to me now thy healing power,
By power of land, the sea, and the sky,
Aid me to easily and safely get by.
By the strength of stone, and the rage of the sea,
Healing energies shall now flow through me.

Traditional Folk Magical Charms

These charms are examples of traditional charms found from Welsh folk magical history. These charms would exist within what could be considered Christian magic, calling upon the Christian God, Jesus, the Holy trinity, and even sometimes the virgin Mary to aid in magical protection and healing. To many neopagan practitioners the concept of Christian magic may be alarming and uncomfortable. For the Witch who walks the crooked path however, we can see the benefit and potency of these forms of magic. After all, the client who would have pursued the help of a *Swynwyr* would have most likely been Christian. Their belief in the Christian God would have aided the charm's potency and efficacy. It may comfort those who feel uncomfortable with the Christian style magic seen in these charms, that a *Swyn* as we would call a charm in Welsh nowadays merely means any spell or incantation that can be spoken aloud, or written into a charm bag. Therefore, the same method of formulating charms but incorporating non-Christian elements can be very effective if used on those, or for those, who do not believe in the power of Christianity. I also believe it would be beneficial to present these examples in this book, as it gives a deeper insight into the inner workings of Welsh traditional folk magic.

A Protection Charm

> *Pan godwy'r boreu yn gynta,*
> *Yn nawdd Beino yn benna;*
> *Yn nawdd Kerrig, nawdd Patrig,*
> *Yn nawdd y gwr gwyn Bendigedig;*
> *Yn nawdd Owain ben lluman llu,*
> *Ag yn nessa yn Nawdd Iessu.*[47]

(As I arise at the sign of dawn, I am mainly under the protection of Beuno. I draw forth the protection of Curing, and Patrick. The protection of the Holy and sacred Man. The protection of Owain, the chief banner of an army. And next, the protection of Jesus.)

Charms of this nature were often referred to as *Gweddion Anarferol*; in English: unusual prayers. These were petitionary prayers with a magical tendency which offered those who utilised them something in return. Protection was a common motif found within traditional charms. Here is another example.

---

47. Suggett, *A History of Magic and Witchcraft in Wales*

A Charm for Protection from Misfortune

> Credo fechan, credo lân, credo i Dduw ac Ifan,
> Rhag y dwfr, rhac y tân, rhag y sarphes goch ben llydan;
> Cerddais fynudd ac o'r fynudd
> A gwelwn Fair wen a rei gobennydd,
> A'i hangel, angel ufudd,
> A Dduw ei hyn yn dedwydd,
> Ar gwr llwyd a'i wisc wen yn llunio
> Llen rhwng pob enaid ac uffern. Amen.[48]

(A little creed, a holy creed, a creed to God and John the Baptist. Protect me from water, and from fire, and from the Devil himself. I walked up a mountain, and from the mountain peak I could see the holy Mary. And her angel, a dutiful angel, and God himself so joyous, and a holy man, in his white robes, weaving a veil between every soul and damnation. Amen.)

In this charm we see mention of protection from the "Sarphes goch ben llydan" or the "broad-headed red serpent," an old Welsh method of saying the Devil himself. It was said that whoever repeated this charm three times before going to sleep would be protected from hell and damnation.

An Animal Protection Charm

This charm was recorded to have been given to a Welsh couple living in the Llanidloes area of Powys, Wales. Looking at the contents of the charm I believe it could be placed upon farm animals, and would have acted as protection to the owner of the animals as well. This charm in particular was recorded in written form, alongside a hexagram with "Tetragrammaton" in its centre, and the letters n, o, d, A, y, a (Adonay) in each point of the star. Both Tetragrammaton and Adonay are Hebrew names of God. The charm also included an "Abracadabra" triangle. An "Abracadabra" triangle is made

---

48. Suggett, *A History of Magic and Witchcraft in Wales*.

up of the word "Abracadabra" in descending lines, and upon each line a letter is removed until eventually only one letter is left, as such:

ABRACADABRA
ABRACADABR
ABRACADAB
ABRACADA
ABRACAD
ABRACA
ABRAC
ABRA
ABR
AB
A

The spelling of Abracadabra alternates between having a "c" or a "k," though in the instance of this Welsh charm it was spelt with a "c." The first usage of the Abracadabra triangle can be traced back to the second-century CE, in a book titled *Liber Medicinalis* by Serenus Sammonicus, a Roman physician.[49] The Abracadabra triangle can be found in various grimoires, and in a lot of folk magical practise stemming from the cunning men of old who operated within what we would now call the "Grimoire Tradition" of magic, meaning they gained much of their magical knowledge from grimoires. The idea is that whilst writing the word "Abracadabra" in this format, the word diminishes as it descends into the shape of an upside-down triangle, and as the word diminishes so too does any ill-fortune, illness, curses, or malevolence.

The written charm was written as follows:

In the name of the Father,
And of the Son,
And of the Holy Ghost,
Amen

---

49. Illes, *The Element Encyclopedia of 5000 Spells.*

And in the name of the Lord Jesus Christ,

My Redeemer,

I give thee protection,

And will give relief to thy creature,

Thy cows,

Calves,

Horses,

Sheep,

Pigs,

And from all creatures that alive be in thy possession,

From all Witchcraft and from all other assaults of Satan.

Amen.[50]

Fetishes of Protection and Luck

Various fetishes, or certain good luck charms, have been utilised by the common folk of Wales for centuries. The standard, well-known tradition of hanging a horseshoe above the front door of the home, or more specifically above the stable or barn door for good fortune, was, and still is in some places, a common sight in Wales. The horseshoe was also considered a ward against malignant spirits and trickster fairies.

The berries of the rowan tree were also considered highly sacred and magical. The virtues of rowan berries are varied; therefore, they can be utilised in an abundance of ways within folk magical practise. The rowan berries can protect the home from certain insects, especially those that feast on wood. They also act as potent protection against mischievous and malignant fairies and spirits. They protect against curses, and the tricks of the fairy folk. Beyond that, it is also said that no illness or disease can come to those who have rowan berries on them or in their home.

A Witch may construct a fetish of a string of rowan berries to hang above the hearth, above the doorways of the home, or even to wear around the neck. The berries could also be placed into charm bags, poppets, Witch bottles and other fetishes, charms, and items of power as added protection.

~~~~~~

50. Isaac, *Coelion Cymru.*

Folk Magic Methods of Healing

As mentioned previously, the people of rural Wales for a long time found it difficult to consult modern practitioners of medicine. There was distrust of the more modern methods of treating ailments, and beyond that, many folk simply could not afford to call for a doctor. It was not unheard of to call upon a *Dyn Hysbys* or even *Swynwyr* (the cunning men and charmers) for help with certain ailments and health concerns. The role of the folk magical practitioner encompasses the role of healer traditionally. People would visit the wise for consultation on matters important to them, on matters regarding the spiritual, and to find lost things. In addition, beyond that, to get remedies and healing for their ills. Here I have outlined a few traditional healing practises collected by Evan Isaac in his book *Coelion Cymru* (*The Beliefs of Wales*). These healing practises were used against common ailments that bothered the common folk of the rural areas. It is important to note that these practises are listed here predominately as examples of Welsh healing practises and charms, and should not be used as a replacement for professional medical treatment.

To Alleviate Sore Eyes

If an individual was afflicted with sore, painful eyes it would be suggested that they wear rings of silver or gold in their earlobes. The silver or gold being believed to have healing properties and virtues that would pass onto the wearer.

Beyond that, there was also a belief in the healing potency of rain water collected in the May. This special water was considered highly beneficial for healing the eyes. It was considered highly beneficial to collect rainwater in May, and bottle it safely away throughout the year in order to have it handy in case of sore or ailing eyes.

Those afflicted with eye pain would be asked to wash their eyes out with the rain water collected in May every morning upon waking up, and every night before sleeping.

Wart Removal

Warts seemed to trouble numerous people, as there are countless traditional magical healing methods surrounding the removal of warts.

One method asks that the afflicted stealthily steal a piece of beef from someone. Once stolen, carry the beef to someplace secret and bury it in the Earth. As the beef decomposes and rots in the dirt, so too shall the wart wither away and perish off of the afflicted. This method is only effective if the beef is stolen, and stolen stealthily at that.

Another method to be rid of a wart is to spit on it first thing in the morning, ensuring that it is the first spit of the day that touches the wart.

A more malicious method of wart removal was effectively a form of hex or curse. You would transfer the warts onto another, unsuspecting party via magical interference. In order to do this you would have to find a handful of "white stones," or quartz stone, and break them up into fragments and dust. You would then collect the fragments and place them into a paper parcel. This paper parcel should then be taken to a crossroads and left there, in plain sight, where an unsuspecting individual might stumble upon it. Out of curiosity, they might open the parcel. Whosoever opens the parcel shall be the victim of this magic, and the warts of the afflicted shall be transferred to them.

To Remove a Stye

The method of healing a stye, a small bump on the eyelid, was rather peculiar. It required the practitioner to count from one to ten, then from ten backward down to one all in a single breath. Upon finishing counting, they would then blow onto the stye. This supposedly healed the stye.

A Concoction to Heal a Heavy Cold

Here is a simple healing remedy given to those suffering with a heavy cold.

Boil buttermilk, and once it is boiling hot mix in a dash of rosemary as well as a small amount of black treacle. Drink this mixture while it is still warm and it will soothe the illness.

Weather Prognostication and Spells

For obvious reasons, weather has long played a prominent role in the lives of the inhabitants of Wales. Weather is often personified within various folkloric tales and whimsical children's stories. The wind is known as *Morus y gwynt*, the rain is *Ifan y glaw*, and beyond this we have *Jac y rhew* (Jack Frost) and *Siôn Barrug* (Hoarfrost). It is no surprise that for good reason many superstitions and methods of prognostication abound surrounding the weather. Prognostication surrounding rain especially was commonplace. It was said that if it were to rain on the fifteenth day of July, then it would surely rain for forty days straight. This belief stems from the folklore surrounding St. Swithun or *Sant Swithin* as he is known in Wales. However, rain prognostication does not stop there. Mist that descended from the sea, red sky at dawn, a ring around the moon, a dog eating grass, trout leaping from the water often—these were all said to be signs that rain was near. Alternatively, red sky at sunset, drops of water lingering on tree branches, mist streaming down from the mountains, and gulls flying out to sea were all said to be signs of fair weather approaching.

Weather Spells

Throughout the varying superstitions and methods of prognostication surrounding weather we also come across peculiar verses written to aid in remembering certain signs of good or bad weather ahead. An example is as follows:

If one desires to decipher whether the weather shall be fair, or if it shall rain, one must simply find a lady-bird (ladybug). Upon finding a lady-bird, coax it to crawl onto your hand. Once it is on your hand, raise your hand up high and recite the following:

Y fuwch fach gota
P'un ai glaw a hindda?
Os daw glaw, cwymp o'm llaw;
Os daw haul, hedfana.[51]

---

51. Owen, *Welsh Folk-Lore*, 347.

(Ladybug, ladybug, which will it be, rain or fair weather? If it shall rain, fall from my hand: if the weather shall be fair, fly away.)

If the ladybug in your hand crawls off of you and falls to the ground, or refuses to fly, this means rain is on its way. However, if instead the ladybug does fly from your hand, then fair weather is to be expected.

The cunning practitioner of magic can use delightful verses, such as the above chant, about the ladybug within spell work. Utilising, or even altering these already-provided folk verses below as an incantation to summon forth the weather one would desire. One might choose to utilise a hag stone (a stone with a naturally occurring hole through the middle) in order to cast these weather spells, holding the hag stone up to the sky, and reciting these incantations, the hag stone acting as a portal to the realm of fairy. In Wales, the *ellyll* are the spiritual embodiments of nature itself; they are the spirits of winds that howl and the rains that fall. The hag stone can offer a method of communicating to them your desires, be that for rain or shine. It would be appropriate to also utilise a Witch's ladder within this context as well, for more potent, powerful workings.

A Spell for Fair Weather

In order to summon fair weather, recite this incantation three times to the skies above.

Bwa'r drindod prynhawn,
Tegwch a cawn.
Awyr goch prynhawn,
Tegwch a cawn.
Awyr las, a ddim mwy o law,
Haul ddisglair, tegwch a cawn.

(A rainbow in the afternoon is a sign that fair weather is near. Red sky in the afternoon is a sign that fair weather is near. Blue sky, and no more rain, shining sun, fair weather will come.)

A Spell for Rain

This incantation is to be utilised in order to summon rain to fall. It may feel counterintuitive to summon rain, especially if you live in a country as wet as I do. However, this does not have to be a spell to summon heavy rainfall. This spell can be utilised in order to summon rain during dry periods, or when one wishes to clear crowds. Most ordinary folk scurry home at the sight of rain, and so it may be beneficial for the Witch to wish for rain before journeying to a special site in order to conduct their rites and workings. Again, recite this incantation three times within your workings.

Niwl o'r mynydd,
Gwres a gynnydd,
Daw niwl o'r môr,
A glaw yn stôr.
Chwipia'r gwynt,
A choda'r baw,
Cyfarchaf i ysbrydion yr awyr,
A glaw a ddaw!

(Mist from the mountain, heat increases, fog shall rise from the sea, and rain is in store. Whip the wind, and raise the dirt, I call to the spirits of the skies, and rain will fall!)

The two spells above are not exactly traditional spells drawn down from the ages, but rather incantations formulated on the backbone of rural folk beliefs surrounding weather prognostication. Though the verses utilised within the incantations are methods of prognosticating the weather, the Witch, asserting their will and desire to the spirits, or *ellyll*, of the weather itself can call forth the continuum of beliefs surrounding these superstitions and exert their desire into reality.

Cursing and Baneful Magic

Modern Witchcraft for the most part operates today within a neopagan, new age expression which is focused almost entirely on light, empowerment, and healing. The topic of curses, hexes, baneful magic, and malevolently intended magical workings raises a brow even among many experienced, knowledge-able Witches. However, when we dig into the rich array of folk magical traditions and lore associated with Witchcraft that stretch far deeper into history than the early twentieth century, we find that the topic of baneful magic is very much a core aspect of Witchcraft's history. Wales' folk magical history in particular houses an array of astonishingly wicked curses that we cannot ignore simply because they do not fit into the confines of what many Witches belief Witchcraft encapsulates today.

Morality is the core issue surrounding the topic of cursing in modern Witchcraft today. However, what was the moral belief surrounding curses and baneful, or even vengeful magic in Wales, historically speaking? The consensus among most common folk was that curses and vengeful magic was absolutely morally sound so long as the desire to utilise malignant forces to instil suffering or vengeance was done with just cause. This is to say that a curse or vengeful magical working required a motivator, and should not be done on a whim. Those who cursed people without just cause were seen as malicious, malevolent Witches and often the accusations of Witchcraft only really extended to individuals who callously and maliciously called upon the aid of magic to work baneful, insidious workings. Neopagan Witches today predominately shun the concept of hexing, cursing, or using magic to fulfil your own goals at the disadvantage of another. However, to claim that curses and hexes are not in the spirit of Witchcraft is to ignore a continuum of traditional magical practises that have been practised for centuries. Baneful and malevolent magic has always been associated with Witchcraft and folk magic. In Wales, we had our *Swynwyr* and our respected magical specialists who were far from being wholly benevolent; they were not averse to delving into baneful magic in the right situation, or for the right price.

Most curses found throughout Wales however, were carried out in a protective, reasonable manner. People would place curses upon intruders into their homes, or those who wished to seek them harm; curses were not performed on those that the common folk did not believe deserved it. They were not taken lightly; nevertheless, they were ruthless and vicious. No one would dare cross an angry Welsh curser, for they would be struggling and suffering for many years to come. As modern magical practitioners, we must reflect on our position on baneful magic, especially for protective or reasonable circumstances.

To try to label these practises as purely evil is naïve and ignorant. Most people who turn to curses do so because they are desperate, tired, and sad. Just as in nature, sometimes the most devastating of storms can bring about the most positive, transformative change.

In seventeenth-century Wales, it was common for people to appear at court under accusations of cursing their neighbours. It was especially common for women to be accused of cursing someone. The majority of curses tended to be performed via an almost performative, ritualistic method of kneeling to the ground, with arms raised skyward. The individual performing the curse would recite a petitionary prayer to God, wishing ill upon their enemy. Not dissimilar to the spoken charms as mentioned in previous pages of this book, however taking on a more malicious, harmful expression. Sometimes women would even bare their breasts as part of the rite of cursing; this acted as an additional sign of disrespect to add fuel, potency, and efficacy to the curse. Fire was a common motif found in curses, as people petitioned within their prayers for wild fires to descend from the heavens, or for their enemies' homes to be engulfed in flames. Those cursing would wish for the destructive powers of fire to seek justice, and cleanse those who had done wrong.

The Llanddona Curse

One of the most famous folkloric legends that details Witches and Witchcraft in Wales is that of the Witches of Llanddona. Legend says that a group of strange, eccentric people were found floating in a boat just off the coast of Llanddona. The people of the small seaside town were reluctant to allow these peculiar folk onto shore, sensing something odd about them. However, they were eventually helped to shore and convinced the people to allow them to stay after impressing them by magically creating a well. It did not take long though for these strange visitors to show their true nature. They were indeed baneful, evil Witches. The Witches plagued the seaside town of Llanddona on the Isle of Anglesey with their baneful magic and manipulative ways. Within the folkloric tales of the Llanddona Witches there is a particular recited curse that goes as follows:

Crwydro y byddo am oesoedd lawer,
Ac ym mhob cam, camfa;
Ac ym mhob camfa, codwm;
Ym mhob codwm, tori asgwrn;
Nid yr asgwrn mwyaf na'r lleiaf,
Ond asgwrn chwil corn ei wddw bob tro.[52]

A translation of this curse would be as follows:

May he wander for many an age to come,
And at every step he takes, a stile,
At every stile, he shall fall,
At every fall, shall he break a bone,
May the bone that breaks not be the biggest, nor the smallest,
But the chief neckbone, every time.[53]

This curse shows just how cruel and prolonged the methods of cursing in Wales could be. It is difficult to find any curse wishing death upon an individual; instead, a curse was more likely to focus on the prolonged lived suffering of the victim.

A Curse upon Intruders

This curse is less malevolent in nature and more so protective. It was utilised to curse any who so dared to enter the home of another against the will of the rightful owner. It is a spoken curse, said aloud.

Melltith Duw i'r neb a ddelo i'm tŷ i om anfodd,
Na chaffo byth cam rhwdd,
Na byth rhywdeb nag iechyd a gymero nhu i.[54]

(I place the curse of God upon any who dare enter my home against my will. He who takes my home from me shall never again take an easy step. Nor will they have prosperity. Nor good health.)

---

52. Isaac, *Coelion Cymru.*

53. My own English translation.

54. Suggett, *A History of Witchcraft and Magic in Wales.*

The traditional cursing style of Wales was not to wish death upon the victims of the curse, but rather to instil upon them a slow, painful demise filled with illness, financial ruin, and the loss of meaningful relationships.

Ill-Intended Written Charms

Though most charms found throughout the history of folk magic in Wales tend to be of a positive nature, invoking protection or healing, charms also had the ability to harm or destroy. The destructive charm was often utilised via the method of written charms placed within charm pouches. These pouches would then be placed in a victim's home, or near where they would often be, such as in a drawer near their workplace. Constructing the charm was fairly simple, as all one need do is find a traditional charm for healing, protection, or a positive desired outcome and then write out the charm backward. The charm being written backward convoluted its positive qualities and inflicted the reversed desire. A charm for healing would become a curse of ill-health, and so forth.

Holy Wells Transformed into Cursing Wells

In the eighteenth century, suddenly wells became notorious not just for offering blessings and good fortune to those who offered coins to them, but also as cursing wells. People would travel from far and wide to give an offering to a cursing well, which in return would curse their enemies. This practise became so notorious and so feared that exceptionally well-known cursing wells, such as *Ffynnon Eilian* on Anglesey, were ultimately completely destroyed. The method of cursing utilised a piece of slate which became known as a "cursing tablet." Upon the cursing tablet, one would place a wax figure meant to represent the victim, as well as their initials. This slate would then be thrown into the well. This was considered an exceptionally effective method of cursing someone; however the well in which you threw the cursing tablet into must be an old sacred well that had been desecrated and transformed into a cursing well. People travelled from across Wales, and even from England, in order to use the cursing well. This is a form of folk magic that was practised widely, and not just by those learned in the magical arts.

To Lift a Curse

Those who suffer the consequences of a malicious curse placed upon them would certainly be hoping to have the curse lifted or broken. The belief surrounding cursing in Wales tended to dictate that only the one who had sent the curse had the power to lift it. The way to lift a curse was rather simple; the victim would seek out the individual who had placed the curse upon them, and would beg for them to lift the curse. The *Rheibiwr* (one who placed the curse) would then, if they felt adequately begged to, mutter a blessing charm or prayer over the victim which would in turn lift the previous curse.

Curse Pots

An insidious tradition found in my native landscape, the Isle of Anglesey, is that of the cursing pot or pipkin.[55] This method of enacting a curse was utilised in order to bring about misfortune upon a particular victim who may have offended the curser. The curse involved writing the name of the victim on a piece of slate, then the curser would take a live frog and stab it with large pins. The frog would then be placed into the pot or pipkin, along with the name of the victim etched into a piece of paper. The slate would be used as a topper or cover to the pot, and subsequently the pot would be hidden in a discreet place. These pots were often hidden in walls or buried in fields. The effects of the curse would be potent and incredibly nasty, and the victim would have no escape from its clutches until they found the pot with their name on. This is a rather cruel and inhumane method of cursing someone. Alternative methods of enacting this curse included throwing the frog into fire, so that the curse could not be broken by the victim.

These curses are presented here as an insight into the various forms of traditional folk magical practises carried out throughout Wales' history. I urge you to truly consider your actions carefully before attempting to carry out any curses yourself. However, they are presented here nonetheless as remnants of Wales' history of magical practises, which of course includes baneful magic.

---

55. From the People's Collection Wales website, *Cursing Pot and Slate Inscription, 19th Century*. This pot can currently be viewed at Storiel in Bangor, North Wales.

Chapter 10
The Virtues of the Natural World

The Earth herself provides the Witch with all the tools we should ever need. It is easy these days, in a world full of consumerism and shiny pretty things, to become distracted and believe that as magical practitioners we need to shell out bags of money in order to attain the most desired of tools. I invite the reader to let go of that idea, and instead to take notice of the most important store you will ever need to visit: the sacred landscape which surrounds you.

In my early days treading my way down the path of magic, I was taught a rather valuable lesson. I remember the day my perspective of the world around me changed vividly. It was when I was a teenager, around sixteen years old. I was sat with a friend and mentor of mine, a Witch who has left a strong influence on the way in which I practise. Back when I was a teenager, my practise was not as strongly developed as it was today and much of my core practises and beliefs stemmed from the few cheap books I could find. I remember we were discussing the fact that the winter solstice was drawing ever nearer, and that I was planning a magical working for the day of the solstice. I explained to her that I was desperately in need of a certain array of herbs, and that unfortunately my parents would not drive me to the supermarket for me to be able to pick up these herbs. She looked at me with shock and bewilderment. She shook her head and said to me:

"Why would you need to go to the supermarket? You are a Witch! And you live in a rural area with an array of magical ingredients at your disposal just in the environment around us. Get your wellies on, go for a walk around the fields and coastal paths, and find what you need. Act like the Witch you say you are."

These words cut deep. As a sensitive teenager, I felt as though I was being attacked. Up until this point, every herb I had used in a spell had come from the supermarket or from my mother's cooking cabinet. At this angsty and sensitive time in my life, I attempted to reject this comment as nothing more than an attack or a rude remark. However, today when I look back at that comment, I realise that it transformed my practise drastically. I may have felt sensitive and upset at the initial remark, and yet I implemented it into my practise. From that week on, I began studying the herbs, plants, and vegetation that grew in my area. I began familiarising myself with the trees, the flowers, and the landscape itself. Every time I went to one of the local beaches along the coastal path, I picked up various stones, pieces of sea glass, and even driftwood; all of these things then played a part in my spell work. It was a message I needed to hear. I was lucky to have the rural landscape at my disposal, and as a Witch I was wasting my time not familiarising myself with it all and making the most of it within my practises.

As my path progressed and I truly embraced the folk practises and magical beliefs of the Celtic landscape, I stumbled upon (and at times invented) methods of interacting with the natural landscape as a devotional to the land itself. A devotional to the continuum of traditions of magic, herbalism, and correspondences that were all Welsh and Celtic in nature.

This next chapter will outline a method of working with the natural world. This acts as a complementary guide to the previous chapter, as everything discussed here will be transferrable into a practical method of working magic. We will discuss herbs, their magical correspondences, and the history of Welsh traditional folk herbal medicine. We will also touch upon the virtues of trees, and their place in the practise of a Welsh Witch. The core aim of this chapter is to provide you with a knowledge of the virtues of the natural world as ascribed to herbs, trees, and plants within the Welsh continuum of magic and folk magical practises. I understand that not all those who pick up this book may be local to Wales, and indeed some of the trees, plants, and herbs we discuss may not even be native to the landscape you currently reside in. Despite all that however, I do believe this information is useful to all those wishing to implement a knowledge of the Welsh traditions of magic into their practises.

————

Almost as pivotal to the imagery associated with the Witch as their large cauldron, book of spells, and broomstick is indeed the Witches' cabinet of strange elixirs, herbs, potion bottles, and magical ingredients. Mugwort, fairy's wand, feverfew, and nettle may sound like a list of ingredients taken directly from a fantasy novel—yet for the modern-day Witch, this is merely a list of useful, magical herbs.

Herbs are so much more than merely tools at the Witche's disposal. Herbs house a spirit of their own, a natural elemental force that can act as an ally to you, if you take the time to learn about them, the lore surrounding them, and their virtues. When utilising herbs in spell work, you are not merely throwing a flower into a pot, but instead invoking the spirit force imbued within that herb to aid, amplify, and transcend your working. Some Welsh Witches may refer to the spirit present within herbs as ellyll. Ellyll, as we already have touched upon in the chapter outlining Welsh fairies, are an elemental grouping of fairy-beings who are the very embodiment of the natural landscape. The important thing to establish here is that herbs are living beings with a spirit and energy of their own. It would be irresponsible for a Witch to harvest and utilise herbs without honouring and respecting the spirit of that herb first and foremost. This is one reason that I personally choose not to use too many store-bought herbs in my practise. The act of going out into the landscape during a significant time, such as when the moon is full, or when the dawn is breaking, and finding and harvesting the herb is not only more focused energy being funnelled into the magical working, but also a method of connecting to the spirit of that herb. However, I am also aware that this is not possible for everyone. Even today as I type out this chapter, the act of venturing out in the dead of night to collect herbs is a rather difficult feat when I currently reside in a more urban area. Sometimes we must admit that the easiest method of collecting and harvesting herbs is indeed to buy them. However, I personally suggest those who can should attempt to grow their own herbs, or harvest them from locations where it is free to do so as much as possible.

Welsh folk throughout history held a strong culture of folk herbal practises. In the art of herbal healing, Wales has long been held in regard as historically being far more advanced than many other nations in knowledge of the virtues of herbs, and the methods of utilising herbs in curing ailments and disease.[56] Herbal healing was such a pivotal aspect of Welsh culture that a tradition of legend and lore began surrounding the physicians of old Wales who were knowledgeable of the various uses and virtues of herbs and plants.

The physicians of Myddfai were a group of physicians highly skilled in herbal medicine practises. The main physician was a man named Rhiwallon who was assisted by his two sons. Rhiwallon was a physician to Rhys Grug, a noble warrior and son of a prince who ruled over a kingdom in the south of Wales.[57] They were aptly named the physicians of Myddfai due to the fact they lived and operated in Myddfai, an area in what is today Carmarthenshire, South Wales. Legend states that their tradition of herbal medicine was passed down to them by a fairy lady from the Otherworld, a lady of the lake who rose from the depths of water to pass on her wisdom.

This legend is known today as *The Legend of Llyn y Fan Fach*. The legend tells the tale of a mortal man who becomes besotted with a lake fairy, and eventually asks her to marry him. The fairy lady agrees to marry the mortal man, and her father bestows upon them fairy cattle as a gift. The only rule of their marriage is that he cannot hit her three times; if he does hit her a third time she will return to her fairy realm via the lake, Llyn y fan fach. Alas, the mortal man does end up hitting the fairy lady lightly on the arm three times: Once whilst they were preparing to go to a wedding, the second time after she began weeping loudly at a Christening, and the third time when she began laughing jovially at a funeral. The three taps on the arm were barely a strike,

56. Hoffman, *Welsh Herbal Medicine*.

57. Hughes, *The Book of Celtic Magic*.

and yet the fairy lady with her Otherworldly perspective saw these as three offenses. Back to the lake she went, and with her she took all the fairy cattle her father had bestowed upon them the day of their union. The mortal man never saw his wife again. However, the mortal man and the fairy lady had children together. The sons of the fairy lady and mortal man often ventured to the lake where their mother would reveal herself to them, and it was during these visits that the lady of the lake bestowed upon them all the knowledge of herbal medicine that she knew. And thus, the physicians of Myddfai came to be the most proficient physicians in all of Wales.[58]

Llyn y Fan Fach is a real lake that you can visit today at the Brecon Beacons National Park, in Carmarthenshire, South Wales. This legend was my favourite tale growing up. I remember excitedly reading it in school, and drawing the lady of the lake as often as I could. As I grew up and began venturing down the path of Witchcraft, this legend became even more relevant. The lady of the lake may indeed be described as an otherworldly fairy lady in most retellings of this enigmatic tale, though she can also be viewed as a goddess of water, liminality, and healing. I often call to the lady of the lake before practising any form of herbal magic.

The Welsh Witches Herbal

Within the next few pages, you will find entries detailing the virtues of herbs within a magical context. These are entries taken specifically from my personal journals and are the culmination of many years of study and practise. Many of the virtues assigned to the herbs that you will see listed below were assigned to them by myself based on a variety of sources. The sources of these virtues may have stemmed from many of my past mentors and teachers, from fragments of information and lore found within the thirteenth-century manuscript of *The Physicians of Myddfai*, or from trial and error. This is a peek into my personal *Llyfr Cyfrin*, mystic book or book of secrets.

I am not an herbalist, nor do I have any medical credentials; therefore for the most part I will only be discussing how these herbs may be utilised within

---

58. This is a brief retelling of this legend. The tale can be found in its entirety in W. Jenkyn Thomas's *The Welsh Fairy Book* as well as many other books on Welsh folklore.

a magical practise and not how they can be used medicinally. I will occasionally mention the medical virtues as assigned to these herbs by the physicians of Myddfai, but this is purely for educational purposes only. Please consult a medical professional before using these herbs for medicinal purposes.

Within this list of herbs, I will provide for you the English name of the herb, the Welsh name of the herb as attributed to them by the physicians of Myddfai underneath, and sometimes its meaning when relevant or useful. If there is more than one Welsh term separated by commas, this indicates that this herb has various names in the Welsh language, and there is often a variation between the names recorded in the physicians of Myddfai, and the modern Welsh word for that herb. This list will then include a guide to the magical virtues of that herb as well as occasionally providing any folk-loric associations of that herb, and sometimes spells or magical workings one could use that herb within.

Agrimony
Y Tryw, Agrimoni
Agrimony is a rather beautiful herb, and is recognisable by its bright yellow flowers and the fact it soars to a height of two feet. Its leaves smell of apricot, and this herb can be found later in the summer months growing in grassy areas, hedgerows, and woodlands. The physicians of Myddfai noted that this herb could be used to cure mastitis. Its length, sturdiness, and beautiful yellow flowers have landed this herb the nickname of "fairy's wand" in some parts of the British Isles.

Within magical workings this plant is useful for divination, dreams, and deep sleep, and is beneficial in workings of counter-magic, to break hexes and curses thrown at you.

Within folklore it was stated that if agrimony were to be placed beneath the pillow of an individual that was asleep, the sleeper would not wake until the agrimony was removed.[59] This is likely why in most folk magical traditions agrimony is a herb imbued with magical virtues associated with sleep and dreams.

---

59. Breverton, *Breverton's Complete Herbal*, 10.

Agrimony Deep Sleep Pouch

If you struggle with sleepless nights, and spend most of your night tossing and turning, take dried agrimony and place it into a small felt pouch. Take this pouch and place it inside your pillowcase. Before sleeping, recite the following incantation three times.

Fairy's Wand beneath my head,
Hear my words as I lay in bed,
Allow me to fall into blissful sleep,
Undisturbed, satisfying, and deep.

Betony
Cribau San Ffraid

Betony, also known as common hedgenettle, is a stunning perennial herb with long stalks and vibrant purple flowers that grow upon it. In Welsh, this herb is referred to as *Cribau San Ffraid*, which means "Saint Ffraid"s Comb." Ffraid is a Welsh Saint and is often referred to as being cognate with the Irish St. Brigid. Of course, this would imply that these herbs may indeed also be connected with Braint, the Welsh goddess of spring and healing.

Betony is considered a holy plant, especially considering its association as being the comb of Ffraid, Braint, or Brigid. Within magical practise, this herb can be used for workings that involve spirit sight, fairy workings, or indeed as a devotional offering to the goddess Braint and her virtues and spiritual functions as a goddess of spring, and of healing. It is a grounding and healing herb.

Burn dried betony on a charcoal disk in a cauldron upon the banks of a river when calling to the goddess Braint, or place a few sprigs of betony on an altar to Braint.

Broom
Banadle, Banadlen

A Witches broom is a tool of cleansing, a tool of spiritual transportation, and a tool steeped in folklore and history. The natural shrub named broom is no different. This plant grows upon heaths and hedgerows and boasts glorious yellow flowers in the late spring. Shape-wise, broom is the perfect natural broomstick.

Within magic the Witch may utilise broom as a literal broomstick, using it to sweep away and banish bad luck and trickster spirits from the working space. It is also a useful herb in workings of attracting love. Hanging the broom in the household or using it to sweep will grant the Witch protection from malevolent entities whilst also attracting love and fostering good relationships.

Burdock
Y Cyngaw

Being a rather whimsical-looking herb, it is not difficult to view this herb as magical. With its spiky-looking, spherical orb-like heads which flower in a vivid purple contrasting against its dark green leaves, this herb is strikingly magical. The physicians of Myddfai noted that burdock was useful as a curative herb against psoriasis. They laid out a method of taking the leaves of the plant, pounding them in a concoction with wine, straining them, and taking three spoonfuls of this mixture each night, morning, and noon. The instructions also state that a decoction of burdock should be the only thing the patient must drink in order to overcome their psoriasis.

Within my magical practise, burdock is used as a protective herb. The root of the burdock when dried can be placed into a pouch along with a written *Swyn*, or charm, and carried in the pocket.

Burdock Protection Pouch

Take the root of the burdock and dry it. Take a piece of red felt and craft with it a pouch big enough to place the burdock root within. Take a piece of paper and write upon the paper this Swyn:

By roots of herbs that cease to grow,
Protect my body and spirit,
I carry this root with me wherever I go,
To invoke its protective spirit.

Roll the paper up and place within the felt pouch with the Burdock root. Sew the pouch closed tightly. Carry this protective charm with you wherever you may wander.

Chickweed
Llysiau'r Dom, Clustiau'r Llygoden
Found throughout the year, the chickweed is a small plant with interesting, star-shaped flowers adorning it. The physicians of Myddfai note its effectiveness as a herb to aid in the reduction of swelling.

Within my magical practise chickweed is a plant that symbolises endurance. It grows year-round regardless of the ever-changing seasons. It is a plant that persists. Because of this, the plant is highly beneficial in magical workings surrounding the strengthening of relationships and bonds.

Dandelion
Dant Y Llew, Blodyn Pi-Pi
Growing up in a rural village surrounded by fields, coastal paths, and lush greenery, dandelions were a common sight. Though the Welsh name for this plant is *dant y llew*, which translates to mean "the lion's tooth," we actually referred to it in my locale as *"blodyn piso gwely"* (bed-wetting flower) or *"blodyn pi-pi"* (wee-wee flower). This was due to the folksy belief that playing with dandelions whilst they were in their yellow flowering stage would cause you to wet the bed. What is interesting however, is that this piece of lore may have scientific basis, as dandelion does indeed hold a strong diuretic quality. Consumption of dandelion can aid the body in flushing out toxins and waste.

Dandelions have always intrigued me. They are among some of my favourite flowers, and yet they are often classed as weeds by many. My Nain (grandmother) once tasked me as a child with ridding her front garden patio of weeds, which required me to pull up an abundance of dandelions. As I grew fond of herbs and plants, I began reading into the benefits of dandelions. Many of my family members taught me that dandelion leaves could actually be eaten as a salad, and that the root makes a lovely coffee or tea.

Of course, another aspect of the dandelion that amazed me in my youth was its transformative quality. This durable, misunderstood plant transformed from being a beautiful yellow flower, to a seedhead that looks like a cotton ball, and when blown on the seeds fly about on the breeze like tiny floral sprites. I spent hours upon hours as a child blowing dandelion seeds into the wind, making wishes, or imagining the seeds were tiny flower fairies.

Within magic dandelion can be dried and burned to use in a spirit summoning incense, and of course when the flower becomes a seedhead this plant can be used as a tool of manifestation. Take the dandelion, hold it up to the sky whilst reciting a spell or manifesting a desire, and blow the seeds into the wind, blowing your desire into the universe.

Pulling on the fact that the dandelion is folklorically known as a plant to cause oneself to wet the bed, and in reality can flush out toxins and waste, it can also be used in magic surrounding removal. The practitioner can utilise dandelions in spells of removal and clearing, such as a spell that aids in removing oneself from the clutches of a toxic relationship.

Elder Flower
Blodau Yr Ysgawen

I have a memory of a teacher in school once telling me during a school trip that using the wood of an elder tree as kindling would invite the devil into your home. Nowadays, as a practising Witch, that warning brings a smile to my face as the elder flower has often been said by many Witches I have had the pleasure of knowing of being a potent herb for spirit summoning. Perhaps in times of old, burning the wood of an elder tree did indeed invite malevolent spirits into the home. In Welsh herbal healing elder flower is used to aid inflammation of the lungs.

In magic, the elder flower is utilised as a plant for summoning familiar spirits, and energising any ritual working.

Eyebright
Golwg Crist, Llygad Crist

The Welsh name for Eyebright is *Golwg Crist* (Christ's Sight) or *Llygad Crist* (Christ's Eyes). The folklore surrounding this plant is apparent in both the English and Welsh; it is a herb that is greatly associated with sight. The physicians of Myddfai noted that eyebright was beneficial as a medicine to strengthen the eyes and sight.

In magical workings eyebright can aid the Witch in peering into the unseen worlds, to see situations clearly, and also to enhance any psychic abilities. Burn dried eyebright in ritual and magical workings when wishing to commune with the hidden realm of fairy, see into the realm of the dead, or enhance your abilities to read the future and see things clearly.

Feverfew
Feddygen Fenyw

Feverfew is a delicate-looking, daisy herb that is a delight to the eyes, evoking the spirit of spring, and of jovial childlike wonder. Medicinally this herb has been used in Wales to aid in healing bruises. However, it is a herb that is often associated with divine femininity. The Welsh name for this herb, *feddygen fenyw*, literally translates to mean "woman's violet."

In magical workings this herb can be used as an incense blend and burnt during devotional workings for a goddess. Bunches of the plant placed upon the altar may also be beneficial when working with divine feminine energies.

Garlic
Garlec, Garlleg

Garlic is a plant that once upon a time I completely despised, as the plant itself reminded me of its taste which as a child I could not stand. As I grew up and progressed as a Witch, it shocks me how frequently garlic is now used in my magical practise. Beyond that I've also gotten over my hatred of its taste, and now implement garlic both for flavour and for its magical qualities into many of my meals.

Garlic is inherently a protective plant. From its associations with warding off malevolent creatures such as vampires and trickster spirits, through to the idea that garlic is a preventative for illness, an idea that many folks from the older generations have instilled onto me all my life. The folksy nature of garlic as a plant of protection means that it is exceptionally useful in magical workings of warding and protecting.

Mistletoe
Uchelwydd

The mistletoe is an exceptionally powerful plant, though exceptionally poisonous too. Within magical workings the mistletoe may be used to promote healing, fertility, or protection. I personally use mistletoe as a decorative charm around the midwinter period; I adorn my altar spaces with it as well as the doorways of my home to protect the inhabitants of the home and usher in good fortune for the year ahead. Take care not to take mistletoe internally.

Mugwort
Y Ganwraidd Lwyd

The one plant I always have well stocked on my shelf is mugwort. I hold mugwort to high regard as being a blessed herb to the Witch. This potent plant works as a protective herb, banishing any malevolent entities and spirits from the working circle or space. It is also a herb that is beneficial for divination, and contact with the realm of fairy and spirits of nature.

When working in nature, mugwort tends to be my herb of choice for burning within my cauldron.

Nettle
Ddynhaden, Danadl Poethion

My childhood home had nothing but miles upon miles of fields and countryside stretching out behind it and in every little corner of every field there grew a huge bush of nettles. We grew accustomed to these pesky plants as children, and quite often I found myself being stung by them. A common practise we utilised was that of taking a leaf of the bitter dock and rubbing it against any patches where nettles had hit us. This soothed the sting and allowed us to continue playing in peace.

Later in life, my mother must have grown exceptionally annoyed at my obsession with nettles. Their abundance around my home meant I was free to pick them whenever I wanted. I would often head out with a pair of gardening gloves and scissors and collect a huge sack worth of nettles to use for various purposes. I used them to make tea and soup, and I dried them to collect in jars for my magical workings.

Nettles are inherently protective; setting out the spirit of the nettles to metaphorically sting anyone who wishes harm has always been an effective magical ward of mine. Beyond that nettles can also be used in magical workings to remove curses and hexes, and their firey, warm nature also instils them with lusty virtues perfect for any workings of a sexual nature.

Nettle Protection Spell

Carefully collect an abundance of nettles and when home wrap them into small bundles. Hang these bundles somewhere warm and dry for a few weeks. Once dry, you can use the dried nettles in an incense blend to burn within the home; however, save a few pieces of the nettle for this next spell. Place the dried nettle leaves into a mortar and crush them with a pestle until the leaves become fine, granulated dust. During the waning moon, take this mixture out to your front door and scatter the dried nettle across the doorstep of your home. Recite the following incantation:

Nettle scatter and guard us well,
Banish the unwanted from where we dwell.

Repeat the same process at every entryway into your home, including windows and fireplaces if possible.

Rosemary
Ysbwynwydd, Rhosmari

Almost every Witch I know today who is fortunate enough to have adequate outdoor space has a pot of rosemary by their garden gate. Rosemary is a protective herb, purging negative influences from its surroundings and fostering a spiritually safe environment. Bundles of dried rosemary often adorn my fireplace whenever I have the chance to pick some sprigs. Rosemary is also beneficial to use in the kitchen; adding it to meals with magical intent promotes bodily protection and blessing.

Sage
Geidwad

Sage is a herb of sagacity, of knowledge, and of wisdom. Its name in Welsh, *geidwad*, literally means "keeper," "guardian," or "preserver." It is this herb we can utilise in our spiritual and magical workings when we wish to further our knowledge, progress intellectually, advance spiritually, and connect to the wisdom of our landscape.

The best method of gathering sage for any magical purpose is to collect it when the moon is full, at the stroke of midnight. In fact, an old Welsh tradition among maidens was to venture out at on *Nos Galan Gaeaf* (Halloween) and gather sage leaves. Upon doing this as a form of ritual, the maiden would then be joined by her future husband at midnight.[60] It has become a custom in my personal practise to gather sage barefoot, wearing loose-fitting clothing, as the full moon is shining upon it. I have found via experience that the sage I utilise after conducting this method of gathering seems much more potent and my workings seem to be exceptionally successful.

Sage may also be used to cleanse or bless a space before conducting a ritual or magical working.

The physicians of Myddfai also record that sage is beneficial for calming the nerves when steeped in boiling water; therefore sage is also calming and is the perfect herb to utilise prior to ritualistic working. Burn sage as an incense, or place sage leaves in a bath prior to invocation or magical working in order to prepare yourself spiritually and physically.

Thyme
Teim, Gryw, Grywlys

Like rosemary, thyme also has a protective quality to it. It can be burned as an incense when dried, or placed in food just as rosemary can. However, thyme also has specific qualities associated with ancestor worship. I burn thyme and sage incense around *Nos Galan Gaeaf*, or Samhain. Thyme aids us in magic that has to do with memory or remembrance, and is a lovely offering in the

---

60. Owen, *Welsh Folk-Lore*, 304.

form of incense to those we remember. Those we remember are never truly dead, and thyme aids us in remembering them.

Beyond its qualities as a herb of remembrance and ancestor veneration, thyme also promotes good fortune, bringing nothing but luck to those who utilise it in their magical practise.

Yarrow
Milddail, Llysiau Gwaedlif

Yarrow was a common plant to find in the fields and lush green areas of the Isle of Anglesey. The white flat-topped flower heads made it instantly recognisable, and it is in abundance from June to November.

In magical working yarrow is highly beneficial in workings requiring any form of divination. In particular, it is highly useful to use during one of the spirit nights—May Day, the Summer Solstice, or *Nos Galan Gaeaf*/Halloween. It is a beneficial herb to utilise when working with the spirits of place, the fairies, or indeed the spirits of the dead.

Connecting with the Spirits of Nature

Though it is far easier today to purchase our herbs from store, and I am certainly not shaming practitioners who do, I must emphasise that I do recommend we attempt to connect to herbs and plants on a deeper level. As I have already mentioned, herbs and plants hold a spirit of their own; they are not tools at our disposal, but useful spiritual allies. If at all possible, I highly recommend growing your own herbs or harvesting herbs from their natural habitat, remembering when doing so to meditate with the plants, ask for their permission to pick them, and thank them for their contribution to your craft. A wise Witch once told me that the elements we collect ourselves and put in the effort to connect to before using them in our practise will always hold a potency that store-bought items never will. I have carried that piece of advice with me throughout my practise.

Blodeuedd, the Floral Maiden

A spiritual ally to turn to when working with the spirit force of plants and flowers is that of Blodeuedd. Blodeuedd is introduced to us within Lleu

Llaw Gyffes' tales; she is not a mere mortal woman, but a woman born of pure magic, transformed by the magicians Gwydion and Math from flowers. Gwydion embarked upon transforming flowers into Blodeuedd so that she may become a wife to Lleu Llaw Gyffes after Lleu's mother, Aranrhod, placed a curse upon Lleu so that he would never have a wife of this mortal world. Later in the tale Blodeuedd is transformed into an owl, and thus her name is changed from Blodeuedd, to Blodeuwedd. Blodeuedd means "flowers," whereas Blodeuwedd means "flower face." Blodeuedd holds the virtues of oak, broom, and meadowsweet, the plants which Gwydion and Math transformed her from, and for the Welsh Witch can be called upon to help with all herbal workings.

✸ EXERCISE ✸
Dedicating Herbal Workings to Blodeuedd

This next exercise acts as a devotional act in honour of Blodeuedd, the floral maiden of Welsh lore. This simple rite can be performed before any herbal workings, whether magical or mundane. Regardless of whether you are preparing to create an oil, a tea, or an incense blend, or perhaps preparing herbs for spell work, or even tending to your herbal garden, conducting this rite dedicates the working to the floral spirit of Blodeuedd.

Begin by making yourself comfortable. Close your eyes and breathe deeply. Become aware of your breath and start incorporating square breathing.

Inhale to the count of four, hold the breath for a count of four, and then exhale to the count of four. Repeat this until you feel calm and at ease, or at least four times.

In your mind's eye, visualise oak, broom, and meadowsweet being gathered by two men. They gather these plants together and place them on the floor in the vague shape of a human body. They stand beside this pile of plants and nod to one another. From the sleeves of their robes they pull out their wands. Take a moment to take in this visual, two mystical looking men looking down at a pile of oak, broom, and meadowsweet with wands in their hands. Take in every detail. Suddenly they begin waving their wands, and incanting a spell of mighty power.

The plants on the floor begin shaking, vibrating, glowing, and transforming. Before your very eyes, what was once a pile of leaves, twigs, flowers, and stalks is now a woman. How does she look to you? Pick out every little detail. Is she pretty? Does she have flowers in her hair? Spend some time getting to know this entity.

Once you feel you have spent enough time with this flower maiden, take a deep breath once more and shift your focus back onto your plans. Open your eyes.

Make your way over to the project you had planned. Look over at your tools, your herbs, and mentally map out what it is you are planning to do. If you are planning on working in the garden, take yourself to a place where you can gently touch the plants surrounding you. If you are working with herbs for a magical purpose, or preparing to make some form of herbal tea, oil, or other concoction, get close to your ingredients. Think about the virtues of the plants, or what they mean to you. When you are ready, recite the following in either Welsh, English, or both:

> *Merch y blodau, Blodeuedd têg,*
> *Cymhortha fi heddiw yn fy ngwaith.*
> *Dal fy llaw ac fy arwain,*
> *Yn fy swyngyfaredd a fy nhaith.*
> *O Blodeuedd, cyfarchaf i ti,*
> *Bydda yma nawr.*
> *Cymhortha fi i ddeall y byd naturiol,*
> *Ac i weld hud ym mhob toriad y wawr.*
> *Floral maiden, Blodeuedd fair,*
> *Aid me in my task.*
> *Guide me as I work my will,*
> *This I humbly ask.*
> *Oh Blodeuedd, I call to you,*
> *Your knowledge and power I have drawn,*
> *Aid me in understanding the virtues of the natural world,*
> *And see the magic in each dawn.*

After reciting this incantation, you may feel pulled to burn a fragrant floral incense in honour of Blodeuedd. My incense of choice to Blodeuedd is usually rose, meadowsweet, or lavender. Once you have offered your devotions to Blodeuedd, go about your herbal workings knowing that the Welsh floral maiden guides you and aids you in understanding the virtues of the natural world.

The Virtues of Trees and Wood

We have already touched briefly on some aspects of tree lore throughout this book; for example, the fact that oak trees are sacred to the fairies of Wales and that rowan berries as well as prickly furze can repel malevolent spirits. In this section however, we will delve into the virtues assigned to certain woods and trees. This guide will enable you to construct your own magical tools utilising these woods and their virtues, tools such as wands, staves, stangs, or even the handles of broomsticks. The leaves, berries, bark, and flowers present on some of these trees may also prove useful for magical workings and rites. Once again, the virtues I assign to these trees stem from a multitude of sources, with folklore and local lore that I learnt via my mentors being the main sources. Much of the virtues assigned to these trees stem from what was written of them in the *Kat Godeu* or "The Battle of the Trees" in *The Book of Taliesin*.[61] The *Kat Godeu* is an intriguing and deeply enigmatic poem that describes a fierce battle where the magician Gwydion summons trees to be the main soldiers in the fight. Each tree in the poem is assigned its own virtue or role in the battle, from alder being the leading tree, to hawthorn dispensing pestilence, and oak causing the Earth to tremor at its every move. Through study of Welsh tree folklore, the *Kat Godeu*, and the traditional uses of various woods in streams of modern traditional Witchcraft, I have compiled this list of virtues, and here I present it from my own magical journals. Once again, the English name for the tree will be given, with the Welsh name below.

---

61. Williams & Lewis, *The Book of Taliesin*, 18.

Alder
Gwern

The alder tree acts as a potent teacher; it imbues us with great knowledge and wisdom as magical practitioners. When we commune with alder, we gain insight into deeper streams of wisdom and can further our own studies into any chosen subject. Specifically, the alder can aid us as we are initiated into the mysteries of magic. A newcomer onto the path of magic and Witchcraft would benefit from constructing a walking staff from alder to hold during meditation. The alder is also associated with Bran the Blessed, and was said to provide Bran with divine wisdom and oracular vision.[62]

Willow
Helyg

The willow is a tree I feel specifically close to spiritually. Willow is deeply associated with the natural element of water, being a tree that grows predominately in moist soils and near rivers, ponds, or lakes. This watery quality makes the willow a tree imbued with the virtues of intuition, emotion, and even deception. A potent tool in glamour magic, or transformative magic, the willow is also a beneficial ally in divination and can aid in healing emotional turmoils.

Rowan
Pren Gochel

As already touched upon in the chapter dedicated to fairies, the rowan tree as well as the berries that grow upon it are protective in quality from malevolent, trickster spirits. It is a powerful tree to utilise in any protective magical working and can aid in lifting baneful magic cast upon you.

Birch
Bedw

The birch is a tree imbued with vitality and can aid the magical practitioner in rites concerning growth, fertility, birth, or transmuting energies. Tools made of birch are useful in workings of manifestation and creation.

---

62. Gary, *Traditional Witchcraft*.

Ash
Onn

With the ash as an ally the magical practitioner can pull on its ability to radiate peace and calm. Ash is beneficial in aiding mindfulness, and a lovely tree to call to during meditative sessions. Beyond its peaceful qualities, the ash is also a tree of liminality and is useful in spirit workings.

Elm
Llwyf

The elm tree can be utilised within workings of love. However, the elm's primary virtue is that of delusion, and so the question must be asked: do we use elm in love spells, or in spells of delusion and deception? As a tool of delusion, the elm can be used in rites involving trickery.

Hazel
Pren Cnau

The perfect tree for those who consider themselves psychic. This tree can further psychic abilities, bring forth visions and aid in divinatory workings. The hazel is also a tree of creativity, and of knowledge.

Beech
Ffawydd

The wood of the beech can be utilised in workings concerning justice. When the scales of justice seem to be tipped against you, draw upon the power of beech to tip the scales in the opposite direction. A tree of security, it is beneficial to have beech wood in the home to radiate emotional and even financial security.

Hawthorn
Gwrych

Though the hawthorn tree is powerful, imbued with the ability of aiding one in communing with familiar spirits, and beneficial in rites of cursing, banishing or destruction, I was warned in my youth to never use the hawthorn tree to make a wand or staff. I was taught that this tree, if cut and brought into the home, would bring nothing but bad luck to whoever cut it. Instead, find a hawthorn tree and work your rites and magic near it. Gain a connection with the spirit of the tree, and it will be a useful ally to you.

Oak
Derw

The oak is an ally of empowerment. One of the first trees I learnt about when beginning my magical studies, the oak tree is found in much of Wales' folklore and mythology. It is said to have been sacred to the ancient Druids, and to the fairies of Wales. Oak gives to the magical practitioner strength, and the endurance to continue their studies and their spiritual journey. With the aid of the oak, one can connect to the magic of the landscape and the continuum of lore embedded in the culture.

✸ EXERCISE ✸
Developing a Relationship with Trees

This is a very simple exercise, yet very much effective and useful for any magical practitioner if carried out with discipline and drive.

Now that you have been given a brief introduction into the virtues of trees, it is time to garner a deep, personal connection with the spirits of the trees around you. Find the trees mentioned here in this book that grow around your home, or nearby. Learn to identify them, sit with them, and meditate with them. Keep a journal and note your experience as you develop a deeper connection with the tree spirits. Continue studying not only the magical virtues of trees, but also their physical properties.

When I visit my local woodland, I walk up to the trees, touch them, sit with them, and sometimes even sing to them. When communing with them on a spiritual level, I begin my communion by reciting the following incantation:

Tree branches stretch to the heavens,
And commune with the realm of sky.
Tree roots stretch beneath my feet,
And commune with the realm of Earth.
Tree thrives on water and light,

And communes with the realms of Water and of Fire.
Tree speaks to nature,
Witch speaks to Tree,
As I speak to you,
My wish is for you to speak to me.

You may utilise this incantation in your practise or use it to construct your own personal petitionary call to the trees. Understand the deeply beneficial practise of becoming one with the glorious trees that surround us. They are our teachers, our guides, and our allies in the natural world.

Chapter 11
The Ever-Turning Cycle

The Welsh Witch whose practise is informed by the folklore and folk practises of the land will always find it beneficial to work with the ebb and flow of the natural world. Within modern Witchcraft the celebration of the Wheel of the Year has become a staple of foundational learning. Newcomers to Witchcraft and modern Paganism quickly note down the eight seasonal festivals generally accepted within the Pagan community and are excited to begin honouring these times of revelry. What many new practitioners fail to do however is ask "Why?" I was guilty of not asking "Why?" early on in my practise; I honoured the eight festivals of the Wheel of the Year without delving too deeply into where these festivals originate, or how they relate to my day-to-day life. This led me to have a severe disconnect with the festivals; I often forgot certain celebrations and would later feel guilty for not observing them. It was only via delving deeper into the lore and custom of my locale and evaluating what role the seasonal festivals play, not only in my modern-day life but in my community and cultural history, that my relationship with the seasons and celebrations began to thrive.

There are eight predominant festivals that most modern Pagans and Witches today celebrate and acknowledge. They are solstices, the cross-quarter days, and the equinoxes. The authenticity behind the antiquity of all eight of these celebrations has long been in dispute. Many people believe that all eight spokes on the wheel of the year have pre-Christian, ancient Pagan origins, whereas some say that a handful of the festivals are either derivatives of Christian folk customs or more modern inventions. It is highly unlikely that every single one of these celebrations does indeed mirror pre-Christian festivals. My observance of the year as a Welsh Witch and Celtic Pagan looks very different to the traditionally observed NeoPagan wheel of the year. My calendar of revelry includes special days that are specifically tied to Wales and Welsh folk history.

In this chapter we will explore the seasonal tides and the various customs, traditions, and holy days of Wales. This will not be a guide to the Wheel of the Year, but instead a look at the traditional customs and traditions that aid us in observing the ebb and flow of the seasons. Providing you with a foundational understanding of not only how the eight common Pagan festivals may or may not relate to a Welsh Witches' practise, but also to smaller celebrations and holy days that are often overlooked yet are deeply important to a more traditional folk practise.

The Welsh landscape is dotted with hills, valleys, mountains, and coastline, and as such the physical environment played, and continues to play, an important role in how the inhabitants of Wales observe and work during the four seasons. Agriculture has always been a grounding element of Welsh culture, and many continue to see Wales as a nation of farming. It is of no wonder then that Wales' calendar is very much influenced by the people's ability to work the land. In many rural areas of Wales agriculture is still a main source of income, including in the area in which I was raised. Many old traditions and customs persist in Wales today that are centuries old and harken back to a time when the weather and working the land divided up most people's days. Unless you live on a farm or somehow work outdoors, the idea of dividing up your calendar based on the ebb and flow of the agricultural year may seem strange; however for a Witch who works with the spirits of the landscape and the natural world it is important for us to closely observe the changes in the season. Understanding the subtle energies of the seasons will allow a deeper connection with the land, the spirits of that land, and the potent energetic forces one can tap into during magical workings.

The Welsh year is divided into various holy days, seasonal festivals, and observances that mirror what is occurring in the natural landscape. However, beyond the observation of the agricultural and seasonal changes throughout the year, the Welsh calendar of revelry also includes three spirit nights. The spirit nights are liminal nights where any boundaries that may exist between the realms of mortals and spirits are blurred. Within this chapter we will explore these spirit nights, sacred holy days, seasonal festivals and outline practical methods to allow you to observe and celebrate your year in a spirit that is traditionally Welsh.

It may be somewhat jarring or uncomfortable for some Pagans and Witches to see saint days and holy days that are specifically tied to the Christian church in this section. I have decided to include them as they are relevant to Wales as a nation, and there is an abundance of folklore and customs surrounding these sacred days. Furthermore, some saints are indeed rumoured among Pagans today in Wales to have pre-Christian origins, and therefore can be looked at as entities or even deities to call upon as opposed to saints, if you do have an issue with working with saints in your practise.

This chapter is separated into the four seasons—spring, summer, autumn, and winter. Let us explore the seasons, the celebrations and the customs that relate to the Welsh Witch.

Spring

The Welsh Springtime

Springtime in Wales was, and still is, considered a time of rejuvenation and fresh beginnings. In the folk calendar the Welsh springtime began in March. An exceptionally popular holy day in modern day Wales that is celebrated throughout the country today is *Dydd Gwyl Dewi*, or St. David's Day. Today St. David's Day is celebrated on the first of March. We celebrate by wearing pinned daffodils on our clothes, baking Welsh cakes or *bara brith* (a traditional Welsh fruit loaf), and celebrating all it means to be Welsh. We are taught about St. David, or as he is called in Welsh *Dewi Sant*, from a very young age at school. There are numerous tales and folkloric stories surrounding Dewi Sant; however the most popular tale tells of a miracle he performed. According to this tale, Dewi Sant was preaching to a large crowd in what is today Llanddewi Brefi, Ceredigion. Due to the large crowd forming, many people could not see or hear Dewi, and so he miraculously made the ground below him rise to form a small hill. The crowds watched as the Earth rose beneath his feet, and he continued preaching with a white dove sat on his shoulder. The village of Llanddewi Brefi is said to rest upon the hill which this miracle took place.

Though St. David's Day is celebrated today on the first of March in Wales, the day believed to mark the time of his death, St. David's Day historically was celebrated on the twelfth of March.[63]

Prior to the invention of electricity, the coming of spring would have been marked as a time of celebration that the days grew longer and more could be achieved in the day. Between the nineteenth and the twenty-first of March, we celebrate the vernal or spring equinox, and it is ever so fitting that the dates the equinox falls upon seems to be rather close to the times at which the beginning of spring was celebrated in Wales historically. The spring equinox is often referred to by Pagans as Ostara. Among the Celtic Druids, this time of year is known as *Alban Eilir*, the highest point of spring. A celebration of the turning of the cycle, when we are jetting full steam ahead into the lighter half of the year. This is the period in the cycle when we honour the fertile nature of the spring, the growth and birth happening all around us. It is a time to slow down, look around us, and take heed of all the bounties our sacred land is receiving before our very eyes. The spring equinox can very much be a time of meditative reflection and solemn pondering. However, it can also be a time to release childlike joy into the world. Take inspiration from the bouncing, bleating lambs of the fields, the ducklings waddling away in the ponds, and bunnies hopping along the colourful, flower-filled meadows. It is the perfect time of year to unleash that childish wonder; embrace our youthful, sprightful aspects, and indulge in some harmless fun and frolics. From a practical point of view this time of year is a fruitful time to "plant seeds" so to speak—this could literally mean planting seeds, tending to the garden, or planting the seeds of manifestation. Pull on the power of blooming flowers to aid in blooming your desires. Burn fragrant and floral incense

---

63. Owen, *The Customs and Traditions of Wales.*

in your home to promote the cleansing essence of the spring to rejuvenate the space in which you are constantly residing. This is a period to fully embrace and absorb the warmth of spring deep into your bones. Awaken your passions. Rekindle the flames of Awen, of divine inspiration.

✪ EXERCISE ✪
Spring Cleansing Ritual

Within my practise, the period around the beginning of March is a time of clearing and cleansing so that I may welcome the budding spring with a fresh and open mind. The first step in achieving this fresh mindset is to conduct a ritualistic spring clean.

Begin by cleaning out your working space. Spend time cleaning out the space in your home in which most of your magical workings and spiritual practises are undertaken. This may be your altar, or perhaps your hearth. Clean the space thoroughly, all the while envisioning that you are releasing any tempestuous emotional energy that has permeated in this space in the past season. When I conduct this ritual cleansing I begin by literally pulling every item off of my fireplace and altar and setting them aside to dust and clean one by one. When the space in which my working tools and books reside is cleared, I dust it and then I take a bucket of boiling water and throw in a few sprigs of rosemary into the water and allow it to sit for a few moments. Once the water is cooled, I then use a sponge and scrub my working space with this new elixir of boiled water and rosemary. All the while I chant:

Ffarwel i'r hen egnioedd, ffarwel i'r gaeaf oer,
Croesawaf egni'r gwanwyn, a nosweithiau cynnes dan y lloer

A close English translation would be:

Farewell to stagnant energies, farewell to winter's embrace,
I welcome the energies of springtide, here into this space

I then allow the space to dry and move on to cleaning each of my individual items. Afterward I spend some time thoughtfully rearranging my items back into the space. Once this is complete, I sprinkle Anglesey sea salt onto the floors near my working space and allow it to sit. Salt is used throughout various spiritual traditions for spiritual and energetic cleansing. Once I feel the salt has sat long enough, whether that means a few minutes or even a full twenty-four hours, I then sweep at it with a broom before usually vacuuming it up, though if possible, you could also sweep it toward and out your front door.

Next, swing open your windows and allow the fresh air to permeate your living space. Breathe the new spring air deeply and set your intentions for the coming of this new season. I usually end this ritual spring clean by taking a long, relaxing bath or shower to cleanse not only my space, but my body too.

Calan Mai: May Day

Calan Mai, the first day of May, is most commonly known as the Gaelic Beltane among modern Pagans and Witches. In Celtic Wales, it is *Calan Mai*, *Calan* being the Welsh word for calends, or the first day, *Mai* being the Welsh word for the month of May. We know this special occasion to be a time of fire, of protective magical workings, and growth. In Wales, the May Day was the first of the year's *Ysbrydnos*—or spirit nights. The two spirit nights of the year were *Calan Mai*, the summer solstice, and of course *Calan Gaeaf*, or Samhain. An Ysbrydnos is a night when spirits, fairies, goblins, and all manners of spectral entities freely move around our mortal realm. These are the times of the year we can connect to the spirit realms with ease, and when protective magic is a must. *Calan Mai*, as well as the summer solstice, are more commonly associated with fairy sightings, visitations, and abductions rather than the spirits of the dead specifically.[64] It is an opportune time of year to place wards, protective charms, and Witch bottles around the home to protect from baneful, mischievous spirits. It is also a great time to honour the spirits of place, especially the spirits of the hearth and home.

Romantic Divination

The custom of *Rhamanta* was carried out throughout Wales at one point in history. The methods by which it was carried out varied from region to region; however the core concept remained the same. *Rhamanta* is a method of romantic divination, via which maidens may conjure an image of their

---

64. Sikes, *British Goblins*.

future spouse. Here are two unique methods of *Rhamanta*; there are so many varied methods that it would be impossible to list all here.

The first method requires the maiden to wait until all members of the household are fast asleep. Once certain she is the only one awake she must go to the hearth. Upon the fire she must place a good heap of coal, and set a fire. Then she must set up a table with a small feast. The traditional feast includes toasted bread with cheese, and whatever else she may have to spare in the kitchen. Once the feast is prepared, the maiden must then stand before the fire and ritualistically unburden herself of her clothing one piece at a time. The final piece of clothing she takes off must then be washed in a bowl of clean spring water. This wet garment is then placed on the back of a chair to dry near the fire. Once this is all done, the maiden must then take herself to bed. As she lies in her bed, she must listen for any sounds coming from the kitchen. It is said, that if this ritual is done correctly, an apparition of her future lover will appear before the feast. If the maiden does hear the apparition of her future spouse, she is allowed to peep a look through a keyhole or a crack in the door. Lore maintains that some individuals who carry out this divination see the spectral apparition of a fearsome creature, and this is a sign they will be unhappy and unloved in their life. This ritual must be carried out upon one of the three *Ysbrydnos*, or, "spirit night" of the year. That is—Halloween, May Day, or the summer solstice.

An alternate method of *Rhamanta* stemming from Glamorganshire asks that a young couple place a shovel against the fire. Upon this shovel they will each place a grain of wheat beside one another. As the wheat grains heat, they will eventually pop off of the shovel. If the pieces of wheat fly in the same direction, together, it is a good sign for the relationship ahead. However, if the pieces of wheat fly off in separate directions, it is an omen that the relationship is doomed to suffer.

Summer

The Summer Solstice

Months have passed since we celebrated the longest night of the year, the cycle has turned, and now we reach the longest day. The Celtic Druids call it *Alban Hefin*, the highest point of summer. In the Welsh language the summer solstice is referred to as *Heuldro'r Haf.* Occurring on the twentieth or twenty-first of June, it is the midsummer festival, a time to celebrate the immense power of our life-giving sun. The fires of passion, of creativity, and of love burn brightly upon this night. It is a potent time for channelling creative projects and working creative magic too. The summer solstice is a time of dancing, of abundance, of feasting, and of powerful, energetic magical workings. It is the peak of the summer, and from here onward the days will grow shorter and colder. When pondering on the summer solstice my mind evokes images of wild, constant dancing to the sounds of drumming and revelry all around. Bonfires are lit in celebration, and magical practitioners gathering in convocation to celebrate the source of all life, magic, and mystery.

In modern day Britain, solstice celebrations can be found across the British Isles. From the gatherings of revelry at the infamous Stonehenge, to calmer, more subdued celebrations atop hills and mountains in Wales near lone-standing stones and stone circles. I have spent many a solstice at local burial chambers, atop cliffs overlooking the sea, and even sleeping under the stars in the depths of the forest. It truly is a time when one feels they should let their hair down, run wild and free in untamed, overgrown nature, and bask in the warm glow of the potent summer sunshine. The power of the summer solstice reminds us to take full advantage of the long summer days, to spend as much time close to nature as humanly possible.

In Wales, bonfires have been recorded at this time of year for centuries, with fragrant wildflowers and herbs being thrown into the fires in celebration. The solstice also marks the second *Ysbrydnos,* or spirit night, of the year. Again tonight, the spirits of the fairies can be seen freely dancing upon the hills and meadows. Be careful not to fall for their beguiling tricks! You would not want to find yourself a victim to their sport.

Perhaps one of the most interesting Welsh traditions at this time of year is that of finding a *glain neidr,* or snake-stone (also referred to as adder stones). Folklore dictates that snakes, specifically the venomous adders that are abundant in many parts of Wales, gather on warm stones near the solstice and hiss at one another. Their hissing creates mystical bubbles, which harden into a powerful stone.[65] To find one of these stones upon the day of the summer solstice was a sign of good fortune upon the finder for the year ahead. These peculiar items, the adder stones, were used in various folk magical practises throughout Wales. However, what exactly constitutes as an adder stone or snake-stone seems to be up for debate. In some descriptions, the stones are said to be glassy, bead-ßlike orbs. In other accounts, they are simply glassy hag stones, or a stone with a hole through the middle. As well as bringing about good fortune, these special stones could protect from baneful magic and allow one to see and be protected from invisible entities.

✪ EXERCISE ✪
A Solstice Ritual

What better time of year to celebrate the potent powers of the sun, the blessings of the source of all life, and the magical nature of our world than at the summer solstice. Here is a ritual that can be adapted to be performed by either solitary practitioners or groups. It is a ritual in celebration of the sun, as well as a ritual to aid us in taking heed of all we hold dear, our accomplishments and our creative endeavours over the last cycle.

This ritual is best performed at sunrise on the day of the solstice, but can be adapted to be performed when best suited. Begin the ritual by empowering the working ground and constructing a working circle, as provided in the practical Witchery chapter of this book.

Once you have called upon the powers of land, sea, and sky and empowered your own inner Witch light, the next step is to honour the strength and power of the solstice sun. Face the direction in which the sun is rising from, and extend your arms out as if inviting the sun to embrace you in a warm hug. Close your eyes and take a deep breath, tilting your head skyward. With eyes still closed, recite these words;

I honour the fire of the sun,
The power of this, the longest day.
May your warm, life-giving essence penetrate my mortal skin,
May your energetic undercurrent inspire me to seize the day.

---

65. Owen, *Welsh Folk-Lore.*

Powers of the sun, warmth of the day,
I honour you today, via the Witches' way.

Now move to the centre of the circle; if working in a group, join hands. Take a moment to reflect on all you have accomplished between now and the last solstice. All your accomplishments, the things that make you proud. Consider the things that make you feel alive. Reflect on how, without the sun, none of these accomplishments would be possible. The sun is our constant life force, which offers us the nourishment and warmth to live. Our sun aids our Earthly mother to sustain us. Ponder on these facts for a moment before raising your hands skyward once more and chanting:

Mighty sun, our giver of life,
We thank you today on this solstice bright,
Your power, your warmth, your loving embrace,
We honour your fire, and enlightening light.

You may wish to repeat this chant a few times. Spend a few moments in deep reflection, honouring the long days that have been and are still to come. From here on out the days will grow shorter. What would you wish to accomplish before the darkness approaches? If you are working in a group, take this moment to face away from one another, allowing each of you to have a moment of quiet contemplation. Just you and the solstice sun.

Alter and change this ritual as you desire. Perhaps you may wish to give an offering to the gods associated with the sun. Some Welsh deities that have solar correspondances may be Beli Mawr, the great father god of the realm of the sky, or Lleu Llaw Gyffes, whose first name *Lleu* etymologically derives from the Welsh word for light or rays of light. Even Rhiannon, the goddess of sovereignty and horses, has some solar correspondences, as in the Mabinogi during her first appearance she is said to move in tandem with the horizon, almost like the setting sun. Perhaps you would like to incorporate any spells or workings of manifestation into the ritual. When ready, close the working space and end the ritual as you see fit.

Autumn

Gwyl Awst

Known most notably within the modern Pagan community as Lammas or Lughnasadh today, *Gwyl Awst* is the celebration of the first harvest. It is celebrated on the first day of August, marking a mid-point between the summer solstice and the upcoming autumn equinox. This day is both a celebration of all we have achieved throughout the lighter half of the year as well as a sign of the coming darker months ahead. After this celebration, we will begin to notice a shift in the seasons as we enter a liminal phase once more. The end of summer draws near, and the crisp mornings of autumn await us.

I must admit that Gwyl Awst plays a rather small role in my personal celebratory year. I know it as the feast of August; it is a time of reflection and of gathering. I, and those dearest to me, gather at Gwyl Awst for a feast and a catch-up. We discuss all we have achieved; we bake bread for the feast, and we ponder over what awaits us in the months ahead. Within my working circles and groups, we perform rituals of thanks to the land for providing the bounties of summer. This time of year is considered a sacred time for the Gaelic deity Lugh, which some have associated with the Welsh Lleu Llaw Gyffes.[66] Overall, the celebrations of August are the last, sparing celebrations of summer and of the height of the sun. It is a time in which we must prepare for what is to come, whilst also taking heed of all we have achieved thus far.

The Autumn Equinox

The autumn equinox much like the spring equinox is a time of balance, and a time of liminality. It is upon this liminal time when we begin to feel the embrace of autumn blowing away the remnants of the warm summer days. Originally, this would have been the second harvest, a literal harvest where the crops grown would be harvested in preparation for the winter. The harvest was an important time of celebration, but also of hard work for the people of rural Wales. In a metaphorical, modern sense, this is a time to harvest all we have learnt and achieved. All the knowledge we have gathered over the last cycle. It is yet again a time to reflect on all we have gained and

---

66. Franklin & Mason, *Lammas: Celebrating the Fruits of the First Harvest.*

lost, to take stock of our bountiful blessings and banish all that which weighs us down.

Most modern Pagans and Witches know this day to be Mabon on the Wheel of the Year. Of course, if you are familiar with Welsh legend and lore, you will know that Mabon is a divine entity from Welsh myth. He is the divine son, the child of Modron, the great mother goddess. Contrary to what many will teach you, the word Mabon is not pronounced May-bon. In my native Welsh language, the word is pronounced "Mah" as in the "Ma" in "March" followed by "bonn" pronounced the same way as the word "gone" but with a "b" at the beginning. I will admit that as a native Welsh speaker, and a Welsh Pagan I am not very fond nor comfortable with this time of year being referred to as Mabon. The deity known as Mabon has absolutely no connotations with this time of year, and indeed the name Mabon being associated with the autumn equinox is a wholly modern concept. There is no evidence to suggest this holiday was ever named Mabon until the late twentieth century, around the mid-1970s to be exact. Of course, antiquity does not equal authenticity and if it simply feels right for you to call this time of year Mabon then by all means continue doing so. However, I felt it imperative to point out that no one in modern Wales outside of the Neopagan community refers to this day as Mabon. It is simply the equinox, or among Celtic Pagans, specifically Druids, it is *Alban Elfed*, the highest point of autumn.

On the day of the equinox may we accept that from this day onward the sun's power will wane, the days will grow shorter and colder. May we harvest all we have grown, and feel at one with the potent ever-changing power of the great cycle.

✹ EXERCISE ✹
A Meditative Equinox Walk

We Witches can often become highly distracted by the notion of powerful magical workings, elaborate spells and rituals. There are times however, when we must take heed, and attune ourselves to the world and the land around us. This exercise can be done whenever needed, and is meant to enhance a sense of oneness with the natural world. The exercise harnesses our observation skills, and aids in heightening our senses to the subtle changes of the turning cycle. For the purpose of this section of the book however, the exercise will be constructed to be utilised as an autumn equinox ritual. Feel free to alter the words, and change them to suit whatever time of year you may choose to partake in this task.

Plan to go for a walk to a local outdoor area that is dear to your heart. It may be a local park, forest, beach or, if a walk isn't something you can easily plan to do, even just planning to take yourself out to your garden will suffice. The aim is to be able to see the outside world and natural plants around you.

Once you are in nature, spend a few moments familiarising yourself with the environment. What colour is the sky today? How does the wind feel against your skin? What is the weather like? What texture is the ground beneath your feet? Are there any sounds or smells that are drawing your attention? Take mental note of every little thing that stands out to you. From the sounds of birds nearby, to the rustling of the trees in the wind. Continue exploring the area, being fully aware of your surroundings. Consider the fact that it is the equinox, and we are in a liminal period where the cycle is turning and the world around us is changing. What aspects of the coming autumn do you see? Have the leaves changed their colour? Does the air feel crisper? Is there a lack of insects or animals around? Try to notice any signs that autumn is near.

Find a place to comfortably relax for a while. This might be a bench, a comfortable patch of ground, or just somewhere that makes you feel at ease. If possible, attempt to ensure it is a place you will not be interrupted by other people. Once you securely feel relaxed, close your eyes and begin the exact same exercise again without utilising your sight. Listen to the sounds around you, smell the local scents, feel the sensations shifting through your body. Simply be. Be at one with the land around you. Take deep, healing breaths throughout this process. Do not worry much about what exactly your body should be doing. Allow yourself to fall into a natural, intuitive rhythm.

Take as long as you need to truly connect with the land, the space around you. When you feel good and ready, continue on your walk and head home, keeping this sense of awareness to the intricacies of life around you. Once you are home, spend a few moments reflecting on the experiences you had. Write any poignant moments or reflections into a journal to come back to later.

Winter

Calan Gaeaf

You are wandering down a misty street; it is still early in the evening yet so very dark. There is an eeriness in the air, and you swear that in the moans and groans of the autumn winds you can hear the faint sounds of screams. In front of you is a small cottage, and near its garden gate you see a small flickering light. You decide to make your way over to the light, to investigate what it is. You cannot help but feel as though someone, or something, is watching you from the shadows. As you approach the cottage, you realise that the flickering light is that of a candle, but the candle has been placed within what looks like a hollowed-out swede or turnip, with a ghoulish face carved into the front. From the ghoulish face, the candlelight flickers with the winds. You open the garden gate and approach the cottage doors, and something sways you to knock at the door. The door creaks open, and from behind it pops out a tall, demonic-looking creature. You scream and run away in fear, as the howling winds surround you and the barren trees lining the streets shiver and shake. It is here, the eve of winter. *Calan Gaeaf* is upon us.

Halloween. What a fantastical holiday it is. Probably the most famous of all the festivals spoken of so far to those outside of Witching circles. In modern Wales Halloween is referred to by Welsh speakers as Calan Gaeaf, a historical term meaning the first day of winter. Of course, the true Calan Gaeaf more likely falls upon the first of November, rather than the thirty-first of October, with the thirty-first being *Nos Galan Gaeaf*, or winter's eve. Modern practitioners of Witchcraft as well as modern Pagans would probably know this spectacular and magical time of year as the Gaelic Samhain. I have seen it mentioned in some books as well as in abundance on the internet that Wales' version of Samhain is spelt the same way as the Irish Samhain but pronounced "Sow-een." This is entirely false. Samhain is a Gaelic word, and Welsh is not a Gaelic language. The word Samhain does not exist in the Welsh language; it never has and never will. However, that does not mean that Wales does not have its own brand of Celtic, spiritual frivolity at this time of year.

Calan Gaeaf is the second and most potent ysbrydnos of the Welsh Celtic year. It is at this time of year the veils, which separate the realms of the spirit, the fae, and mortals are lifted and blurred. The spirits of our ancestors, spirits of the dead, and all manners of ghoulishly fantastical creatures run rampant at this time of the cycle. For those who live an unenchanted life devoid of magical practises, this may be a time of pure fear and superstition. Indeed, throughout history the people of Wales have warned against visiting church-yards, crossroads and liminal spaces on the eve of Calan Gaeaf.[67] For the Witch however, who dwells in the liminal spaces and works in tandem with the realm of spirit, this is a time of potent magical potential. The Witch's Calan Gaeaf rites would only be enhanced by the energies of the season, making the very places most avoid the best places to be in order to honour this sacred time.

Ancestral Magic

It is at this time of the cycle we honour our ancestors of blood and bone. Those who came before us, and whose actions and choices initiated the very possibility of our existence. With the veil between our realm and the realm of the dead virtually non-existent, this is the most opportune time of year to show those ancestors your devotions and thanks to them for all they have passed down to you.

A Note on Difficult Ancestral Connections

We are not all privileged to have deep, lasting connections with our families nor beautiful, fond memories of our ancestors. I understand and am aware that connecting to our ancestors can be a difficult, painful process for many. If you have a strained relationship with your ancestors, have difficulty con-necting to your ancestors due to a variety of reasons, or simply have negative connotations surrounding your ancestors, then rest assured you can avoid any ritual ancestral worship altogether. If, however, you still wish to honour

---

67. Hutton, *Stations of the Sun.*

your ancestors without tapping into those painful traumas associated with them, then my best advice would be to keep it vague. Rather than honouring specific ancestors, call to your ancestors "of blood and bone, who would wish me no harm or ill will." You do not have to honour people for their bigoted, harsh, and harmful way of life. Instead, honour the magic of chance that led to your creation, the magic that allowed you to be who you are today. Honour that you have fought your ancestral curses, and have probably won. This can be a difficult time, but know that you are loved, you are valid, and you have guiding spirits that look upon you with nothing but love and trust.

⊗ EXERCISE ⊗
Ancestral Altar

One method of honouring our ancestors is to ensure they are at the forefront of your mind throughout this season. You can do this by setting up an altar in their honour. Start by clearing a table or empty space, and place cloths of black, orange, red, and/or grey down. At the centre of the altar place a tall candelabra or candlestick holder, and if possible, place black or pure white candles into it. You may add additional candles surrounding the edges of the altar if you feel drawn to do so. The next step is to find photographs of family members that have passed away. As many as you can find. If you do not have access to photos of your ancestors, you could speak to the living elders of your family and construct a family tree, with the names of the dead in clear sight. If this is not possible either, then place anything that reminds you of your ancestors. This could be old photos of the region in which you know they once lived. Alternatively, perhaps it could be mementos left by the long-lost members of your family. The important thing is that this altar should make you think of those that have come before you. Place as many items as possible that relate to your ancestors onto the altar. Next, place items of remembrance onto the altar. On my ancestor altar, I choose to place decorative ornamental skulls, pinecones, and an array of flowers ranging from black lilies to freshly picked hawthorn flowers.

Keep this altar up for as long as you deem fit. I personally set up my ancestor altar in mid-October and do not take it down until mid-November.

If you wish, you could also place an offering bowl onto the altar and offer your ancestors an offering of their favourite beverage, or of bread. Come to this altar daily and light the candles in remembrance of them. Gaze upon the images and/or paraphernalia you have placed which remind you of them. Feel their presence, the blood they have passed down to you.

Living Calan Gaeaf

Calan Gaeaf was my favourite time of year as a child, and still is to this day. My family would decorate the house with elaborate, spooky decorations and would often have fun-filled revelries at this time of year. Calan Gaeaf is very much a living, breathing celebration even in modern Wales, and remnants of old traditions remain. I remember being taught in school about the *Hwch ddu gwta*—the tailless black sow. A Halloween ghoul who sits in the shadows waiting for unsuspecting victims to pass by. This creature was a ghoulish manifestation of a folk devil, a tale meant to scare children and ensure they would not stay out too late during the Calan Gaeaf revelries. I have fond memories of wandering my seaside village with a group of friends, when we heard what sounded like growls coming from a darkened alleyway and a friend screamed in terror "*Y Hwch ddu gwta!*" ("The tailless black sow!") Which of course led to an array of frightening shrieks and screams as we all ran for the safety of our homes. Yes, Calan Gaeaf was always a time of joy and fear perfectly intertwined as one. We dressed up, bobbed for apples, attended parties, and told ghost stories through the night. These traditions I still attempt to keep in my life to this day. Carving pumpkins is a global phenomenon nowadays; though in many Welsh speaking parts of Wales we still refer to pumpkins as a *bwgan rwdan*, which would translate to be "swede/ turnip ghoul." This may be a remnant from the days when instead of pumpkins, the people of Britain would carve their jack-o-lanterns out of turnips or swedes. The vegetable swede of course, not Swedish people; we are not that barbaric.

Indeed, the season of Calan Gaeaf is very much the season of the Witch. It is a time of year to truly revel in your magical nature, embrace your darker aspects, and mingle with the various spirits that haunt our darkened streets at night. Calan Gaeaf and the Halloween season could easily be viewed as a solemn, reflective period to honour your ancestors and batten down the hatches for the coming darker period ahead. However, it is also a time for absolute frivolity and perfectly harnessed chaos too. What other time of year would you be able to recite a prayer in honour of your ancestors, whilst lighting black candles and wearing frivolous costumes, fishnet tights, and over-the- top makeup? You can do just this and remain within the very nature of Calan Gaeaf.

A Calan Gaeaf Feast

Calan Gaeaf is among the few holidays that I prepare a feast of sorts for. My partner and I prepare a *cawl* at this time of year, a type of stew. The perfect meal to welcome the coming winter. Our *cawl* consists of potatoes, carrots, swede, onion, vegetable stock, and an array of herbs and spices. We bake bread to accompany this *cawl* and have a feast by candlelight. Pulling inspiration from an old Welsh *Calan Gaeaf* tradition, we also bake an extra bread roll as an offering for the ancestors. Before sitting down for our meal we place a candle in the window alongside the extra bread roll and recite these words:

> *Bendithiwch eich teulu,*
> *Offrwm bara i chi ar Nos Galan Gaea.*[68]
> *(May'st thou bless thy whole family,*
> *This we offer you on the eve of Calan Gaeaf).*[69]

We would then light the ancestral altar before tucking in to our meal. It is a great time to invite either your blood family or your chosen family to feast with you as well. Honouring your connections to both the living and the dead.

The Winter Solstice

For a long while now, Earth has been silent and still. The cold embrace of winter clutches our earthly mother. The bitter cold winds of the north carry the souls of the dead; hear their voices echo through the barren branches of

---

68. My own translation.

69. As found in Hutton's *Stations of the Sun.*

the trees. It has been a long period of gestation, a time for reflection and an appreciation of the still. Alas, a change is near. Soon, the longest night will be upon us. The sun shall rise for the shortest day of the year. The solstice. Day by day, after the solstice has been, the light will grow stronger. Guiding us to the warmer, spring days ahead. Therefore, we celebrate the rebirth of the sun. Soon the Earth will be flourishing once more. We acknowledge the darker part of the year, learning all we can from it. Nevertheless, today is a celebration of light, of warmth, of rebirth.

The winter solstice usually falls on the twenty-first or twenty-second of December. It is the shortest day and the longest night of the year. Looking at it from an astronomical perspective, it is the day that the sun is at its lowest point in the sky. For many modern traditions and streams of Witchcraft and Paganism, this is the time of year when we celebrate the metaphorical death and rebirth of the sun. From the winter solstice onward the days grow longer, paving the way for the warmer spring and summer months ahead. For the Witch, the winter solstice is the perfect opportunity to reflect all that has happened over the last cycle. Counting our bounties and blessings, mourning those we have lost, sweeping away any unwanted or unneeded aspects of our lives and looking ahead to a brighter, warmer future. It is a time to honour all the wisdom and insightful knowledge you have gathered during the dark period of gestation and bring them out into the world ready to transform them from merely being thoughts and ponderings into real, effective actions. It is the most beneficial time to set intentions and to manifest what you wish to achieve over the cycle to come.

Though most practitioners today choose to celebrate the winter solstice on the day the actual solstice occurs, this celebration is more than just a day. All the celebrations of the cycle are. They are seasons that fill us with useful insights into who we are and how we interact with the world, as well as who we wish to be moving forward. My personal winter solstice celebrations begin in early December and continue well into mid-January. The day of the solstice is a day of pure revelry. It is usually spent with loved ones, fellow Witches, and dear friends. We drink, feast, dance, sing, and be merry. The period leading up to the day of the solstice is a time of reflection, pondering, stillness, and gathering. Whereas the days following the solstice are spent manifesting, weaving magic, and setting intentions for that which I wish to happen. It is very much a celebration of stillness being transformed into potent, powerful action.

Many people new to Paganism find it easy and comfortable to draw parallels between the various Pagan celebrations of the solstice in Europe with the modern Christian Christmas. I find the conversation surrounding the notion that Christians "stole" the winter solstice celebrations from Pagans petty, overdone, and redundant. As people evolve and change, of course older practises will be absorbed into newer belief systems. Modern Pagans can be just as guilty of appropriating traditions and practises from Eastern philosophy, and various spiritual traditions from around the world. Therefore, I steer the conversation away from bashing any religions or belief systems. Yes, the Christmas tree very much has pre-Christian origins but is now a part of various people's winter celebrations and is no less authentic to those individuals regardless of their religious inclination.

Growing up in North Wales, the holiday we celebrated around the time of the winter solstice was indeed *Nadolig*, the Welsh Christmas. To this day, I continue many of the traditions that my family practised at Nadolig, incorporating them into my modern Witchcraft practises. I still decorate a tree as the main focal element of the home, though nowadays I decorate it with pinecones, wooden ornaments, herbal charm pouches, and natural items rather than plastic baubles. Gift-giving is still an integral part of both my winter solstice celebration and the morning of Nadolig on the twenty-fifth of December. For the solstice, I gift my closest Pagan and Witch friends and my partner with books, journals, and useful tools to aid in celebrating the cycle ahead. Then for Nadolig gifts we simply go wild and gift whatever will show our appreciation for one another the most. It may seem odd for a Witch to still celebrate in accordance with how many Christians practise today, but Nadolig has been an important holiday in my family for generations. By continuing the traditions of Nadolig, which emulate the importance of family, of ancestry, of the home, and of love, I am continuing a family tradition that is close to my heart. Though Christians predominately celebrate Nadolig in modern-day Wales, my family have not been particularly religious in a long while. Our Nadolig traditions did not include any mention of Jesus or the biblical tales associated with this time of year. Much of my personal Paganism and Witchcraft is a celebration of my ancestry and heritage, and it would be entirely disingenuous of me to completely abandon longstanding family traditions that have little to nothing to do with Christianity. Nadolig is a time of merriment, of familial warmth, where we listen to and sing along to merry music, feast together as a family, and shelter from the cold together. That tradition is something I can easily and happily continue and incorporate into my Paganism and Witchcraft. Look into your family or ancestors' winter traditions too; there is no need within modern magical and spiritual practise to completely abandon what you are accustomed to in favour of something completely alien.

Both the winter solstice and Nadolig are a celebration of perennial life. Of life that exists beyond the mortal constraints of life and death. Though the world around us seems bleak and barren, we know that soon nature will return to its bright and vibrant glory. It is a reminder that though our bodies will one day die, our soul, as well as the memory of who we once were, will live on. In addition, if you are inclined to believe in the concept of reincarnation, the winter period is a perfect metaphor for death leading up to an eventual rebirth. A perfect symbol of the divine power of perennial life is that of the evergreen. Holly, pine, and ivy are among the various evergreen trees and plants that we may turn to as symbols of perennial life. A reminder that even in the darkest depths of winter, life can still flourish. We may choose to decorate our homes and altars with sprigs of evergreen, and use pine scented oils and incense to bring the joys of winter into our homes at this time of year.

The Mari Lwyd—Wales' Most Peculiar Winter Tradition

Envision yourself lounging at home on a cold, winter night. You have a warm drink beside you; you are snuggled up under blankets when suddenly, there is a knock at the door. You open the door and find yourself staring down a great, skeletal horse being. The being is almost human in stature, donned in a long white robe. You cannot help but stare at the sinister skeletal horse's head looking directly at you. It is adorned with colourful ribbons, has glass eyes, and its jaw is gnashing furiously. You take a deep gulp; your blood runs cold, as this demonic entity looks you up and down. Behind the skeletal horse figure is a small party, some dressed up in very strange attire. Out of nowhere they all erupt into a chorus chanting loudly:

Gentle friends,
Here we are,
Harmless fellows are we.
We ask you allow us entry,
Might you have food and drink for me?[70]

Suddenly, you are locked into a battle. A battle of verse. If you cannot turn these folk away, whilst rhyming the entire time, then they are entitled to enter the home and partake in food and drink with you. This is not a scene from an ancient folk tale of a fairy, horse, demon visitation, quite the contrary; it is an insight into the colourful tradition of the Mari Lwyd.

The Mari Lwyd is a Welsh Christmas tradition, mostly found in the south of Wales. The general idea is that a party including an individual carrying a decorated horse's skull on a pole, concealed by a white sheet, and would sing outside a house, petitioning a plea to allow them entry for some food and drink. The home owners would sing back listing reasons why they cannot enter. Think of it as a mixture between the modern trick-or-treat and an epic Welsh rap battle. Upon gaining entry into the house, the party would be given food and drink, and the frightening mare named Mari would chase the residents of the home. It was a joyous occasion. Once the skeletal mare and her party were to leave, they would place a blessing upon the house and its inhabitants, wishing them good fortune for the New Year ahead.

This peculiar tradition was first recorded in the year 1800, though it could have older, ancient origins.[71] There is certainly a pre-Christian feel to the entire ritual. The presence of the Mari Lwyd itself, this looming skeletal horse figure, denotes a feeling of otherworldly fairy lore. The Anglesey Druid order incorporate the Mari Lwyd into a select few of their rites, particularly that of the rite of Alban Arthan (the Celtic, Druidic term for the winter solstice). Reading and hearing about the Mari Lwyd is exciting as is but seeing the

---

70. My own words, based on the traditional introductory verse spoken by those participating in the tradition of the *Mari Lwyd*.

71. Hutton, *Stations of the Sun*.

Mari in person is something else entirely. This is a Welsh tradition I surely do not wish to see lost to the mists of time, hence my reasoning for including it here.

Reborn in Flame

The winter solstice may be an opportune time to reflect on the joys and necessity of the darkness; however, at its heart the solstice is a celebration of light and fire. We honour the sun's return, and look ahead to the bounties that await us in the warmer months to come.

⊛ EXERCISE ⊛
A Ritual for Awaiting the Dawn of the Solstice

This ritual is an easy, solitary ritual. It is a way of honouring the light and reflecting on that which you wish to manifest in the cycle ahead. For this ritual, you will need:

- A notebook
- A pen
- Twelve tea light candles
- One pillar candle
- A flat surface that you can safely place candles onto
- Your positive intentions

This ritual is intended to be performed on the morning of the winter solstice, just as the sun is rising. You will rise shortly before the dawn and prepare for this ritual. Set up a flat surface that you can easily and safely light candles on. Preferably, either this surface will be outdoors or near a window that faces the rising sun. Place the pillar candle in the centre of the surface, with the twelve tea light candles surrounding it in a circle.

As you wait for the sun to rise, light each of the candles one by one. Leave only the final pillar candle unlit. Within your notebook, write thirteen intentions for the coming year. These can be anything you wish! Perhaps you wish to be more disciplined, or would like to make new friends. Come up with thirteen small but significant desires.

Once the dawn breaks and you see the sun begin to peer over the horizon, light the final pillar candle, saying aloud:

Upon this dawn,
We celebrate the sun reborn.

Sit facing the rising sun and close your eyes. Breathe in the solstice air, and contemplate on the past year. Reflect on who you once were. Take a deep breath in, and as you exhale release any pent-up emotions that no longer serve you from the previous year. Take another deep breath, this time visualising that you are breathing in new beginnings. Opening up your spirit to the freshness of the coming cycle.

When you are ready, you will open your notebook, and read aloud to the rising sun each of your intentions for the coming year. As you say each individual intention, you will blow out one candle, leaving the middle pillar candle until last. Think of it as similar to blowing out candles on a birthday cake. Each candle you blow out is you manifesting your intentions.

Once all the candles are out, sit and watch the solstice sky shine as the sun continues to rise. Ponder the potentiality of the cycle ahead, and honour the sun as it is finally born anew from this period of gestation.

Happy New Year!

There is much debate over what constitutes as the "Pagan new year" among Neopagans circles today. Some say it is Samhain that marks the eve of the New Year, whilst others prefer to celebrate the dawn of a new cycle on the winter solstice. Call me boring, but I celebrate the New Year on the first of January. I am a modern Witch living in the modern world, and this is how many of our ancestors have marked their calendars for generations now. The cycle of the seasons is a never-ending, turning wheel; therefore it has no real beginning and no real end. If I had to choose one period during the changing of the seasons as a time to celebrate a new year, it would certainly be the period after the winter solstice. Here we honour that the days will grow longer, and the gestating period of the winter months are ending as spring creeps its way toward us. It just feels natural this way. It just so happens as well that Wales is a land ripe with New Year traditions. One of my favourite

Welsh New Year traditions is that of the *calennig*. Though not really cele-brated as much today in modern Wales, at least not in my area, I remember hearing folk talk about the *calennig* in my youth and so made it my mission to learn more about it.

The *calennig* was originally a time when the poorest in the community would go door to door, asking for a gift for the New Year. Traditionally the gifts would be that of cheese and bread.[72] Eventually this custom became popular with children and beyond merely asking for a gift, those participat-ing in the *calennig* would carry a New Year's apple. Those who were kind enough to give generously a gift of food, or even money, to those going door-to-door would be blessed with good fortune for the coming year.

The *calennig* New Year's apple was an apple that stood atop three sticks; the apple would be stuffed with fragrant herbs at the top and then covered in flour as well as nus, oats, or wheat. A fourth stick would then be shoved into its side so that those partaking in the *calenning* could carry this strange object. The Christian interpretation of this New Year's apple was that it rep-resented the gifts of the three wise men from the biblical nativity tale. There have been theories that this tradition is pre-Christian, or specifically Druidic in nature.[73] That the three sticks holding up the apple like a tripod represent the rays of the sun, or the rays of the Awen. The apple itself representing the sun overcoming the darkness of winter, which is represented by the nuts or grains stuck onto it. There is very little evidence to support these theories; however, it is an interesting and fantastical theory that sparks much inspira-tion. Modern Witches could easily adapt this tradition into a solstice blessing. The New Year's apple would look splendid adorning a modern Witch's altar, representing bountiful blessings for the coming cycle as well as a method of honouring the traditions of the past.

Purification by Water of Well and Sprig of Evergreen

This purification spell is based on a quaint Pembrokeshire tradition carried out at dawn on New Year's Day. The custom was traditionally carried out by

---

72. Hutton, *Stations of the Sun*.

73. Sikes, *British Goblins*.

children, and they would go about the practise blessing all they came into contact with as they wandered around the streets.

Collect a fresh cup of spring water, preferably from a local well upon the morn of the New Year. Next, take a sprig of evergreen and dip into the cup of water. Sprinkle your present company with the water by waving the dipped sprig of evergreen toward their faces. Sing aloud whilst splashing them:

Here we bring new water from the well so clear,
For to purify you, this happy new year,
Sing levy dew, sing levy dew,
The water and the wine,
with seven bright gold wires,
And bugles that do shine,
Sing reign of fair maid, with gold upon her toe,
Open you the west door and turn the old year go,
Sing reign of fair maid, with gold upon her chin,
Open you the east door and let the new year in![74]

This acts as a spell of good fortune, and purification for the New Year ahead.

The winter solstice evokes potent ideas of potentiality of the cycle ahead, new beginnings, and rebirth. It is a time to reflect, to prioritise what is most important, and to set intentions for the months ahead. Now that we have explored the winter solstice, the cycle turns and we move to the next celebration.

Dydd Santes Dwynwen: Saint Dwynwen's Day

One of the more prominent holy days or saint days celebrated primarily on the Isle of Anglesey and in the Gwynedd region of North Wales but that is becoming more and more popular throughout Wales as of late is *Dydd Santes Dwynwen* or Saint Dwynwen's Day, celebrated on January the twenty-fifth. Dubbed as the Welsh equivalent to Valentine's day, which may be strange as Valentine's day is also celebrated by many in Wales, the modern celebration of Dydd Santes Dwynwen consists primarily of showing your adoration and

---

74. Adapted from the traditional song "Levy-Dew." J. Boys Smith, "Custom on New Year's Day in Pembrokeshire," *Archaeologia Cambrensis* 4, no. 14 (April 1849): 141, http://hdl.handle .net/10107/2991655.

love to your significant other, friends, or family. Cards, gifts, chocolates, and flowers are usually sent to those you wish to share your love with on this day. Some folk even gift Welsh love spoons on Dwynwen's feast day, though today folk tend to purchase love spoons in stores rather than following the older tradition of carving the spoon themselves as a proposal gift.

This celebration was specifically prominent in my local area due to the fact we were but a few miles away from *Ynys Llanddwyn* (Llanddwyn Island), a small tidal island near the town of Newborough. Dwynwen set up a convent on Ynys Llanddwyn and now every year on Dydd Santes Dwynwen couples and families embark onto the island either as a romantic walk, or in honour of Dwynwen. The last time I visited Ynys Llanddwyn on Dydd Santes Dwynwen upon the beach were numerous single red roses, right near the water's edge, as if someone were offering the flower to the spirit of place.

For the Welsh Witch, Dwynwen is a potent and powerful ally to call upon to aid in magical workings that deal with matters of the heart. As well as being the patron saint of lovers, Dwynwen's tale is filled with heartache and pain and she ultimately sacrifices her place in society and her ability to marry in order to help others. Dwynwen aids us in reflecting on our heartache, healing our past traumas, and moving forward in love and in life.

The story of Dwynwen is one I have memorised since I was a child. Dwynwen was a princess, the daughter of a great king. Dwynwen had fallen madly in love with a boy named Maelon, but unfortunately unbeknownst to Dwynwen, her father had already arranged for her to marry another. When Dwynwen learnt of her father's arrangement, she rushed to tell Maelon. Upon telling Maelon the news, Dwynwen was devastated when he became extremely angry and turned her away, telling her he never wished to see her again. Dwynwen wept and ran deep into the forest. There deep in the trees she prayed to God for his help. Suddenly, an angel stood before Dwynwen and offered her a potion that would heal her aching heart and allow her to forget Maelon. Dwynwen, in her heartbroken state rushed to drink this potion, but she would soon regret the decision to do so. It was not long before Dwynwen discovered that Maelon had been transformed into a block of ice as a consequence to her drinking the potion. Dwynwen fell to her knees and began sobbing, and begged for a miracle to occur. The angel who had gifted

Dwynwen the potion appeared before her once more; this time they offered her three wishes. Dwynwen's three wishes were that Maelon be thawed, that all true lovers be aided by God to live their happily ever afters, and finally she wished that she would never marry and instead live a blessed life dedicated to helping struggling lovers. All three wishes came true.[75]

I have heard whispers and rumours from many Welsh Pagans in my time that the story of Dwynwen may indeed hold pre-Christian origins and that Dwynwen may indeed be both a saint and an older goddess or spirit related to lovers and heartache. These are but rumours; however we as Pagans and Witches can still call upon the spirit of Dwynwen in our practises if we so wish it. Dwynwen has become a powerful spirit of Welsh lore, elevated as the very embodiment of love and healing from heartache in Wales.

✵ EXERCISE ✵
Healing Heartache Potion

This is a recipe for a herbal potion or tea calling upon the healing power of Dwynwen that can either be drunk by yourself, or perhaps given to those who may be struggling with a broken heart.

For the tea you will need:

- Loose lavender tea
- Loose rose tea
- Locally sourced honey (or honey alternative)

Mix half a teaspoon of loose lavender tea with half a teaspoon of loose rose tea, and place them in a tea strainer or straight into a teacup. Pour boiled water into the cup and allow to steep for two to three minutes, depending on how strong you would prefer it to be. Once the tea is strained put half a teaspoon of honey into the tea and stir clockwise. Whilst stirring, recite the following:

Dwynwen caredig, ysbryd cariad y tir,
Cymhortha fi heddiw, a fyddai"n hapus cyn bo hir.

---

75. This is my own retelling of the tale, as I remember it being told from my childhood.

Generous Dwynwen, loving spirit of the land,
Aid me in my healing, hold out your caring hand.

Once the tea is cool enough to drink, sip gently and feel the calming embrace of Dwynwen as well as the soothing potency of the tea.

Gwyl y Canhwyllau: Candlemas, or Gwyl Braint

Softly, a stirring begins beneath the Earth. The goddess of spring awakens, warming the land with her healing energies. The first signs of spring make their appearance, despite the fact that frost continues to coat the meadows and fields. During the winter solstice we celebrated the fact that soon, light will return, now we begin to see the gentle stirrings as the seasons change.

This time of the year is marked in more conventional Pagan calendars as Imbolc, celebrated usually on the first of February. In the Welsh Witches' calendar however, it is known as *Gwyl y Canhwyllau*, or *Gwyl Ffraid*. Ffraid is the Christian saint equivalent of Braint, the Welsh goddess of healing and of the spring tide. To our Celtic brethren in Ireland this time of year is heavily associated with Brigid. In Christian Wales, this celebration is known as *Gwyl fair y canhwyllau*, the virgin's feast of candles. It was a time of blessing candles. Some theorise that the focus on candles, a reverence for light and fire at this time of year have pre-Christian origins.

My native landscape was *Ynys Môn*, the Isle of Anglesey. The Afon Braint is a river that flows through my island home. Within my personal practise I refer to this time of year as *Gwyl Braint*. It is at this time of the cycle I honour the goddess in her manifestation as Braint, the goddess of Spring and healing. I honour Braint by constructing an altar in her honour in my home, and celebrate the ushering in of the spring, which is just around the corner. It is a time of healing, and a period of awaiting. Divination is heavily associated with this time of year, especially divination in fire or candlelight. This is an opportune time of year for practising your divination skills by candlelight.

✪ EXERCISE ✪
A Shrine for the Goddess Braint

As this time of the cycle is associated with the healing goddess Braint, it is an opportune time to dedicate a shrine in her honour. Any shrine you create in devotion to deity should be deeply personal to you and your practise; however, for reference, here is a vague guide as to how I set up my Braint srhine.

I begin by setting up a table with a white tablecloth, usually made of silk or lace. Ensure it is a pure white in colour, the colour of winter snow. I then place a vase with freshly picked snowdrops in it at the centre back of the altar. If snowdrops are not easily accessible to you, learn about your local flora, investigate what flowers bloom and grow at this time of year in your area. The more rooted to your land and your region your practise is, the better. I use snowdrops as they grow in abundance in my region, and at this time of year, they are the first things to shoot through the frosty or snow-covered grasses. A sure sign of the budding of spring softly approaching. Following the snowdrops, I then place a goddess figure onto the shrine in representation of Braint in front of the snowdrops. This does not need to be a literal statue or figure of Braint, but rather something that represents her spirit. Around the edges of the shrine, I place a number of candles. In the very centre of the shrine, I place a bowl with freshly collected river water. If fortunate, I am sometimes able to collect from *Afon Braint* itself, Braint's blessed river that runs through the isle of Anglesey. I understand this is not possible for all, and so any fresh running river water or even collected rainwater could work. Alternatively, I also sometimes place a cauldron in the centre of the shrine and use it to burn incense made from herbs that represent purification and healing. Finally, I then cover the rest of the shrine with various paraphernalia that represent healing to me. For my tastes, this usually includes pebbles from the beach, or quartz, and white feathers.

This is but an example of how I set up my shrine. Now it is your turn to get creative; construct your shrine to your personal tastes and practises. You can then use this altar as a focal point to dedicate any devotions to the goddess Braint or practise any rites and magical workings with healing intentions. It may also prove useful to keep a journal or notepad on or near the altar to note down things such as changes in your local natural environment, and reflections on how you feel now that the cold and dark embrace of winter is simmering to an end.

And thus, the cycle repeats itself, the seasons continue to move and change. We have explored a few of the annual celebratory events throughout the year and how they may relate to a Welsh Witch's practise. My hope is that this sampling of festivals, traditions, and lore that permeates throughout the four seasons allows you to truly immerse yourself in the marvellous opportunities to observe the ever-changing nature of our world.

Conclusion

More and more people today are being drawn to the magic and empowerment that is found within the various traditions, streams, and practises of Witchcraft. With such a variety of individuals forging their own unique, authentic paths, it is becoming increasingly important that there is just as wide a variety of accessible information available to all. The main drive I had to write this book was due to a lack of representation of a practise that aligned with my beliefs, my ancestry, my land, and my needs. I was told long ago that if I could not find the book I wanted on the shelves, then I needed to write it myself. I am proud that I was able to do this, and I hope that this book will inspire practitioners to do just the same. If this book inspires just one person to begin, or alter, their own spiritual and magical tradition then I will be absolutely thrilled. As it stands, I am glad I wrote this book mostly for myself.

This body of work initially aimed to simply explore the richness of lore, belief, and customs associated with what could be understood, via a modern context, as Witchcraft throughout history in the Celtic region of Wales. There have been numerous investigations into pre-Christian beliefs and practises specific to Wales over the years, usually with a Druidic expression. However, as we have deduced from the contents of this body of work, Wales also has a rich history of magical practises, folk belief, and old customs that can easily inspire and inform a modern magical practitioner. I hope that I have adequately explored the themes of Witchcraft and magic in Wales, at least enough to spark a desire in other practitioners to now conduct their own research. My hope is for readers to question the things I have written here, extend their knowledge further, and indeed incorporate some of the practises into their own magical practise just as I have done with mine. My explorations are but the tip of the iceberg; there is so much more to explore and discover. At the very least, the aim of this book was to be a springboard to help those with a Celtic practise to carve out the initial framework of their practise. I would have given anything for more books of this nature as I began my tentative first steps into the inner workings of magic and Witchcraft. A book that not only explored Witchcraft and magic, but also how that magic relates to my land. My goal and hope was that this book would not only aid in furthering the studies and practises of those with specific Welsh ancestry, or a pull toward Celtic magical practises, but that also it would act as a reference for eclectic Witches all over. You do not need Welsh or Celtic ancestry to be able to appreciate and delve into the practises mentioned in this work, I hope.

Overall, I also feel deeply privileged and proud to have been able to present the magic of Wales to all those who have picked up this book. As I have mentioned in past chapters, we are a land that is often overlooked, underappreciated, and misunderstood. Despite our rich collection of myth, legend, folklore, and indeed magical practises, Wales is still a relatively untouched area within spiritual and magical circles.

A main lesson I have learnt over the course of my continued studies into Witchcraft and magic, is that authenticity does not need to stem entirely from a place of antiquity. What this means is that magical practises do not need to have ties to ancient, old-world practises in order to be authentic and effective. This might seem like a hypocritical stance to take, considering a large portion of this body of work delves into the historiography of Witchcraft and magic in Wales. However, what I have learnt is that our practises can be very much informed and inspired by history, but at the end of the day, we are modern Witches living in a modern world. In order for our magic to be effective in working in this modern world, then our practise must also have a modern sensibility. Tradition is lovely, and keeping in touch with our history is exceptionally important. Ignoring the present, and living entirely in the past however, is a recipe for disaster. This is why countless times in this book I have made an effort to repeat that the majority of the exercises, spells, and rituals found in this book have little to no antiquity behind them. A few were inspired slightly by older practises, but overall they were an insight into my own deeply personal exploration into what works for me. I truly hope that no practitioner would ever pick up this book and assume that they are expected to follow each spell, rite, and practise word by word. The aim of including those exercises and practises was to offer an insight into how I have intertwined my theoretical knowledge of magical practises native to my land with a modern understanding of my own personal spiritual and magical needs. Now it is your turn to explore your magical and spiritual needs yourself. Older practises and traditions can work in brilliant tandem with modern sensibilities.

Where to Go Next

Where does one go from here? You might be asking yourself that now that you have reached this final chapter. Well, my friends, the end is merely the beginning. My advice to you now is to venture out into the world and begin formulating your own unique, individualised approach to magic. Perhaps the contents of this book have inspired you to delve deeper into certain aspects of Witchcraft, or certain aspects of the Celtic pathway. There are a few other authors beyond me who deal with similar themes in their works, and I very much recommend that you seek them out. However, the fact of the matter is that at the end of the day you will not truly gain an insight into your own spiritual and magical needs unless you set out to actually incorporate the practises and aspects of Witchcraft that speak to your soul into your life. Go back through the various chapters of this book and start truly partaking in those exercises I carefully provided. Read the recommended reading section found within the next few pages of this book. Find what works for you, and what does not. Make note of it all. Challenge what you have learnt; find better, stronger answers to your questions. No single author holds all the answers to the questions you must have about how the world and the universe might work. Now it is time for you to ponder on those questions yourself.

Now it is time for you to forge your own authentic, unique magical practise. Regardless of whether you are entirely new to the craft, or you are continuing a lineage of traditions, you are a unique individual with your own unique perspective on the world. Your path is merely as old as you are. I, as well as any other authors you may have read up to this point have offered you the initial framework. Now you need to fill in the gaps.

Stand in your power and be the Witch that you know you are.

Bendithion swynol i ti, gyfaill.
Magical blessings upon you, my friend.

Recommended Reading

I am certain that you are now pondering what to do next, or if you are a dedicated bookworm like myself, you will undoubtedly now be pondering what to read next. Here I have provided a list of a few of the books I recommend to those who approach me asking specifically for recommended reading. Some focus solely on Celtic and Welsh Paganism, Witchcraft, and magic. Others focus on Witchcraft in a broader sense.

Books on Welsh and Celtic Paganism, Witchcraft, and Magic

The Mabinogion by Sioned Davies

The Book of Celtic Magic: Transformative Teachings from the Cauldron of Awen by Kristoffer Hughes

From the Cauldron Born: Exploring the Magic of Welsh Legend & Lore by Kristoffer Hughes

A History of Magic and Witchcraft in Wales by Richard Suggett

British Goblins by Wirt Sikes

The Welsh Fairy Book by W. Jenkyn Thomas

Further Recommended Reading on Witchcraft

Traditional Witchcraft: a Cornish Book of Ways by Gemma Gary

Weave the Liminal by Laura Tempest Zakroff

For Welsh speakers:

Coelion Cymru by Evan Isaac

Glossary and Guide to Welsh Pronunciation

Here you will find a glossary of various prominent words and terms mentioned in this book and their meanings. The words featured here are words from my native Welsh language, and I have provided a guide to the phonetic pronunciation for those who do not speak Welsh. I have also created a YouTube video alternative to this glossary, which can be found on my YouTube channel Mhara Starling, so that you can hear these words spoken as they are meant to be pronounced.

A note: The Welsh alphabet consists of most of the letters in the English alphabet but excluding some letters, and including other letters.

The Welsh Alphabet

a, b, c, ch, d, dd, e, f, ff, g, ng, h, i, l, ll, m, n, o, p, ph, r, rh, s, t, th, u, w, y

A non-native speaker, or someone unfamiliar with Welsh, may find themselves stumped at the additional letters of: *ch, dd, ff, ng, ll, ph, rh,* and *th.*

To those whose first language is English, it may seem strange to consider what seemingly appears to be two letters together as one singular letter. However, individual letters they are. Each of these letters create a specific sound as follows:

ch: A throaty sound, emanating from the back of the throat. Similar to how a Scottish person would pronounce the *ch* in *Loch*. It is not an S sound, nor a sound similar to the *ch* in English words such as Cheek.

dd: The sound of this letter comes from the front of the mouth. Similar to the sound of *th* in English words such as *there, them*, and *this* but not like the *th* sound in English words such as *thick* or *thin*.

ff: This is a hard F sound as in the English words *fight, freedom*, or *full*. The singular *f* in Welsh is a *V* sound as in *video*.

ng: Thing of *ng* as the same sound found at the end of English words such as *thinking, listening*, or *singing*.

ll: The double L letter is one of the most complex Welsh letters. There is no English counterpart. It is a sound similar to that of a hiss.

ph: Simply pronounced similarly to the *ph* in the English word *phrase*.

rh: Very similar to a rolling R sound when used within words. Roll your R and then exhale or sigh while doing so.

th: Pronounced as the *th* in the English words *thick* and *thin*.

A common joke that many non-Welsh speakers like to make regarding the Welsh language is "where are the vowels?" As tongue-in-cheek this joke may be, it actually makes very little sense. Welsh has its own set of vowels, and in fact we have more vowels than the English language does. Here are the Welsh vowels:

a, e, i, o, u, w, y

"A" is pronounced "ah" such as the "a" in English words such as "cat," or "bat."

"E" is pronounced similarly to how the "e" would be pronounced in English words such as "ten," so more of an "eh" sound than an "ee."

"I" is pronounced the way one might pronounce "e" in English, or in words such as "see."

"O" in the Welsh alphabet is pronounced almost like saying the word "awe" quickly, similar to how the letter "o" is pronounced in "on" or "from."

"U" can be a tricky one! It almost sounds like "ee" but your tongue should make a "U" shape when saying it.

"W" is an "ooh" sound. Similar to how a double "O" would be pronounced in English words such as "cool" or "loon."

"Y" is pronounced "uh," similar to the sound you might make in English when saying the "u" in words such as "but," "cut," etc. In Welsh "y" can be both a vowel and a consonant.

For a more in-depth guide to Welsh pronunciation please see my YouTube channel, which is under the channel name "Mhara Starling." Now for a glossary of the common words, names, and place names found within this book and relevant to Welsh Celtic Paganism and Witchcraft. The phonetic method of pronouncing them is in brackets, though note I have left the *ll* and *dd* as they would be in Welsh due to a lack of English equivalent sounds.

Afagddu (Ah-VAHG-thee) An alternate name for Morfran, the son of Cerridwen. Afagddu means "utter darkness." Named so due to his repulsive appearance.

Afon (AH-vonn) The Welsh word for "river."

Alban Arthan (Al-Bann ARTH-anne) The Druidic/Celtic name for the Winter Solstice.

Alban Elfed (AL-bann ELL-ved) The Druidic/Celtic name for the autumn equinox.

Alban Hefin (AL-bann HEV-een) The Druidic/Celtic name for the summer solstice.

Annwfn (ANN-oovn) The Welsh Celtic otherworld or underworld.

Aranrhod (Arh-ANN-rod) Sister of the magician Gwydion, a goddess often associated with the moon in modern Paganism.

Awen (AH-when) The spirit of pure, divine inspiration.

Awenydd (AH-When-ee*dd*) A historical Welsh soothsayer.

Awyr (AH-weer) The sky in Welsh.

Bendigeidfran (BEN-dee-GAYD-vran) A blessed king from Welsh mythology, brother of Branwen, son of Llŷr and often said to be a giant. Also known more commonly as *Brân* (BRA-nn).

Bendith Y Mamau (BEN-deeth UH Mam-aye) A humanoid race of Welsh Fairies/otherworldly beings.

Bendithion (Ben-DITH-ee-on) The Welsh word for *Blessings*.

Blodeuedd (blod-AY-e*dd*) A woman made of flowers by the magicians Math and Gwydion. When transformed into an owl is renamed as *Blodeuwedd* (blod-AY-we*dd*).

Braint (BRR-aeent) The Welsh goddess of spring and healing connected to the isle of Anglesey.

Branwen (BRAN-when) The sister of Brân and daughter of Llŷr. She married the king of Ireland and was abused horrendously. Her brother crossed the Irish sea to rescue her.

Bwbach (bOOb-ach) A household spirit or fairy.

Calan (Kal-ANN) Calends. The "first" day of something, such as the first day of winter or the first day of the month.

Calan Gaeaf (Kal-ANN Gay-av) The first day of Winter. The Welsh equivalent to Samhain or Halloween.

Calan Mai (Kal-ANN My) May day, Beltane.

Calennig (Kal-ENN-eeg) A Welsh winter tradition to bestow blessings upon people for the new year.

Cerridwen (care-REED-when) The Welsh Witch goddess, goddess of inspiration.

Chwedlau (*Ch*WED-lie) The Welsh word for *fairy tales* or *fables*.

Coblynau (kob-LUNN-aye) Fairies of the mines, a type of goblin.

Consuriwr (Con-SEER-ee-oorr) A conjurer.

Creiddylad (Krey-DDUL-add) A minor character in the fourth branch of the Mabinogi.

Creirfyw (Krey-UHR-view) The beautiful daughter of Cerridwen, her name meaning *the finest*.

Cŵn Annwfn (KOON ANN-oovn) Welsh hounds from the otherworld or underworld. Pure white hounds with blood-red ears.

Cylch Cyfrin, y (uh Kill-ch KUF-reen) A secretive group of magical practitioners who operated on the isle of Anglesey in the early twentieth
century. The *"y"* at the beginning is the Welsh word for "the."

Cymraeg (Come-RAeeg) Literally: *Welsh* the Welsh language.

Cymraes (Come-RA-ees) A Welsh woman. The male equivalent being a
Cymro (Come-RAW).

Cymru (Come-REE) The Welsh word for *Wales*, the country.

Dewin (Deh-WEEN) The Welsh word for *Wizard*.

Dinas Emrys (DEAN-ass Em-rees) A place in Wales associated with the
Wizard Merlin.

Doethgrefft (DO-eeth-greft) The Welsh word for *Witchcraft*.

Dwynwen (Do-IN-when) The Welsh patron saint of love and relationships.

Dyfed (DUV-ed) A county in South Wales, also the kingdom which *Pwyll* is
a prince of.

Efnisien (Ayv-NISH-yen) The half-brother of Brân and Branwen, a wicked
man engulfed in darkness.

Ellyll (Ehll-EE-ll) A sub-group of fairy, elemental beings.

Ellylldan (Ehll-EE-ll-DAN) An orb of fairy light, similar to the English will-
o'-the-wisp.

Eryri (Eh-RURR-ee) A mountainous region of North Wales, Snowdonia.

Ferch (Verr-CH) The Welsh word for daughter, for example: Gwen *ferch* Ellis
means Gwen, the daughter of Ellis.

Ffraid (Pronounced similarly to the English word *fried*) Another name for
Braint, the goddess of spring and healing.

Ffynnon (FUN-on) The Welsh word for a well.

Glain Neidr (Gline NAY-durr) Snake stones, adder stones. A type of stone
used in Welsh folk magic.

Gwerddonau Llion (Guh-WHERE-thone-aee *ll*-EE-on) The emerald isles of
enchantment, a fairy realm/island that exists somewhere in the Irish sea.

Gwion Bach (Gwee-ON bach) A boy tasked by Cerridwen to stir her mystical cauldron, who eventually becomes imbued with the Awen.

Gwrach (GOO-rach) The modern Welsh word for *Witch*, originally meaning something repulsive or hag.

Gwrachyddiaeth (GOO-rach Uh-THEE-eyeth) An informal modern Welsh term for *Witchcraft*.

Gwragedd Annwfn (GOO-rag-eth ANN-oovn) A category of humanoid Welsh otherworldly beings, fairies.

Gwragedd/Dynion Hysbys (GOO-rag-eth / DUH-knee-on Huss-bus) Cunning women/men.

Gwydion (GWID-eeon) A prominent magician from Welsh mythology.

Gwyl (GOO-ill) The Welsh word for *festival* or *holiday*.

Gwyl Awst (GOO-ill OW-st)—The last word *Awst* pronounced like *joust* but without the *J* - The Welsh equivalent of the first harvest or Lammas.

Gwyl y Canhwyllau (GOO-ill UH Can-HWEE-*ll*-aye) Candlemas, or Imbolc.

Gwyllgi (GOO-*ill*-Gee—the "Gee" would be pronounced with a hard "G" as in words such as *Great, Gullible*, etc. And not as in the words *Giraffe* or *Giant*). A fearsome spectral hound from Welsh folklore.

Gwyllion (GOO-ee*ll*-EE-on) A mountain fairy native to Wales.

Gwyn ap Nudd (GWIN Ap NI-dd) God of the wild hunt, a psychopomp, ruler of the Celtic underworld and often referred to as king of the fairy.

Hiraeth (HERE-ayeth) Often translated as meaning *homesickness*. A longing for a place, feeling, or person which is either out of reach, or non-existent.

Huw Llwyd (Hugh *ll*OO-id) A Welsh conjurer from the tale of the Cat Witches.

Hwch Ddu Gwta (HOO-ch Thee GOO-tah) A Welsh phantom, folk devil. A tailless black sow that haunts people on Halloween.

Llanddwyn (Ll-AN-thween) An island in Anglesey which has connotations to the goddess/santes Dwynwen.

Lleu Llaw Gyffes (*ll*-ay *ll*-aw GUFF-ess) The son of Aranrhod, his name meaning light of skilful hand.

Llyn (LL-in) The Welsh word for *lake*.

Llŷr (LL-ir) The mighty Celtic god of the sea.

Mabinogi (mab-INN-Og-ee) The collection of Welsh myths.

Mabon (MABB-onn) The divine son, son of the great mother goddess Modron. Not to be confused with the modern Neopagan name for the autumn equinox.

Mari Lwyd (MAREE LOO-id) A Welsh winter custom, the name Mari Lwyd is ascribed to a skeletal horse figure which goes door to door at winter.

Math (Pronounced just as the *Math* in *Mathematics*) A semi-divine king and magician from Welsh mythology.

Modron (MOD-Ron) The great mother goddess.

Môr (Pronounced similarly to the English word *More* with emphasis on the "O") The Welsh word for *Sea*.

Morda (MORE-Dah) A blind man tasked by Cerridwen to stoke the fires beneath her cauldron.

Myrddin (MER-Theen) A Welsh name for the famous wizard *Merlin*.

Nadolig (Nah-DAW-leeg) The Welsh word for *Christmas*.

Nos Galan Gaeaf (NOS kal-ANN Gay-av) The eve of winter, Halloween or Samhain.

Offrymu (Off-RUM-ee) The Welsh tradition of offering something, usually for magical purposes. An offering.

Plentyn-newid (PLENN-teen Nay-weed) A Changeling.

Pwyll (PWEE-ll) A prince of the kingdom of Dyfed, husband of Rhiannon, he is who traded places with the king of Annwfn in the first branch of the Mabinogi.

Rhamanta (Rha-MAN-tah) A Welsh method of romantic divination.

Rheibes (*Rh*-aye-bess) A female sorceress who practises baneful, harmful magic (curses).

Rheibwr (*RHay*-bOOR) The male equivalent of *Rheibes*.

Rhiannon (*Rh*ee-ANN-onn) A Welsh horse Goddess associated with sovereignty.

Swyn (Sue-in) literally: *Charm*. A Welsh form of magic, also a magical practitioner.

Swyngyfaredd (Sue-in-GUH-VAR-e*dd*) Witchcraft, the practise of magic and sorcery.

Swynwr (Sue-in-OOH-uhr) A male practitioner of Witchcraft and magic.

Swynwraig (Sue-in-OOH-rye-guh) A female practitioner of Witchcraft and magic.

Swynwyr (Sue-in-weir) A gender-neutral term, and plural term, for Welsh magical practitioners.

Swynydd (Sue-in-ee-*dd)* A gender-neutral term for practitioners of Witchcraft and magic.

Taliesin (tal-YES-inn) He who was born of Awen. A prominent prophet and bard from Welsh mythology.

Tân (Tahn) The Welsh word for *fire*.

Tegid Foel (TEG-id Vo-yal) The husband of Cerridwen.

Tir (TEER) The Welsh word for *land*.

Tylwyth Teg (Tull-WITH Teg) A Welsh term for *fairies* but also literally translating to mean *the fair family*. Humanoid otherworldly beings.

Ynys Môn (Uhn-ISS Monn) The Isle of Anglesey.

Ysbryd (Uhss-BREEd) The Welsh word for *Spirit*.

Ysbrydnos (Uhss-BRUHd-noss) Spirit night. There are three spirit nights in Wales—Beltane, the summer solstice, and Calan Gaeaf/Samhain. A night when spirits roam freely among mortals.

Bibliography

Bevan, Gareth, and Patrick Donovan, eds. *Geiriadur Prifysgol Cymru (A Dictionary of the Welsh Language)*. Cardiff: University of Wales Press, 2004.

Boys Smith, J. "Custom on New Year's Day in Pembrokeshire." *Archaeologia Cambrensis* 4, no. 14 (April 1849): 141. http://hdl.handle.net/10107/2991655.

Breverton, Terry. *Breverton's Complete Herbal: A Book of Remarkable Plants and their Uses*. London: Quercus, 2011.

Burns, William E. *Witch Hunts in Europe and America: An Encyclopedia*. Westport, CT: Greenwood Press, 2003.

Coleman, J. A. *The Dictionary of Mythology: An A-Z of Themes, Legends and Heroes*. London: Arcturus Publishing Limited, 2008.

Conran, Tony. *Welsh Verse: Fourteen Centuries of Poetry*. Bridgend: Seren, 1967.

Cooper, Lucy. *The Element Encyclopedia of Fairies: The Ultimate A-Z of Fairies, Pixies, and Other Fantastical Creatures*. London: HarperElement, 2014.

Daimler, Morgan. *A New Dictionary of Fairies: A 21st Century Exploration of Celtic and Related Western European Fairies*. Croydon: Moon Books, 2020.

Davies, Sioned. *The Mabinogion: A New Translation by Sioned Davies*. New York: Oxford University Press, 2008.

Ellis, Joseph. *"Conjurations, Enchantments and Witchcrafts": To What Extent Was the Execution of Gwen Ferch Ellis (1594) a Turning Point in the Welsh Perception of Common Magic? An Exploration of the 'Cunning Folk' of Wales at the Turn of the Seventeenth Century*. PhD diss., The Open University Module A329: The Making of Welsh History, 2019. Accessed April 8, 2021. http://oro.open.ac.uk/62650/3/ELLIS_A329_RVOR.pdf?fbclid.

Forest, Danu. *Gwyn Ap Nudd: Wild God of Fairy Guardian of Annwfn*. Hampshire: Moon Books, 2018.

Franklin, Anna and Paul Mason. *Lammas: Celebrating the Fruits of the First Harvest*. St. Paul, MN: Llewellyn Publications, 2001.

Gary, Gemma. *The Devil's Dozen: Thirteen Craft Rites of The Old One*. London: Troy Books, 2015.

Gary, Gemma. *Traditional Witchcraft: A Cornish Book of Ways*. London: Troy Books, 2019.

Hoffman, David. *Welsh Herbal Medicine*. Abercastle: Abercastle Publications, 1978.

Holland, Richard. *Wales of the Unexpected*. Llanrwst: Gwasg Carreg Gwalch, 2005.

Hopwood, Mererid. *Straeon o'r Mabinogi*. Ceredigion: Wasg Gomer, 2011.

Hughes, Kristoffer. *The Book of Celtic Magic: Transformative Teachings from the Cauldron of Awen*. Woodbury, MN: Llewellyn Publications, 2014.

Hughes, Kristoffer. *Cerridwen: Celtic Goddess of Inspiration*. Woodbury, MN: Llewellyn Publications, 2021.

Hughes, Kristoffer. *From the Cauldron Born: Exploring the Magic of Welsh Legend and Lore*. Woodbury, MN: Llewellyn Publications, 2012.

Hughes, Meirion and Wayne Evans. *Rumours and Oddities from North Wales: A Selection of Folklore, Myths, and Ghost Stories*. Llanrwst: Gwasg Carreg Gwalch, 1986.

Hutton, Ronald. *Blood and Mistletoe: The History of the Druids in Britain*. Hampshire: Yale University Press, 2011.

Hutton, Ronald. *The Stations of the Sun: A History of the Ritual Year in Britain*. Oxford: Oxford University Press, 1996.

Hutton, Ronald. *The Triumph of the Moon: A History of Modern Pagan Witchcraft*. Oxford: Oxford University Press, 1999.

Hutton, Ronald. *The Witch: A History of Fear: From Ancient Times to the Present*. Ceredigion: Yale University Press, 2017.

Ifans, Dafydd and Rhiannon. *Y Mabinogion*. Ceredigion: Wasg Gomer, 2007.

Illes, Judika. *The Element Encyclopedia of 5000 Spells*. London: HarperElement, 2004.

Illes, Judika. *The Element Encyclopedia of Witchcraft: The Complete A-Z for the Entire Magical World*. London: HarperElement, 2005.

Isaac, Evan. *Coelion Cymru*. Aberystwyth: Cambrian News, 1938.

Owen, Elias. *Welsh Folk-Lore: A Collection of Folk-Tales and Legends of North Wales*. Burnham-on-sea, Somerset: 1996.

Owen, Trefor M. *The Customs and Traditions of Wales*. Cardiff: University of Wales Press, 2016.

Rhiwallon of Myddfai. *The Physicians of Myddfai*. Lavergne, TN: CreateSpace Independent Publishing Platform, 2012.

Rowlands, William. *Chwedlau Gwerin Cymru*. Oxford, University Press Oxford, 1923.

Sikes, Wirt. *British Goblins: Welsh Folklore, Fairy Mythology, Legends and Traditions*. London: Sampson Low, Marston, Searle & Rivington, 1880.

Stewart, R. J. *Celtic Gods, Celtic Goddesses*. New York, NY: Sterling Publishing Co. Inc, 1990.

Suggett, Richard. *A History of Magic and Witchcraft in Wales*. Gloucestershire: The History Press Ltd., 2008.

Thomas, W. Jenkyn. *The Welsh Fairy Book*. Cardiff: University of Wales press, 1995.

Williams, Rowan and Gwyneth Lewis. *The Book of Taliesin: Poems of Warfare and Praise in an Enchanted Britain*. United Kingdom: Penguin Books Limited, 2019.

Zakroff, Laura Tempest. *Weave the Liminal: Living Modern Traditional Witchcraft*. Woodbury, MN: Llewellyns Publications, 2019.

Zakroff, Laura Tempest. *The Witch's Cauldron: The Craft, Lore & Magick of Ritual Vessels*. Woodbury, MN: Llewellyns Publications, 2017.

Online Resources

Cadw. "Barclodiad Y Gawres Burial Chamber." Accessed March, 17, 2021. https://cadw.gov.wales/visit/places-to-visit/barclodiad-y-gawres-burial -chamber.

Casgliad y Werin Cymru. "Cursing Pot and Slate Inscription, 19th Century." People's Collection Wales. Accessed April17, 2021. https://www.peoples collection.wales/items/1237.

Celtic Source YouTube Channel. "The Celtic 'Otherworld'?" Accessed April, 12 2021. https://youtu.be/Y5WiifupG-4.

Visit Wales. "The Welsh Dragon and the Welsh Flag." Accessed April 18, 2021. https://visitwales.com/info/history-heritage-and-traditions/dragon -spirit-legend-welsh-dragon.

Index

To Write to the Author

If you wish to contact the author or would like more information about this book, please write to the author in care of Llewellyn Worldwide Ltd. and we will forward your request. Both the author and publisher appreciate hearing from you and learning of your enjoyment of this book and how it has helped you. Llewellyn Worldwide Ltd. cannot guarantee that every letter written to the author can be answered, but all will be forwarded. Please write to:

Mhara Starling
℅ Llewellyn Worldwide
2143 Wooddale Drive
Woodbury, MN 55125-2989

Please enclose a self-addressed stamped envelope for reply,
or $1.00 to cover costs. If outside the U.S.A., enclose
an international postal reply coupon.

Many of Llewellyn's authors have websites with additional information and resources. For more information, please visit our website at http://www.llewellyn.com